Growth with Justice

A COMPENDIUM OF PAPERS
PRESENTED BY THE PARTICIPANTS
OF NATIONAL SEMINAR ON
GROWTH WITH JUSTICE

AT UNITY DEGREE COLLEGE
LUCKNOW, INDIA

APRIL 10, 2016

COMPILED BY

Masood Rezvi

PUBLISHED BY
LEAD Trust

(Lucknow Educational And Development Trust),
Flat No. G/C-6, Shahid Apartment, Golagunj, Lucknow (U.P.), India
Email: leadtrust.lko@gmail.com
Website: www.leadtrust.net

1st Edition 2016

ISBN: 1519227078
ISBN-13: 978-1519227072

DEDICATION

To all those persons, who yearn for an equitable and sustainable
growth and development of the human species -
The *Homo sapiens*.

CONTENTS

ACKNOWLEDGMENTS

We, the trustees of LEAD Trust, thankfully acknowledge the patronage provided to us by Honourable Mr. Justice Imtiyaz Murtaza and Prof. B. N. Singh.

We are extremely thankful to our guests of honour especially Dr. Anis Ansari, Prof R. S. Yadav, Prof. M. Verma, and Mr. H. K. Mazhari as also to all the learned scholars who have taken the trouble of writing these papers and to the delegates and audience participating in the seminar.

We want to put on records our very special thanks to Prof. Anjum Abrar for his help and guidance in organising the event.

We are also highly obliged to the Management, the Principal Prof. A. B. Siddiqui, the faculty, the students and the staff members of Unity Degree College for providing us all the infrastructural support for the seminar.

We are also thankful to M/S Create Space Independent Publishing Platform, USA and M/S Amazon for providing us such a convenient platform for publishing the book and a smooth and frictionless vehicle for its global distribution.

Last, but not the least we are extremely thankful to those who supported us financially by giving an advertisement in this compendium. Even a small financial support was a big moral boost for us.

A QUESTION FROM THE PAST DECADE

"...while rapid GDP growth rate is a necessary condition for the nation's well-being in the 21st century, it is by no means a sufficient condition. Economists have long accepted that the market may be a very efficient allocator of resources to maximise output but not an adequate dispenser of social justice. Altogether expectations of a GDP growth rate of 8-9 percent as has been suggested recently depend very materially on the commodity producing sectors of agriculture and manufacturing industry performing much better than now and in a more consistent fashion. This is, of course, possible; but the chances of achieving such a growth rate require the stepping up of domestic investment rather steeply and an all round increase in factor productivities, together with more employment of labour. What really are the prospects in this regard?"

(K S Krishnaswamy in Economic & Political Weekly March 13, 2004)

1 INAUGURAL ADDRESS
(By: Honourable Mr. Justice Imtiyaz Murtaza[*])

*G*rowth and Justice are the two fundamental necessities of the human society. The impetus for growth is an insatiable instinct of the human race and perhaps the most fundamental drive which distinguishes it from all other known forms of life. The desire to grow has been the fuel for the engine which has brought us to this stage of developmental supremacy over all other living creatures. From the primitive nomads not much different from chimpanzees, we have grown to a stage where we are capable of listening to the birth cries of a black hole far, far away in the fathomless universe which took place million years ago.

In this journey, however, we have reached a juncture, where we all must address a few fundamental questions. And the most basic of these questions will be - whether our growth can be called a healthy growth? A very common layman analogy will perhaps clarify the seriousness of the question. If we see a pot-bellied young child gaining weight very fast, but not growing the limbs and other organs proportionately, and who is in a habit of messing up and soiling his own living room, destroying the furniture and breaking the window panes, will we say that the child is healthy? No, never! Without any medical examination, even the most ordinary onlooker will tell that the poor child has become unhealthy physically and mentally.

[*] *Former Senior Judge, Honourable High Court of Judicature at Allahabad (Lucknow Bench), Chairman Unity Technical Institute Society and Unity Degree College, Chairman Justice Murtaza Husain Educational Charitable Trust and Patron LEAD Trust.*

Some recent reports disturbingly tell that the gains of the human race are now becoming comparable to the plight of that sick child.

There have been reports and claims, and of course, which can be observed even by a common person, that the distribution of resources is becoming very heavily lopsided. It has been reported that 50% of the world resources are being owned and controlled by only 1% of the population while the other 99% of the population is making itself content with the remaining 50% of the resources only. There are also reports that, not an ordinary doomsayer or a clergy, but a scientist of the stature of Prof. Stephen Hawking has prophesied that the planet earth is going to be destroyed within a couple of centuries or so! Brother Masood Rezvi has dwelt upon the subject passionately in his recent book *"Tightening Noose of Poverty"* published by the LEAD Trust.

The situation clearly calls upon for an immediate attention on distributive justice. The law-framers, the judiciary, the academia, the technocrats, the urban planners and developers, the rural experts, the media, the bureaucracy, and of all, we the people; must seriously work towards a reliable standard of Growth with Justice. Distributive justice has to be ensured on the legal front, economic front, sociological front, educational front and technological front etc, for a long term survival, development and well-being of the human species.

This seminar is a joint effort by the LEAD Trust, Unity Degree College and Justice Murtaza Husain Educational Welfare Trust in this regard. I congratulate the organisers, the Trustees, the Principal and faculty members of Unity Degree College for collecting an impressive galaxy of experts, thinkers, academicians and practitioners in different relevant fields to brainstorm on the subject, and wish that this effort will not end with this seminar but will continue for the times to come. I am sure this humble effort will go as a milestone in the annals of the history of growth with justice.

2 THE LEAD TRUST AND GROWTH WITH JUSTICE – AN INTRODUCTION
(By: Mr. Masood Rezvi[*])

*W*hat is the ultimate fruit of education?
Wisdom!

And what is wisdom?

Let's first try to understand what is NOT wisdom.

Wisdom is neither a measure of the amount of information and data stored in our brain cells nor of the dexterity with which we can perform tasks which were originally invented and perfected by others.

Wisdom is, rather, the ability to absorb and input information and data from the outside as well as from within our own selves; sift, arrange, classify, doubt, question, reject, accept and connect each and every item of such data with each other to find, invent and create holistic solutions hitherto unknown to the humanity; learning, unlearning and relearning in the way.

Wisdom gives us out of the tunnel vision.

Our mother land India, since times immemorial, has been the most fertile ground for supporting and nurturing wisdom. Great thinkers and wise people - from the architects of the Harappan civilisation to the saints, thinkers, philosophers, astronomers, physicians, mathematicians, physicists and what

---

[*] *Managing Trustee, Lucknow Educational And Development Trust (LEAD Trust) and Member GB Unity Technical Institute Society.*

3

not of the ancient ages to the planners, engineers, bards, poets and *Sufis* of the medieval era to thinkers, lawmakers, and scientists of the modern age right up to the brilliant son of India Dr. A. P. J. Abdul Kalam - have been gifted by India to the humanity. Some of the brightest jewels, humanity could produce. In fact, while standing here before you at the Unity Degree College, I remember one of such persons I had a chance to work with and he was the Honourable Late Mr. Justice Murtaza Husain, the founder secretary of Unity Technical Institute Society and Unity Degree College. These people were wise people and original thinkers, and not just educated people – as is generally understood from the word 'educated' by many.

We felt the need of an organisation – under the patronage of Honourable Mr. Justice Imtiyaz Murtaza, the illustrious son of Honourable Late Mr. Justice Murtaza Husain – separately and exclusively concentrating on providing a platform where scholars and learned thinkers from different walks of life interact with young men and women so as to quicken the seeds of wisdom into their minds, while the original organisation the Unity Technical Institute Society concentrates on its noble goal of providing technical and job-oriented education to people from the weaker sections of the society. Thus, Lucknow Educational And Development Trust (LEAD Trust) came into being in October 2015.

Under the visionary guidance of Honourable Mr. Justice Imtiyaz Murtaza as also of Dr. B. N. Singh within a short span of six months of its existence the Trust has the following achievements to its credit:

1   Organised *Kisan Goshthi* (Farmers' Meet) at Unity Girls School at Village: Sidhnath, Asiwan, Mianganj Unnao, in which Prof. B. N. Singh guided farmers about the cultivation of wheat and rice and answered their queries.

2   Helped in the free distribution of biofortified wheat seeds to some farmers on a trial basis under HarvestPlus programme by Centre for Research and Development, Gorakhpur.

3   Published the book *"Tightening Noose of Poverty"* by Masood Rezvi, which is available in Large Font Edition and Abridged Edition, both in paperback and Kindle

format, internationally on Amazon.

4   Is holding the seminar Growth with Justice and has published this book which is again available both in paperback format and in kindle format, internationally on Amazon.

This seminar is the first in the series. We will be organising such seminars biennially in addition to workshops, conferences and brainstorming sessions on relevant contemporary sub-themes and issues. We will be encouraging the younger generation to think and write, almost any genre, from books of scientific and technical utility to, novels, short stories, poems etc., and will give them debut by publishing their work and promoting it globally.

We will be working on technology transfer to farmers and artisans and encourage innovative developmental technology and business strategy for Growth and Development of the economically marginalised classes, without any discrimination whatsoever.

We, definitely invite you, ladies and gentlemen, to kindly support us generously, through purchasing our publications, subscribing to our events, writing for us, inviting us to hold such events in your city, town or village; inviting others to join and donating to us for building our own financial base if you so desire.

With these words, I thank you very much for your support and for your benign presence and move out of your way to let you get immersed in the wisdom of all the thinkers and writers who are presenting their papers in the seminar.

sponsored

Best wishes from:

3 URBANISATION A KEY FACILITATOR TO ECONOMIC GROWTH

(By: Mr. H. K. Mazhari*, IAS(Rtd.))

Abstract

Urbanisation is the manifestation of changes brought about in the rural landscape due to changes in the means of production of goods and services accompanied by movement of people with skills to perform the activities in the changed means of production. Each country has its own definition of an urban area mostly on the basis of the economic activities like manufacturing, the population engaged non-primary activities, the number of people living per unit area and the public agency responsible for the affairs of the city. In India, the urban areas are defined based on the minimum population of 5000 persons and ¾th of male population engaged in manufacturing and other non-

---

* Hussain K. Mazhari is by training a Civil Engineer and a City Planner having obtained his Bachelor of Engineering Degree from National Institute of Technology Allahabad and Masters in City Planning from Indian Institute of Technology Kharagpur. He is also an Alumni of International Institute of Aerial Surveys and Earth Sciences Enschede, Netherlands. He is a fellow of Institute of Town Planners India and life member of Indian Institute of Public Administration New Delhi.
 He has nearly 45 years of experience of working in the field of Urban Planning, Urban Development, Urban Management and Urban Governance. After his retirement from the Indian Administrative Service as Commissioner and Secretary Urban Development, Government of Meghalya, he took to consultancy and worked as a free lance consultant in projects funded by Multilateral Agencies like Asian Development Bank besides projects supported by Japan Bank for International, Cooperation where he worked as Institutional Expert, Team leader, Urban Utility Management Specialist, Urban Governance Specialist.

*agriculture activities and the area has an urban local body like
the municipal corporation/ municipal council or a Nagar
Panchayat. As per census 2011, there are 7933 towns. Urban
areas in India have grown nearly 3times during 1901- 2011.
The recent census shows a decline in the growth of very large
metro cities but much higher growth in one million plus cities
and smaller towns.*

*The paper focuses on the provision of urban infrastructure and
gives an overview of the present status and deficiencies for the
quality of urban life depends on the quality of urban
infrastructure and level of service delivery. It attempts to
understand the reasons for the poor quality of life in urban
areas and analyses the entire gamut of urban planning, urban
development, urban management and urban governance and
briefly mentions how the deficiencies can be improved. It
suggests the participation of the people in preparation of
master plans, design and implementation and maintenance of
the urban infrastructure and service delivery absence of active
participation is the main reasons for tardy implementation of
urban plans and lacklustre enforcement of development
control. It highlights the importance of the role of urbanisation
as a key facilitator for economic development measures; it is
only by having well-planned sustainable, resilient and
efficiently managed and well-governed towns and cities that we
can expect higher and sustainable economic growth.
Investment in the cities and towns are in fact investment for
economic growth, prosperity and welfare of the people.*

1   Urbanisation in India

Urbanisation is the process of change in production of
goods and services from Agriculture to non-Agriculture
activities with the dominance of manufacturing and services.
The outcome of this change is manifested in terms of changes
in the landscape of the rural areas when it goes through the
process of transformation from a rural to an urban area. Each
country has its own definition of an urban area mostly on the
basis of the economic activities like manufacturing, the
population engaged non-primary activities, the number of
people living per unit area and the public agency responsible
for the affairs of the city. In India, the urban areas are defined
based on the minimum population of 5000 persons and 3/4th of

male population engaged in manufacturing and other non-agriculture activities and the area has an urban local body like the municipal corporation/ municipal council or a Nagar Panchayat. As per census 2011, there are 7933 towns. The growth rate of urbanisation has been steady with some decline in the growth rate in the past decades. Though India has historically been witness to the development of many cities in the ancient and medieval period there are a few townships built after Independence. The ancient cities of Mohanjadro and Harpa are examples of the well-planned development of urban areas with proper urban infrastructure. A few like Patliputra (now Patna) and Kashi (now Varanasi) are still most vibrant cities in the country. Post independence a few cities as State Capitals in the States, industrial and Institutional townships got developed with the support of the Central and or State Governments. The private sector's support was and still very limited in building the cities, notably ones being Tata Nagar in Jharkhand and Modi Nagar in Uttar Pradesh. The Institutional townships were, by and large, secluded development and mostly as large campuses cut off from the areas outside the townships. Development within and outside the Institutional townships had different levels of urban infrastructure and services which have remained so despite some development in areas outside such townships. This has led to a situation where the urban planning and development of infrastructure and urban services and urban environment, is far superior, within the planned city than that outside. This is noticeable in almost all the planned cities and also those which have grown organically. Even old cities have areas for rich and middle class and that of the areas with people who are not economically so better off.

1.1 Status of Urbanisation in India

Despite the shortcomings in our cities, the urban population has gone up from 28, 61, 19,689 to 37, 71, 05,760 during 2001-2011. The number of towns as per 1901 census has increased from1830 to 7933; the percentage of population living in the urban areas has gone up from 10.8% in 1901 to 31.16% in 2011. Census of India has made six classifications of towns. Table 1.1 gives the details of the towns classification by population size. It is apparent from the said table that large portion (70.2 %) of the urban population reside in class 1 (As per census classification of 2011) towns with a population of one lakh and above with the major chunk (42.6%) in the cities with a population of 1 million and above. Class II towns to VI towns with a population of 50,000 to 100000(1 lakh) and the smallest towns Class VI with a population of less than 5000 make rest of the urban population. Urban and Regional Development Plan Formulation Guidelines Volume 1of Ministry of Urban Development Government of India, while dealing with the urbanisation in India refers to the population figures of 2001 and 2011 census which shows that the three urban agglomerations namely Greater Mumbai, Delhi, and Kolkata have crossed 10 million marks in population but with much-reduced growth rate. The million-plus population cities have shown a growth rate of over 48% during 2001-2011, but their number has gone up from 35 to 43 and five cities viz Chennai, Bengaluru, Hyderabad, Ahmadabad, and Pune have attained 50 lakh population. Table 1.1 below gives the population of cities for 2001 and 2011 and the urbanisation trend.

Table 1.1: Population Trend 2001-2011

Class	Definition (Population)	Census 2001			Census 2011			Decadal Growth 2001-2011	
		No of towns	# population	% of Urban Population	No of Towns	Population	% of Urban Population	No of Towns	Population
(1)	(2)	(3)	(4)	(5)	(6)	(7)	(8)	(9)	(10)
Class 1	*Greater than 1 lakh	394	1963	68.7	468	264.9	70.2	18.8	34.9
Of which									
Below Million	1-10 lakh	359	88.0	30.8	415	104.2	27.6	15.6	18.4
Million city	Plus 10 lakh	35	108.3	37.9	53	160.7	42.6	51.4	48.4

Of which									
Mega Cities	**Plus 1 crore	3	42.5	14.9	3	48.8	12.9	0.0	14.8
Class II	50,000 - Less than 1 lakh	496	27.8	9.7	605	41.3	11.0	22.0	48.7
Class III	20,000 - Less than 50,000	1388	35.2	12.2	1905	58.2	15.4	37.2	65.5
Class IV	10,000 - Less than 20,000	1561	19.5	6.8	2233	31.9	8.5	4.3	63.8
Class V	5,000- Less than 10,000	1041	6.7	2.4	2187	15.9	4.2	110.1	138.7
Class VI	Less than 5000	234	0.7	0.2	498	2.0	0.5	112.8	180.1
Total		5161	286.1	100	^7933	377.1	109.8	53.7	31.8
Statutory Towns		3799	265.1	92,7	4041	318.5	84.5	6.4	20.2
Non- +Statutory Towns		1362	21.0	7.3	3892	58.6	15.5	185.8	179.0
Total Urban Population		5161	286.1	100.0	7933	377.1	100	53.7	31.8

Source: Table extracted from URDFI Report Volume 1, Ministry of Urban Development, Government of India.
Population figure is in millions except in column 2 where population is in lakhs
* One lakh means 100,000
** One crore means 10 Million or 100 lakhs
+ Statutory Towns are those notified by the competent Authority and meets the definition of the urban areas as laid by the census of India. ^ There appears to be some discrepancy in the data for the number of towns, urban population, and percentage of the urban population for the year 2011. The data as in the above is considered for the purpose of this paper.

The growth of cities in the population of 1 million plus has shown a growth rate of 48.4% which is close to that of the class II towns with the rate of 48.8%. The smaller towns have registered growth rate from 63% to 180%. These towns are growing at very high rate without having any planning framework and in absence of the institutional mechanism to prepare and implement the Development Plans resulting in the chaos that we see in such areas notwithstanding the fact that towns and cities having approved Development Plans and Administrative and Planning Machinery are only a shade better than the non-statutory towns. Only the level of chaos varies.

1.1.1 Urban Infrastructure

The quality of life in any habitat is defined by the urban infrastructure which includes physical, social, economic and financial infrastructure in tune with the macro and micro environment ensuring humane urban environment. Most of our towns and cities offer urban infrastructure and service delivery which are not in conformity with the norms as approved by the Ministry of Urban Development Government of India or as prescribed by the competent Authority in the States.

1.1.2 Urban Water Supply

As per the High Powered Expert Committee (HPEC) Report Urban Water Supply and Sanitation in 2011, India's 71.2% urban households had access to drinking water within their premises up from 65.4% in 2001; 20.7% had a water source within 100meters from their premises and the rest beyond 100meters.The piped connection is 50.2 % that is only half of the urban population gets water supply through municipal pipelines. Metering is only to the extent of 13.3%, Non – revenue water or the water that is not accounted for and wasted is 32.9% Against, the approved norms of water supply of 135lpcd, on the average 69.2 lpcd is supplied, duration f water supply is on the average is 3.1hours as against 24 hours and quality of water is 81.7% and not 100% as required under the water service delivery level norms of MOUD. Inadequate coverage, intermittent supply, low pressure, poor quality and high water losses are the main reasons for deficiencies in the water supply apart from the inability of the concerned agencies to recover the cost of operation and maintenance.

1.1.3   Urban Sanitation

MOUD study on urban sanitation conducted for 423 cities in 2010 revealed that none was found to have healthy and clean environment; open defecation continues with 12.6% households practising it. Only $1/3^{rd}$ of the waste water is treated the rest is discharged into the nearest water bodies causing water pollution of the streams, lakes, ponds and rivers besides contaminating the ground water reserves. A study on sustainable Solid Waste Management in India by Ranjith Kharvel Annepu sponsored by Waste-to-Energy Research and Technology Council, Columbia University Earth Engineering Centre in January 2012 estimated that urban areas in India generated 188,500 tonnes per day. Big cities collect 70-90 % whereas small towns collect less than 50% of the generated waste. Even if we take an average value of the two categories of cities as 60%, more than 75400 tonnes of the solid waste lies scattered in dumps and on the city roads or inside the municipal bins towards the end of the year total accumulation is more 2.75 lakh crore tonnes. The study has also brought out the fact that 2% of the uncollected waste is burnt and 10% of the solid waste is burnt or caught in the landfill fires. The Urban Local Bodies (ULB) are not in a position to collect 100% of generated waste, transportation, processing and final disposal are also not as per the norms of Manual on Municipal Solid Waste Management MOUD and the Solid Waste (Management & Handling) Rules2000.

1.1.4   Urban Housing

Housing shortage in urban areas as per the report of the Technical Group (TG-12) of the Ministry of Housing and Urban Poverty Alleviation (MUHAPA) on housing shortage is estimated to be18.78 million housing unit of which households in homeless category is 0.53Million (3%); households living in *Kutcha* (housing units made with local materials such s mud and bamboo and other materials which are serviceable only for short period) is 0.99 million or 5%, households living in obsolescent houses 2.27million or 12% while households living in congested houses requiring new houses is 14.99 million making 80% of the housing shortage. Table 1.2 below gives the distribution of the housing shortage category wise.

Table 1.2 Housing Shortages

*Category	Distribution of the Housing Shortage among different Economic Categories as on 2012	
	No in Millions	In percentage
EWS	10.55	56.18
LIG	7.41	39.44
MIG And Above	0.82	4.38
Total	18.78	100.00

Source: Report of the Technical Group on Urban Housing Shortage (TG-12) MHUPA, Government of India

* EWS is an Acronym for Economically Weaker Section of the Society, LIG for Low-Income Group, MIG and above for Middle-Income Group.

During the 11th plan, there was surplus housing stock in view of the enhanced realty estate activities mostly in the large cities and targeted to the middle and high income; empty housing units in the National Capital Region (NCR) is noticeable. The private developers with its profit motive had no interest to put money in the construction of housing units for the low-income group though there was huge demand as the returns were not attractive enough. They made houses for middle and the high-income group kept them vacant for many years with the hope of getting it sold when the market is good. The public sector effort is tardy and simply cannot meet the requirement because of various reasons some of which are also true for private developers. TG-12 has adequately dealt with each of the factors that did not encourage the developer both public and private to develop housing for the people who require it the most namely the pavement and slum dwellers, a household in the EWS and LIG category. The reasons are I) Unavailability of Urban Land II) Delay in approvals from Multiple Authorities III) Rising Construction Cost IV) Lack of Skilled Manpower V) Financing Constraints for Low-Income Group (VI) Unlimited financing avenues for developers VII) Archaic Government Laws and Unclear Guidelines VIII)

Disputable Tax Regime.

1.1.5 Urban Transport

Urban India's transportation is characterised by low car ownership as compared to Industrialised countries but the higher concentration in the metropolitan cities, inadequate road capacity, poor traffic management and mixed traffic without any segregation of motorised and non-motorised transport besides poor driving habits and enforcement of traffic rules. The outcome of all the said factors is traffic congestion, cities from the mega to the small towns are laden with heavy traffic load leading to acute congestion affecting adversely the economy as well as the health of the population living in the cities and their vicinity. A comparison of the data on the registered vehicles category wise in India during 1951- 2011 reveals a high increase from 0.3million vehicles to 141.8 million; the highest increase registered is in the two wheelers from 8. 8% of the total it increased to 71.8% of the total vehicles. The ratio of cars, jeeps and Taxis has reduced from its share of 52% to 13.6%. There is a reduction in the share of buses, goods vehicles as well; however there is an increase in the share of the vehicles categorised as others which include, tractors, trailers and vans from 1.3% to 8.5%.

Table 1.3: Comparison of India's Vehicle Population

Year End (March)	As Percentage of Total Vehicles					Total (Millions)
	Two Wheelers	Cars, Jeeps, Taxis	Buses	Goods vehicles	Others	
1951	8.8	52.0	11.1	26.8	1.3	0.3
1961	13.2	46.6	8.6	25.3	6.3	0.6
1971	30.9	36.6	5.0	18.4	9.1	1.8
1981	48.6	21.5	3.0	10.3	16.6	5.4
1991	66.4	13.8	1.5	6.3	11.9	21.4
2001	70.1	12.8	1.2	5.4	10.5	55.0
2011	71.8	13.6	1.1	5.0	8.5	141.8

Source: Ministry of Transport, Government of India (2012)

Though the data is inclusive of both the rural and urban areas, it is nevertheless indicative of the trend in the changes in the composition of the vehicles category wise reflecting indirectly on the modal split of the traffic in the country. The predominance of the private mode of transport whether two or four wheelers does indicate preference of the people to have a dependable means of transport at their disposal and an indicator of the poor public transport which most of our cities offer barring a few large cities in the country. The modal split in each town is different depending on the size, availability of public transport and other options that the city offers. Urban Transport Working Group, National Transport Development Policy Committee 2013 suggested Modal Split for different city size suggesting higher percentage to non-motorized for smaller towns higher to large cities. While adoption of the above may result in additional road capacity due to the higher load being taken over by the public transport, there is need to improve the road capacity, by having increased road network and parking spaces, besides proper traffic management.

1.1.6   Urban Power Supply

During the past five decades or so the country has faced power shortage both the rural and urban areas have had power outages for hours together, the worst suffers were the urbanites and the urban economy. The reasons for the power shortages are attributed to i) Increased demand due to higher economic growth ii) Increase in population iii) Inadequate Distribution System iv) High Transmission losses v) Power theft vi) Poor tariff collection vii) Political Intervention and free electricity to farmers vii) Slow pace of reforms no withstanding the progress made since liberalisation of economy in 1991. There has been a huge increase in the generation of power and power availability has increased considerably. As per the Ministry of Power records, against the energy requirement of 830594 MU the power availability 746644 MU a deficit of 83550MU (10.1%) in 2009-10, with the peak demand of 119166MW and availability of power 744644 MW and deficit of 83550(12.7%). The power requirement during 2014-15 was 10, 68,923MU, availability at 10, 30785 with a deficit of 38,138MU (3.6%); the peak demand being 148166MW and power made available was only 141160MW leaving a deficit of 7006(4.7%). Though the data is for both urban and rural areas, it does reflect the deficit fairly for urban areas consume nearly $2/3^{rd}$ of the total power. The urban area needs electricity for Infrastructures like water, waste treatment, transportation and housing besides commercial, industrial and domestic use and for the provision of social infrastructures like education, health care and other social and cultural infrastructure in the absence of adequate quantity and quality power the above services do get affected.

1.1.7   The Chaos in Urban India

Indian cities and towns do not offer the quality of life that one expects in the 21st century. The reasons are not far to seek. It is the way we plan, implement and maintain the urban infrastructure and carry out the urban planning and urban designs. Urban Planning, Urban Development and Urban Management issues have not been addressed well and were not a priority till some time back.

1.1.8   Priority of the Five-year Plans for Urban Development

The first five-year Plan 1951-56 gave the lowest priority. Urban Development was a part of Housing Ministry. National Commission on Urbanisation set up in the mid-eighties submitted its report in 1988 dealing with the urban issues and making far-reaching recommendations on investment in selected towns with economic growth potential. Though this report was not implemented it did lead to some deliberations both at the Government level and outside. The GEM towns as the commission termed for 329 towns had the potential for growth and expected to provide economic momentum for development. The post-1991 plans did enhance the outlays for the urban sector but urbanisation was not a part of the stated objective of any of the five-year plans before or after 1991. It was only in the 12th five-year that as part of the plan policy "Reinventing the process and management of urbanisation" were included as a priority nearly two years after the Government took up massive investment on the improvement of urban infrastructure under the flagship programme Jawaharlal Nehru National Urban Renewal Mission (JNNURM). This did help the selected 63 cities in augmenting their urban infrastructure services despite the fact that many projects remained incomplete due to various reasons. Recently Government of India have announced the development of 100 smart cities with an investment of Rs 2 lakh crore over a period of 10 years thereby giving strong signals that urbanisation and urban issues need to be addressed and urbanisation is one of the priorities for investment both for Government and private investors.

1.1.9   Urban Planning

Urban chaos is partly due to poor planning or absence of spatial planning while taking investment decisions. Post-independence, a few cities were developed as capital cities, Industrial Townships and Institutional campuses. Almost all the cities were planned as low-density development areas exclusively for those associated with the main function of the city concerned and lived in exclusive enclaves. This kind of development was preferred over-inclusive city development resulting in two distinct areas in the same city, one within and the other outside where the level of infrastructure and urban services were far below.. The need for skill and unskilled labour in the towns did attract the surplus labour from rural areas that had no opportunities for employment to move and take shelter in unauthorised colonies or slums since they could not afford any regular housing. The emphasis in all the Master plans was on producing a land use plan and to use it as a tool for development control. This approach to planning was essentially due to the fact that most of the Planners involved during the 3rd and 4th plan were products of the British and American universities where land use planning and zoning regulations were and are still the tool used for plan enforcement and implementation. Zoning and Land use Plan was against the way towns in India had grown and developed over the years, the cities had mixed land use and moderate to high-density development. The top-down planning approach and non-participation of the people in the planning process have city plans which do not reflect aspiration of the people hence devoid of the ownership so vital for any plan, proposal or project. People for whom the plans are made do not own them, the Government of the day and in actual practice, the Government officials take over the ownership and decide how the city should be planned. The real owners of the plan and the city, the people should be involved in the planning process right from the beginning to the conclusion of the process. The millions of urbanites cannot and should not remain indifferent and let the officials of the Urban Development and that of the Development Authorities decide their fate. An emerging trend of hiring consultants for preparation has further alienated the people from planning processes for they very often do not have the adequate local knowledge and local people may not be very comfortable in sharing their ideas on shaping the city of their vision. The poor and the poverty issues and informal sector of the economy are not addressed adequately. The slums and the old areas of the cities are at the best suggested for conservation and very few proposal is made for improving the living conditions resulting in an exodus of the residents to other residential areas and commercialisation of the old city.

1.1.10 Urban Poverty and Slumming of Indian cities

Master Plans of most of the cities have not dealt head on with the problems of urban poverty and slumming of urban areas big or small; it has not taken an inclusive view. The urban poverty alleviation programme taken up by Government Agencies and the ULBs have had some effect in reducing the level of urban poverty but those at the bottom of the urban poverty ladder have not benefitted, the rag pickers and the casual labour, the elderly and the young among them are required to struggle to manage two square meal a day and a place where they sleep for the night. They are not only deprived of a reasonable livelihood but are regularly harassed by the law enforcing agencies and the local ruffians. There is no attempt to integrate the nearly 25-30% of the urban poor in the Master Plans, such areas designated as a slum, blighted areas in the plan, without much consideration to the root cause of the rural poverty which sends a large number of mostly unskilled labour to the hostile environment of the cities. Urban Planning exercise has been limited to urban areas and not in the context of their Regional setting; the Rural and Urban areas have been divided into two separate entities for planning purposes with different planning strategy leading two different levels of development with a higher level of socio-economic growth in the urban areas. This differential causes a large number of people to migrate to cities for search livelihood for sustenance. This, in turn, results in slumming of cities. There are recognised or identified slums where the ULBs or the State

Governments make some efforts to provide basic services under Slum Improvement Schemes which are neither properly implemented and nor maintained well; the non-identified slums do not have the above services available purely on technical grounds people are made to suffer. The poor and the underprivileged continue to live in sub-human conditions.

1.1.11 Urban Development

Development of urban infrastructure is similar to laying the foundation for the construction of a building. It is the level of the infrastructure that defines the quality of life in the urban areas. The same is designed by the professionals on the basis of

Manuals prepared by the concerned Ministries of Government of India, the Bureau of Standards and guidelines issued on different aspects of planning and designing of the urban infrastructure. Despite the designs made in accordance with approved norms, it is observed that even the infrastructure be it water supply, waste water treatment, solid waste disposal, transportation, housing, power supply remains strained and the level of services gets reduced. It is not possible to pinpoint exactly the reason/s; it may perhaps be due to underestimating the designed user population and or the construction practices and shortage of skilled manpower, non-enforcement of quality control measures. Gurgaon city known as millennium city built in the eighties is facing an acute shortage of water, waste water treatment, solid waste disposal, the roads are choked with traffic and parking lots seem to overflow with cars lined up trying to find a place, this is happening to one of the newest city in the country one can imagine the plight of older cities which were not designed for the present population and with latest codes and guidelines. The problem of deficiencies in urban infrastructure and service delivery is not confined to large cities but across the various sizes and character of cities and towns.

1.1.12 Urban Management

Poor Urban Management has been one the root causes of the poor service delivery. There are multiple agencies responsible for operation and maintenance of infrastructure and urban services, all of them working in isolation and often at cross purposes. It is a common sight to see the road surface being dug up for laying water lines or for repair and maintenance (O&P) immediately thereafter comes the workers from the power supply distribution company for laying new lines or for O&P; as soon as they leave the local Municipality maintenance staff is there to check the manhole and digging of the road surface around it. This is followed by a visit from the telephone line service providers. In short one finds one or the other O&P staff of half dozen or so agencies responsible for service delivery. It is ironical that this happens soon after the road is resurfaced or repaired by PWD or ULB. The people are not informed of such works except a few city service providers do so for major disruption of services through newspaper advertisement. It smacks of insensitivity to the inconvenience to the people.

1.1.13 Urban Governance

Urban Governance in India in the form of a Municipal Corporation was established first in Madras in the year1687 followed by the Municipal Corporations in Bombay and Calcutta. The corporations were then administered by Government officials. It was only in the year 1882 that some kind of democratic structure was put up. With time, more and more Municipal Corporations and Municipalities were established. Though there were elected members of the Municipal Boards and the Councillors of the Corporation with Chairperson and the Mayors the executive powers for managing the city affairs was vested in the Government official who was not accountable to the Mayor/ Chairman as the case may be but to the Government of the day. This continued even after India got independence. It was after 45 years of independence that through the 74th Constitutional Amendment constitutional provision for transfer Functions and Fund and Functionaries were ensured. Despite the 74th Amendment, only a few State Governments transferred the functions to more Urban Local Bodies (ULB) as per the 12th schedule of the constitution. Implementation of JNNURM gave another push to the reforms, for sanction and release of fund to the states under the scheme was linked to the urban reforms which also included the transfer of functions to the ULBs. However till date, most of the States have issued a necessary notification but the transfer of functions, fund and functionaries were only partly made and the State Government continues to muddle with the civic affairs. The Municipal Commissioner continues to be an appointee of the State Government and hence accountable to it. The State Governments are continuing with the Parastatal Agencies and even creating new bodies to carry out the functions which under the constitution comes under the jurisdiction of the ULBs offering excuses that they do not have neither the necessary expertise nor the infrastructure not realising that so are the new Agencies created; the efforts required to make the new bodies functional could have been made for the ULBS. The intention of the State Government is not to shed their Authority even when it comes to functions under the 12th Schedule of the Constitution.

2   Urbanisation and Economic Development

The developed world's economic growth and prosperity bear testimony to the general perception that urbanisation plays a key role. It is proposed to study the relevant data both for a few developed countries as well as the data on a few states in India. The scope is however limited to the per capita income and other factors not considered.

3   Urbanisation and per Capita Income

Urbanisation is a key facilitator for economic development as borne by experience as well as studies and the data which bring out a strong relationship; countries with higher level of urbanisation have shown high growth rate of their per capita income / GDP as per the table 2.1

Table 2.1 Urbanisation and Per Capita Income in World Cities

Country	*Urban Population in Percentage, 2014	#GNI(GDP) per capita in Us Dollars,2014
USA	81	55200
United Kingdom	82	43430
South Korea	82	27090
South Africa	64	6800
China	54	7400
India	32	1570

Source: *Statistical Portal World Bank data. #GNI as per Atlas Method

Perusal of the data does indicate a correlation between urbanisation rate and the GNI (GDP) but this may not be universally true as is the case with South Africa, where despite having the higher rate of urbanisation (64%) her GNI is less than that of China with a lower rate of urbanisation of 54%. While urbanisation may be a key facilitator, there are other factors which contribute to the economic growth such as the business policy and the priorities to Development Agenda including the governance issues besides supportive infrastructure for business enterprises and availability or otherwise of skilled manpower. This needs further study and is outside the scope of the paper.

Table 2.2 Urbanisation and Per Capita Income in Indian Cities

States	Urban Population in Percentage 2011	Per Capita Income in INR2013-14	Ranking in order of urban population in percentage	Ranking in terms of Per Capita income of selected States
Andhra Pradesh	33.49	81937	10	13
Assam	14.08	44263	19	16
Bihar	11.30	31199	20	20
Chandigarh	97.25	156951	2	4
Delhi	97.50	212219	1	2
Goa	62.17	224138	3	1
Gujarat	42.8	106831	7	8
Haryana	24.25	133427	14	5
Himachal Pradesh	12.80	92300	20	11
Karnataka	38.57	84709	8	12
Kerala	47.72	103820	5	9
Maharashtra	45.30	114392	6	6
Madhya Pradesh	20.30	51798	16	18
Meghalaya	20.08	61548	17	17

Odisha	16.68	52559	18	16
Punjab	37.49	92638	9	9
Rajasthan	24.89	65974	13	15
Sikkim	24.93	176491	12	3
Tamil Nadu	48.45	112664	4	7
Uttar Pradesh	22.28	36250	15	19
West Bengal	31.89	70059	11	14

Source: *Census of India 2011# Press Information Bureau, Government of India, and Ministry of Statistics & Programme Implementation. Ranking of urbanisation and per capita income are based on the above-sourced data.

Perusal of table 2.2 reveals that urbanisation rate and the per capita income of the 21 states included in the table does reveal a trend of higher rate of urbanisation and per capita income but there are exceptions like Goa which recorded the highest per capita income but the rate of urbanisation is not the highest (Rank 3). Other states follow closely the two, the rate of urbanisation and the per capita income; however there is also a deviation for the state of Sikkim and Himachal Pradesh. Sikkim with only 24.93% rate of urbanisation has third highest per capita income while Himachal Pradesh with 12.8% urbanisation rate has a rank of 20 and 11 in order of per capita income. This may be due to higher share of tourism due to its natural and pristine beautiful landscape and culture and tourism infrastructure and friendly people who welcome the tourists as important guests to the state. It needs to be supported by data and further research which is outside the scope of the present study. It is appropriate to say that the rate of urbanisation and per capita may not be directly proportional to each other but has a strong relationship which does facilitate economic growth as borne by the data in Table 2.1 and in Table 2.2.

4   Urbanisation as Facilitator for Economic Growth

Urbanisation as a facilitator is aptly explained in the report prepared by Mickinsey Global Institute 2012 which reasons the role of the cities to their attractiveness to both skilled labour and productive businesses due to wage difference between urban and rural areas, the report says " The income gaps reflect the capacity of the cities to attract skilled workers and productive businesses and economy of scale that enable workers in cities to be more productive and reduce the cost of supplying basic services. Mickinsey research in India suggests that it can be 30-50% less expensive for large cities to deliver basic services including water; education and health than it is in more sparsely populate rural areas. Cities attract people with skills to power growth."The same report further adds "Unlike many countries that are grappling with ailing population and rising dependency ratios, India has a young and rapidly growing population- a potential demographic dividend. But India needs thriving cities if that dividend is to pay out. The report estimated that cities could generate 70% of the new jobs created to 2030 produce more than 70% of the Indian GDP and drive a nearly fourfold increase across the nation."

5 India Needs Inclusive and Sustainable Cities for Economic Growth

India's desire for higher growth and its sustainability would depend largely on how the concerned Authorities / Agencies plan, develop, manage and govern their cities well since they are the ones to trigger and take to the higher trajectory of growth. India needs to ensure that the cities are sustainable, resilient and is well managed and have highly efficient governance and above all inclusive. A city is sustainable if it is planned and developed without impairing environment; it is resilient if it is in position to absorb any future shocks due to climate change or any adverse environmental factors, its infrastructure is operated and maintained well to provide adequate level of urban service delivery and above all it is an inclusive city. The Planners need to plan for compact cities with high density of mixed land use development and use the latest technology for design maintenance of the urban infrastructure and ensure that people are involved in the entire process of development of cities. The government should ensure that lack of resources does not come in the way of developing towns and cities by devising investment policies which may attract private sector investment. The more we invest in the sustainable, resilient and inclusive cities, or smart cities which are the flavour of the season the more it will lead to higher economic and inclusive growth that is what we the Indians are looking up to.

Acronym:

EWS	Economically Weaker Society
GEM	Generator of Economic Momentum
GOI	Government of India
HPEC	High Powered Expert Committee Report on Urban Infrastructure 2011
LIG	Low-Income Group
LPCD	Litre Per Capita Per Day
MIG	Middle-Income Group
MOUD	Ministry Urban Development
MOEF	Ministry of Environment & Forest
MUHPA	Ministry of Housing & Urban Poverty Alleviation
MU	Million Unit
MW	Megawatt
NCR	National Capital Region
O&P	Operation and Maintenance
ULB	Urban Local Bodies
URDPFI	Urban and Regional Development Plans Formulation and Implementation Guidelines 2014

Bibliography:

1. Census Population Tables 2011
2. Cities and Rise of Consuming Class Mickinsey Global Institute 2012

3. India's Urban Awakening Building Inclusive Cities Sustaining Economic Growth, Mickinsey Global Institute 2010

4. India's Urbanisation Econometric Model Mickinsey Global Institute

5.   High Powered Committee Report on Urban Infrastructure, Ministry of Urban Development Government of India 2011

6. Manual on Municipal Solid Waste Management, Ministry of Urban Development Government of India 2000

7. Manual on Water Supply and Treatment, Ministry of Urban Development, Government of India National Transport Development Policy Committee 2013

8. National Transport Development Policy Committee 2013

9. Report on National Commission on Urbanisation 1988

10. Report of the Technical Committee on Housing Shortage(TG-12), Ministry of Housing & Urban Poverty Alleviation, Government of India

11. Sustainable Solid Waste Management in India by Ranjith Kharvel Annepu, study sponsored by Waste to Energy Research & Technology Council, Columbia University Earth & Engineering Centre January 2012

12. Sustainable Solid Waste Management in India by Ranjith Kharvel Annepu, study sponsored by Waste to Energy Research & Technology Council, Columbia University Earth & Engineering Centre January 2012

13. Urban and Regional Development Formulation of Plans & Implementation, Ministry of Urban Development Government of India

14. Statistical Portal World Bank Data. Data World bank.org

4 INDIA VS. BHARAT: THE URBAN-RURAL DIVIDE

(By: Prof. B. N. Singh[*])

Abstract

*I*n 2014, around 67.6% of the Indian population lived in rural areas (Bharat) and rest 32.4% in urban areas (India). The rural population has declined from 80% in 1971 to present level, and it will further decline in coming years. It is around 876 million rural people, which is highest in the world. China has the second lower population of 621 million (46% of total population) rural people. There is a decline in percent rural population, but the total rural population is increasing in India, while in China, the number is declining[3]. In Uttar Pradesh state, the rural population i.e. 79% is higher than the average rural population in India. Towns / cities having more than one million population are classified as urban, and there are 1,500 cities in India (>5,000 population), and 73 cities have more than one million population (2015).

Bharat lives in villages. There are 6.4 lakh villages in India (2011).Their main occupation is farming; while in cities, the main occupation is business, construction, education and non-agricultural activities. In a village, there has been always communal harmony, and everyone knows others from

[*] Prof. Singh is former Director Central Rice Research Institute Cuttack, former Director Research Birsa Agricultural University Ranchi and Director Centre for Research And Development Gorakhpur. Email: baijsingh65@gmail.com.

generation. They participate in all village festivities like marriage, death, and other celebrations. In urban areas, people are not concerned even with their neighbours. The caste system has divided the villagers, and most of the agricultural field work are done by lower caste people. Upper caste women do not go to fields, and only men visit the fields. Women carry most of the work like transplanting, weeding etc. Earlier bullocks were used for ploughing, but now most of the ploughing is done by tractors. Even small and marginal farmers also use tractors for field work. Combines/ harvester and threshers have replaced threshing by cattle. There are wide gaps in living standards of rural and urban people. Sanitation, education, medical facilities, pollution, roads, employment opportunities, electricity supply, industries, communication (phone & emails), technology and transport (rail and bus) services divide India from Bharat. Urban India is flooded with both public and private schools and colleges, Universities etc. Urban areas are also characterised by high population density (>400 persons per sq. km). Urban areas generate 63% of the GDP. Both urban and rural areas have rich, middle class, and poor. The urban poor are economic migrants from rural areas, who do not have a house, and live miserable life by the roadside, and slums without decent living standards.

Total households in the country are 244 million, out of which 179 million (73%) are rural. There are 140 million farmers, and there is 141 million ha of cultivable land (2012). There are 84 million marginal (>0.5 ha), 24 million small (0.51 to 1 ha), one million medium and large farmers (>10 ha) and rest landless. As per SECC (Socio- Economic and Caste Census, 2011) report, 40% of rural household are now landless and a major part of their income comes from manual labour and sharecropping. In eight states of North-East, the landless households are 59%. In 2011-12, 25.7% rural population in India was under below poverty line (BPL) category. The Indian society is divided based on caste (Upper, Backward, Scheduled, Scheduled tribe, and Other Backward Caste), religion (Hindu, Muslim, Christian, Sikh, Jain, & Adivasis), and languages (22 languages and 750 dialects). This paper is based on the living in rural areas, especially in Gorakhpur district after staying for 45 years in urban areas across the globe.

30

1 The Major Differences

Some of the major differences in urban India and rural *Bharat* are as follows.

1.1 Sanitation:

The major problem in rural areas is sanitation. Around 90% of the rural households have no latrines. So open defecation is a major problem. In the rainy season, it is worst compared to summer months. They defecate on the road side, and it becomes difficult to travel on roads during the daytime, and even in the evening, it is more difficult, when women are sitting on the roadside, easing their bowels in full public view. In urban areas too, there is a serious problem with urban poor and if you happen to travel by train, it is difficult to look outside in the morning. Education and more toilets through public- private partnerships are needed. Sulabh International and other NGO's should come forward to build more toilets in India at cheaper costs. They should be properly maintained as "Pay and Use" types.

1.2 Sustainable Agriculture & Droughts:

Drought and floods are the major constraints for sustainable agriculture development in India. Rabi crops can be grown after floods and there will be better harvest after floods; but during droughts, both Kharif and Rabi crops are affected and farmers are unable to get harvest for their family needs. Since 2000, there have been 6 major drought years at the national level: in 2002, 2004, 2009, 2012, 2014 & 2015. The extent of drought varies across states, regions, and districts in different states. In 2015, there was 14% rainfall deficit on all India basis. Total of 340 districts (out of 640) in 18 states had 20% fewer rains, and there was 22% water shortage in key reservoirs of the country. Many farmers could not harvest any grain. A National Policy for drought prone areas needs to be implemented (Table 1).

Public Distribution System (PDS) provides wheat and rice grains from Central pool to each state for people of Below Poverty line (BPL) and Antyoday families. The study shows that there is 50% leakage in the distribution of PDS grains to the beneficiaries. Uttar Pradesh and Bihar have largest numbers of poor i.e. 22 and 13 percent, and there is leakage of 15.3 and 9.6%, respectively. This is diverted to open market instead of reaching to intended beneficiaries[2]. The gap between PDS and open market price is wide, so there is a need to assure 100% grain availability to needy people.

1.3 Farmers' suicide:

There has been an average of 1,400 farmers' suicides between 2009 to 2013 in India. Farmers in 8 states viz., Maharashtra, Telangana, Andhra Pradesh, Karnataka, Punjab (Malwa region), Uttar Pradesh (Bundel Khand region), Odisha, and Madhya Pradesh commit suicide either due to their crop failure or inability to pay the borrowed money from moneylenders or Banks. Cash crops like Cotton, Soybean, Chili, Tobacco and Sugarcane requires a lot of pesticides, and other inputs to raise the crop. Drought, hailstorm, pest attack, and spurious pesticides (whitefly in cotton crop in Punjab during 2015 Kharif) damages the crop and huge losses incur to farmers. National Food Security Act (NFSA) has not yet been implemented in many states. In Uttar Pradesh, probably they did not implement and probably it will be implemented from March 01, 2016. Politicians, Bureaucrats, Judiciary, and Media must monitor sincerely the availability of food grains to needy people, and no one should die due to hunger. The farmers of this country are producing enough food to feed the whole world. Proper policy on foodgrain procurement and distribution is needed.

1.4 Pollution:

Urban India has severe air pollution due to carbon mono and dioxide smoke from Diesel vehicles. In coal belt of Jharkhand, West Bengal, and other states, Industrial coal burning also causes air pollution. In 2013, 1.4 million people died due to air pollution in India. *Bharat* is generally less air polluted, but now straw burning after paddy and wheat harvest, wood and biomass burning has increased air pollution in rural areas. Ban diesel vehicle in major cities, and encourage more CNG vehicles.

1.5 Education:

The literacy rate of urban population is higher i.e.85% as

compared to rural 68.9% (2011)[3].Children of farmer's are mainly engaged in agricultural related works, and their study is only part time. Children of landless, scheduled tribes and scheduled caste start their day by collecting firewood and fallen leaves from orchards for cooking the food of the day. They are also involved in grazing of goats and cattle and don't go to school. The problem is more with a girl child. Evening classes should be encouraged for such children. In Uttar Pradesh, the government education is worst, as there is no English teaching from grade one, and teachers are not sincere for teaching. English should be made compulsory from beginning. The public institutions should be under a public-private partnership, where land should be provided to build more schools, colleges and Universities under the control of both with minimal fees. With Private Universities, the fee is so high that rural people can't afford.

1.6 **Housing:**

Rural household requires more space for a living than their urban counterparts. They need shelter house for their animals, space to keep dry paddy and wheat straw. Enough houses with proper sanitation should be encouraged on subsidy basis.

1.7 **Job opportunities:**

MGNREGA (Mahatma Gandhi National Rural Employment Guarantee Act) is now 10 years old, but it has little improved the quality of life of rural landless people. It has increased the minimum wages in rural areas, and this has led to lesser opportunities for rural employment. This has further led to migration in urban areas and more urban poor with slums. Villages should be connected directly with transport to towns/cities so that people return home after work in urban areas.

1.8 **Healthcare:**

Good and specialised hospitals are only located in urban areas. No MBBS Doctor wants to go in rural areas. The problem is acute during night time, and patients are left at the mercy of God (s). Government hospitals in rural areas also lack good doctors. A Paramedical doctor with three years basic training should be trained to live and stay in villages.

1.9 **Pesticide borne diseases and organic farming:**

In Bhatinda, Punjab cancer population has increased many folds amongst cotton farmers due to excessive use of pesticides. There are 66 pesticides that have been barred/ restricted for use in farming in other countries[3]. There are 13 pesticides which should be immediately banned in India (Table 2). Endosulfan insecticide, which caused so much damage to newborn babies in Kerala, is still in Supreme Court of India. The Verma Panel has suggested phasing out 6 moderately hazardous pesticides viz., Alachor, Dichorvos, Phorate, Phosphamidon, Triazophos, and Trichlorfon. Many extremely hazardous pesticides which are banned in Europe, US, and country of their origin due to its harmful effect on human and animal health, soil and environment, but being widely used in India.How come "Central Insecticides Board", Ministry of Agriculture, Govt. of India register such pesticides for use in the country? Vegetables, fruits, spices, cotton, brinjal, and rice consume most of the pesticides. Consignments of grapes have been returned from the European Union due to high pesticide residue. Organic farming by growing with no pesticides, and inorganic fertilisers, should be encouraged. More Neem & Karanj plantation and use of green manures should be encouraged to farm. Its seed has insecticidal properties and safe to use.

1.10 **Roads:**

Still roads in villages are not pucca/ cemented. During the rainy season, roads get waterlogged and the vehicle can't move on such roads. There is a need to collect villages with towns/ highways. Roads should not be built by contractors; it should be under government-appointed polytechnic engineers so that quality is maintained.

1.11 **Electricity:**

The electricity supply in rural areas is minimal. Electrically operated pumps can't irrigate the field for days. Only Diesel pumps are reliable, but costly. Punjab government provides a subsidy for electricity to a tune of Rs 5,000 crores each year, and free power to farmers. In Uttar Pradesh, in 2015 Kharif season, there was no water in canals and farmers field dried, with no harvest in Sonbarsa block of Gorakhpur district.

1.12 **Grain Procurement and Sugarcane arrears:**

Except Punjab and Haryana state, there is no procurement of food grains on MSP (Minimum support price) in Eastern Uttar Pradesh. The Sugarcane crop arrears are well known. No payments even after two to three years. The paddy is sold @ Rs 950/- to 1,000 a quintal, as the Government does not purchase it. Rice is dumped from Haryana and Punjab in Eastern Uttar Pradesh so that rice millers do not buy paddy from farmers. Farming is nonprofitable, but farmers have to do farming, as they can't sit idle. It is only his employment. Why not rice millers are linked to purchase paddy and supply rice to PDS, Antyodaya and NFSA directly to villagers. This will assure local farmers to sell rice at least on MSP. Only for cities and major towns rice should come from Punjab and Haryana, and to deficit states. Green revolution in Eastern India will be only possible through assured purchase of paddy, wheat, pulses, oilseed, and sugarcane from farmers at MSP. Otherwise, farmers will remain poor in this region.

1.13 **Drinking water:**

In rural areas, the drinking water is mainly through farmer's ground water hand pumps and wells. Tap water is rare, while in urban areas, the water supply is mainly through taps. Arsenic and fluorides are other problems in drinking water. There is a need to supply safe drinking water in villages.

1.14 **The quality of life:**

The overall quality of life is poor in rural areas and urban slum dwellers. Sincere efforts are needed to improve the hygiene, healthcare, food and nutritional security, education, roads, sanitation to improve the quality of life of millions of Indians. India is the home of over 800 million malnourished people and needs immediate attention.

Table 1: National strategy to mitigate drought in drought-prone areas

SN	Strategy	Follow-up
1	Water harvesting	In low rainfall areas, 20% area of each plot should be devoted to harvest runoff in each field. It should be at least 10 feet deep. This water should be used for life-saving irrigation of crop.
2	Mechanisation through custom hiring	Subsidy on tractors, Rotavators, Ridge and Furrow planters, Zero till seed drills, Harvesters and Threshers, Combine etc
3	Cultivation of drought tolerant crops and tolerant cultivars	**Food Crops**: Jowar (*Sorghum*), Pearl Millet, Ragi, Kodo , Upland rice, Barley, Rainfed Wheat **Pluses**: Pigeon pea, Urd bean, Moong bean, Gram, Lentil, *Lathyrus*, Cowpea, Guar etc **Oilseed:** Sesame(Til), Rape Seed & Mustard, Taramira, & Castor
4	Seed Production and seed availability	Enough seed production at district, state and national level, and its availability on time.
5	Dry land Horticulture	Growing Ber, Aonla, Custard apple, Guava, Lemon, Lime etc with drip irrigation
6	Animal Husbandry & Improved Pasture development	Goatery, Sheep rearing, Backyard poultry, Desi milch animals, Camel. Pasture should be grown with drought tolerant fodder legume, forage and tree crops.
7	Employment	Enough funds through

	opportunities	MGNREGA for own and community water harvesting structures.
8	Access to food	National Food Security Act (NFSA) to all people in all drought-prone villages & areas.
9	Crop Insurance	Individual Farmer's crop insurance and easy payment through banks.
10	Credit availability	Kisan Credit Card (KCC) and availability of credits on 4% or less interest through Banks, Waive loans during drought years/ seasons.
11	Avoid Cash Crops cultivation	Avoid growing cash crops like Cotton, Soybean, Tobacco, Chili, & Sugarcane in large areas.
12	District level planning for drought, flood and natural disaster mitigation	There is a need to plan at the district level for household food security in affected areas in collaboration with ICAR KVK, CRIDA, Progressive farmers and others.

Table 2: Extremely hazardous pesticide banned in farming, but used in India [1]

SN	Pesticides	Type	Recommendation
1	Benomyl	Fungicide	Wheat, Groundnut, Tobacco, Grapes
2	Carbaryl	Insecticide	Paddy, Cotton, Sorghum, Okra, Cabbage & Cauliflower
3	Diazinon	Insecticide	Household use

4	Fenarimol	Fungicide	Apples
5	Fenthion	Herbicide	Pea
6	Linuron	Herbicide	Pea
7	Trifluralin	Herbicide	Cotton, Soybean
8	Tridemorph	Fungicide	Groundnut, Mango, vegetables & Roses
9	Thiometon	Insecticide	Brinjal
10	Sodium cyanide	Fumigant	Cotton
11	Methyl parathion	Insecticide	Paddy, Cotton, Urd bean, Mustard, & Wheat
12	Methoxyethyl mercury chloride	Fungicide	Sugarcane, Potato
13	DDT	Insecticide	Mosquito control,

2   Conclusion and Outlook:

Although India is producing enough rice and wheat, and food secure, but it imports pulses and edible oils .There is a need to develop sustainable food and nutritional security system for household food security so that hunger and malnutrition can be reduced in rural areas and urban poor. More job creation activities should be taken in villages. To mitigate drought damage, the subsidy should be given for small farm ponds through MGNAREGA. There is a need to educate the rural children and adult people to practice hygiene and sanitation, avoid open defecation. Rural toilets should be encouraged at the individual family level, and financial support should be provided for public toilets in urban areas through Sulabh on Pay and Use basis. National Food Security Act (NFSA) should be implemented in each States, and free food distribution should be taken in acute shortage areas to avoid hunger deaths. NGO's should also be involved in free distribution of food. Organic food and crop cultivation should be encouraged to reduce pesticide use. Reduce air pollution through the use of CNG vehicles, and avoid straw burning in rural areas. Food and Education should be provided to all. Healthy citizens are the greatest asset of any country, and there should be given on water harvesting structures. Subsidy should be provided to Rural National Healthcare policy to cover each individual in rural areas. In addition to "Smart Cities", effort should be made for "Smart Villages" with electrification, road, school and Colleges, Post office, Banks etc. Climate variability and climate change have added fuel to the fire, and the country needs new sustainable development models for better India.

References:

1   Nigam, Aditi. 2016. Ban 13 pesticides, phase out 6 by 2020, suggests Verma Panel. Hindu, Business Line February 03, 2016.

2   Parashar B.K. 2016. UP tops in pilferage, diversion of PDS grains. Hindustan Times Lucknow March 12, 2016. p2.

3   www.google.com

5 AN AGENDA FOR 21ST CENTURY INDIA

(By: Dr. Anis Ansari*, IAS (Rtd.))

Abstract

*T*he biggest challenge that India faces is the concentration of political, economic and educational power in a small elite minority, both among Hindus & Muslims etc.

This elite minority comprises high income, urban, educated, high caste, male, Hindu population. The victims of this inequality include poor, rural, less educated, low caste, female and non-Hindu sections of the society. Since political, economic and educational strength is concentrated in a small proportion of the population, this is being challenged consistently by the deprived majority. It is a natural consequence of democracy that each of the deprived sections should be demanding an adequate share in the political, economic and educational institutions in proportion to their share of the population.

The principle that the board of directors should be representative of the shareholding pattern among the shareholders has been well-recognized and acted upon substantially in the private and corporate world. However, in

* Former Vice-Chancellor, Khwaja Moinuddin Chishti Urdu, Arabi-Farsi University, Lucknow. Email: anisansariias@gmail.com

the public and political domain, this sound principle has been consistently resisted and overcome by the powerful elite minority. The demand and pressure of the deprived majority and the resistance and retention of monopoly by the elite minority has been resulting in various consequences for the people and democracy of India. For example, in order to retain an undue share in public life, the high caste elites of all the communities, have used the strategy of bringing up communal and cultural issues to create a solidarity of people based on religion and culture. This is done deliberately to create a feeling of homogeneity among followers of a religion and outsiders so that the issues of political, economic and educational deprivation of the deprived majority of the community are glossed over. Wealthy and corporate families have tried to have dominance over political and government organizations in order to exploit public natural resources like coal, petroleum, forest, land, water etc. at cheaper prices leading to crony capitalism. This imbalance has also resulted in having a dual system of education with affluent families and middle classes having education in better managed private educational institutions while the vast majority of rural poor is forced to depend on poorly managed govt. schools with low quality of teaching. The concentration of wealth in minority elite has also had the consequence of corruption and price rise in essential commodities.

In order to make India a better place for all the sections of citizens to live peacefully and happily it is essential to make organized efforts to reduce the concentration of wealth, political power and education in the elite minority which will require a good platform to work for greater equality so that the deprived sections of citizens can get a near level playing field. As the problem has persisted for long the remedial efforts will have to be planned and sustained on long term basis. The leadership in such an organization must rest with the dedicated elements from the deprived majority itself.

The agenda for the deprived sections should include the major segments of the deprived majority such as poor, rural, less educated, low castes, females and non-Hindu minorities. While detailed programmes for improving the lot of these deprived sections will require continual and hard collective deliberation, a few suggestions can be made to form the basis for further deliberations.

1 Political Powers for minorities

The present political system is highly oriented towards the elite Hindus. Representation of Muslims, especially their OBCs and Dalit segments, in political and government organizations is very insignificant. There is a bias against them in the society. Efforts should be made to create a consensus that all the major communities should be adequately represented in Parliament, Assemblies, Legislative Councils, Zila Panchayats, Nagar Panchayats and other government institutions. In this context abolition of religious discrimination perpetrated under Para 3 of Constitution (S.Cs) Order, 1950 must be the first step. This paragraph restricts the benefit of reservation guaranteed to a member of Schedule Castes under Art. 341 of Constitution only to such citizens who are Hindus, Sikhs or Buddhists and exclude Muslim and Christian Dalits unconstitutionally.

2 Concentration of Wealth

Since 1980's and more so from 1990's, economic liberalization has resulted in a concentration of wealth in fewer families and organizations. It is necessary to introduce feasible and economic policies which ensure equitable distribution of wealth among all the segments of society. Taxation policies need to be relooked. This will also require creating infrastructure and policy framework for the revival of handlooms and power looms, handicraft and other small and medium enterprises. Agriculture sector requires lots of intervention for making it a remunerative vocation.

3 Educational Opportunities

We will have to work for making our public education system more result orientated. Transferring the responsibility of school education to elected Panchayats and Nagar Panchayats may be one such solution. The issues of language policy and diffusion of skills require detailed consideration.

4 Low Castes Empowerment

Members of other backward classes and SCs & STs constitute more than 80% population of the country. Yet their share in the wealth, education and political powers is very low. It is desirable to reduce the inequality of opportunity in such groups. Although reservation for OBC, SCs & STs has helped in mitigating their problems yet the benefits of reservation have flown only to a small section among OBCs and SCs. Therefore reservation policy for these group needs to be modified in such a way that the benefits flow to the rests among the deprived groups also. It should be worthwhile to subdivide the 27% reservation for OBCs into two groups of relatively advanced OBCs and extremely backward classes.

Presently 23% of the Plan (investment) funds are earmarked for benefitting the members of SCs & STs. A similar Special Component Plan can be initiated @ of 27% for the members of the OBCs. This would result in adequate funding of infrastructure, education & health schemes for the benefit of the OBCs.

5   Women Empowerment

Despite being half of the population, women have suffered in the public domain. There is a need to work for providing them reservation in Parliament, Assemblies and Councils etc. and jobs. The proposal to provide reservation to women in Parliament has been hanging due to the fear of the OBC groups that relatively advanced women of urban and high caste background will appropriate most of the seats reserved for women. This fear is not baseless. Therefore, a sub-quota of 27% for OBC women and 23% for members of SC would be a balanced approach to resolving the issue.

6   Enforcement o Rule of Law

Our Constitution stands for long-established human values guaranteeing justice and equality before the law for all the people living in the country. Article 14 and 21 guarantee fundamental rights of equality before law and right to life and personal liberty for all. Article 25 guarantees freedom of religion and under Articles 29 and 30 religious and linguistic minorities have been guaranteed the right to promote their language and culture and the right to establish and administer educational institutions of their choice. Despite these, a strong bias has existed against Muslims, members of STs and SCs, women etc. resulting in loss of life and property in riots etc.

Since independence many commissions and courts have confirmed the enormous losses of lives and property of Muslims and other weaker sections. There is an urgent need to enforce laws strictly against the perpetrators of such crimes and suitable damages should be paid to the heirs and relatives of the victims. This will ensure a much-needed sense of security and confidence towards ruling establishment and justice system, which will go a long way in the overall development of the community.

7   Support to Weaving and Handicrafts

A large section of Muslim & scheduled caste population comprises weavers and other artisans who are engaged in weaving and other traditional handicrafts such as chikan work, leather, glassware, brassware, etc. The entire handicraft sector needs more govt. support in terms of adequate supply of raw materials at a reasonable price, market support, diversification and modernization of technology including waiver of their debts. Therefore, a comprehensive administrative and financial package should be provided to revive these handicrafts.

8   Agricultural Sector

Agricultural sector suffers from two major problems of low productivity and overloading of people dependent on the sector for their livelihood. Concerted efforts are required to remove these bottlenecks to make the sector a remunerative vocation. This will necessitate policy framework and infrastructure development in the rural areas such as roads and communication networks, supplies of inputs and processing capacity. A competitive minimum wage rate for the landless labours, go hand in hand.

9   Conclusion

To sum up, there is an urgent need to develop leadership and create an organization, representing poor rural, low caste, less educated and non-Hindu minority groups in the country. The leadership of such groups should start with working among the deprived sections at grass root level to begin with for at least two years. After awareness and goodwill have been created among the affected sections strong pro marginalized, group's organization would be called for. Such an organization can last long because it will take long years to achieve the ideals.

6 AN ANALYSIS OF TRENDS IN EMPLOYMENT, WAGES AND PRODUCTIVITY IN INDIAN AGRICULTURE

(By: Dr. Ajay Singh Yadav[*])

Abstract

Agriculture plays a significant role in overall socio-economic development. Despite a fall in its share in GDP, the importance of agriculture has not diminished due to the high dependence of the rural workforce on agriculture for employment. Agricultural labour constitutes an overwhelmingly predominant share in the rural workforce. Present study analysis relationship exists between employment, labour productivity and wages in agriculture. Analysis of trends in Employment, Wages and Productivity in Indian Agriculture clearly indicate that with the progress and development of Indian economy, the workforce is moving away from the agriculture sector. There is a continuous decrease in the percentage of cultivators in rural population. Agricultural labourer per cultivator is also continuously decreasing, indicating the scarcity in agricultural labourer. The study suggested that with the decreasing labour force in agriculture, increasing yield or productivity is the key to growth, which has

[*] *Assistant Professor, Department of Commerce, Unity Degree College, Lucknow, India e-mail : ajaysinghyadav80@yahoo.in*

to be accelerated. *Shortage of labour and finding solutions thereof should become a major focus.*

1.   Introduction:

India is primarily an agricultural economy. Agriculture is the largest source of livelihood and half of India's population is wholly or significantly dependent on agriculture and allied activities. Agricultural growth has always been an important component for inclusiveness, and recent experience suggests that high GDP growth without high agricultural growth is likely to lead to an acceleration in inflation in the country, which would adversely affect the larger growth process (GOI, 2011).

The contribution of agricultural sector to GDP has continued to decline over the years, while that of other sectors, particularly services, has increased. In 1970-71 agriculture contributed about 44% of GDP, which declined to 31.4% and 14.6% in 1990- 91 and 2009-10 (at 2004-05 prices), respectively (CSO, 2011). Nevertheless, agriculture remains a major source of employment, absorbing about 52% of the total national workforce in 2004-05, down from about 70% in 1971. The share of agricultural exports in total export value declined from about 18.5% in 1990-91 to about 10.6% in 2009-10, while share of agricultural imports to total national imports increased from 2.8% in 1990-91 and reached a high of 8.2% in 1998-99 and declined to about 4.4% in 2009-10 (GOI, 2012) . The importance of agriculture in a country like India is not likely to decline due to concerns for food security, employment, rural poverty and availability of wage goods (Vyas, 2003).

Despite a fall in its share GDP, the importance of agriculture has not diminished for two major reasons. First, the country achieved self-sufficiency in food production at the macro level and second, the dependence of the rural workforce on agriculture for employment has not declined in proportion to the sectoral contribution to GDP. This has resulted in widening the income disparity between the agricultural and non-agricultural sectors (Chand & Chauhan, 1999).

The cropping pattern in India has undergone significant changes with a significant shift from the cultivation of food grains to commercial crops. The use of modern varieties, irrigation and fertilisers were important aspects of higher growth in crop production in the country (Kannan & Sundaram, 2011). Many recent studies indicates that productivity gains from the Green Revolution technology have reached a plateau in many regions, for example, Intensive cultivation in northwestern India has resulted in salinity and water logging, groundwater depletion, loss of soil nutrients, formation of soil hardpans and building up of pests and diseases (Narang & Virmani, 2001).

One of the most distinguishing features of the rural economy of India has been the growth in the number of agricultural workers, cultivators and agricultural labourers engaged in crop production. The phenomena of under-employment, under-development and surplus population are simultaneously manifested in the daily lives and living of the agricultural labourers. They usually get low wages, conditions of work put an excessive burden on them, and the employment which they get is extremely irregular (Padhi, 2007:23).

Agricultural labour constitutes an overwhelmingly predominant percent in the rural workforce (GOI, 1989). Agriculture accounts for almost 60% of aggregate employment in India. Employment in agriculture is rural-based (97%), but it is depressing to note that in the rural sector the rate of growth of agricultural employment is abysmally low (0.01%) and was insignificant during the '90s. The corresponding growth during the '80s was moderate and significant (1.18%) (Jha, 2006).

It is an established trend that as an economy matures, there is a movement of agricultural workers from low productivity agriculture to higher productivity sectors. However in India, the trend has not been limited to just declining share of agriculture in total employment but also has led to a significant decline in an absolute number of people employed in the agricultural sector. A comparison across two time periods, 2004-05 and 2011-12, indicates that while there was an increase in the size of the total workforce in the country, the size of the agricultural workforce reduced by 30.57 million people. The share of the agricultural workforce in the total workforce declined from 56.7% to 48.8% in the same period. This brings to the fore that fewer people are being added to the workforce in agriculture and highlights the net migration to other sectors.

Judicious balance in the availability and use of various farm resources is one of the important dimensions in augmenting the efficiency of a farm production unit. Undersupply of a given resource would act as a constraint on maximizing returns from production activity, and its oversupply might push its use to a point where marginal returns to this factor would be low. Farm labour in Indian agriculture exhibits distinct characteristics of oversupply and undersupply, depending on the intensity of seasonality in its requirements (Hebbar and Bisaliah, 1987). According to Census 2011, out of total agricultural workers i.e., 263 million, the total agricultural labour population in India is 144.3 million and the cultivator's population is 118.7 million. The total population of agricultural labour has increased in 2011 as compared to 2001 Census. However, according to National Sample Survey, an additional 13 million left agriculture in two years, between 2009-10 and 2011-12, a historic shift in employment away from agriculture (Thomas, 2014).

The major factors which affect the labour absorption in agriculture are irrigation, changes in net sown area, cropping intensity or changes in gross cropped area, technology involving (seeds, chemicals, fertilizers and mechanization), soil, climatic conditions, and institutional factors such as tenancy and finally wage rate itself (Reddy and Venkatanarayana, 2013).

After liberalisation of the Indian economy in the early 1990s, India's GDP growth rates have been picked up and there is a sign of speeding up of structural transformation in Indian economy with the share of agriculture in GDP reduced to 12%. However, still more than half of the labour force depends on agriculture, which shows that the structural transformation in employment is slower and productivity differences between agriculture and the non-agricultural sector are growing. The high economic growth has not been able to translate itself into an increase in the wages and earnings of the workforce. The majority of the labour benefited from the increased growth rates in GDP through its effects on the raising wage rates and productivity gains mainly in urban centres, however, the trickle down effects of these benefits to rural areas is questionable. Many observe that since last decade, labour shortages in rural India have become an issue. Farmers in rural areas blaming it on Employment Guarantee Scheme (MGNREGA), but there is no concrete evidence to prove this, some are also claiming that the faster growth of the economy and non-farm sector are the main reasons, which is, in fact, is a good sign (Reddy, 2013).

There are studies reporting deceleration in the productivity growth in agriculture. Real wages in agriculture, however, maintained an increasing trend. The increase of real wages in agriculture in the context of growth in agricultural income and a stagnation of agricultural employment is important. In this situation the **kind of relationship that exists between employment, labour productivity and wages in agriculture** needs to be investigated.

2. Objectives:

- to study the cropping intensity, the sex ratio in the labour market, the prevalence of child labour and methods of wage payment.

- to study the wage differentials among male, female and child labourers, the number of days available to them in various agricultural operation;

- to find out the relationship between wage rate, labour productivity and level of employment;

3. Review of literature:

Bhalla (1993) has examined the wage determination and labour absorption in Indian agriculture. The study reveals that the labour-absorptive capacity of Indian agriculture as a whole has declined. The real wages of agricultural labourers has shown an upward climb.

Shiyani & Vekariya (1999) in their paper have examined the gender differences and the role of women in groundnut and wheat production in South Saurashtra zone of Gujarat. The results of the study indicated that the women played a greater role in the production of groundnut and wheat. The share of female labour used in groundnut and wheat production were 46% and 31% respectively of the total human labour utilization. Harvesting and hand weeding were the two major operations performed predominantly by women in the cultivation of both the crops accounting for 49% and 55-61% respectively.

Tomer *et al.* (2000) conducted a study to examine the family and hired labour employment in various crops and regions of Haryana state. The study was conducted in irrigated and semi-irrigated zones of Haryana. The study revealed that per hectare labour use was higher in the irrigated area. Hired labour (casual and contract) use was higher than family labour use in the irrigated zone. Hired labourers were mostly migrants from labour surplus states. The migrant labour caused a reduction in the wage rate in the rural labour markets of the state.

Sharma (2001) opined that the factor, which influences agricultural wages often vary from region to region. The major factors responsible for wage determination and variation are a land-labour ratio, cropping-intensity, cropping patterns, the incidence of child labour, per worker productivity, the percentage of non-farm employment and proportion of large farm in a region. Further in the context of economic reforms some factors like agriculture productivity nonfarm diversification, investment and supply of labour has played very important role in the determination of wage rate while wage income of the rural /agriculture labour is determined by the number of days employed in a year and the wage rate. Trends in the number of employed days available to the agriculture labour show that the total number of employed days increased in all the state though in some states the period to the other.

Sharma & Kumar (2003) reported that increase in casualisation and feminization of labour is due to male migration and decline in the customary and dependency relationship, whereas an increase in mobility of labour is because of development in the means of communication and road infrastructure.

Bhalla (2008) concluded in his study that the increase in the growth rate of employment can be attributed to the rapid increase in labour force because of the favourable age distribution of increased population as India is passing through a demographic phase, where a bulk of the population is in the working age group of 15 to 59.

Chandrasekhar & Ghosh (2008) found that the employment and unemployment growth rates are higher for the rural areas than for the urban areas. The reason they found, in this case, is that rural areas mostly have labour intensive economic activity, which leads to high employment rate in these regions. But at the same time, most of them are primarily engaged in the agricultural sector which is seasonal. This leads to high unemployment rates in the rural areas.

Sreedhar & Kumar (2012) opined that employment in agriculture is mostly seasonal and intermittent in character. The labourers suffer from seasonal unemployment. During the periods of peak agricultural activity, the demand for labour is high and during the offseason they have to face acute unemployment problem. In the areas where multiple cropping is practiced, the labourers get employment throughout the year with a minimum period of unemployment.

Nithyashree & Pal (2013) analysed the recent trends in the growth of agriculture, income and employment in India. The study reported a shift from the households' self-employment in agriculture and agricultural labours towards self-employment in the non-agricultural sector, which has accentuated labour scarcity in the rural areas. The study suggested that appropriate policies should be evolved to promote skill development and generate employment opportunities in the non-farm sector in the rural areas in order to increase livelihood, food and nutritional security, reduce the regional disparity and alleviate rural poverty in the country.

Reddy (2013) assessed trends in rural wages along the Lewis continuum through wage rates data. Results of the study show a clear rising trend in real wage rates since 1995 and then accelerated from 2007 onwards at least in developed states like Punjab, Haryana and Tamil Nadu. Less participation in public works program in Punjab and Haryana also indicates no surplus labour. This confirms that at least developed states in India crossed the Lewis Turning Point. The acceleration of real wages even in slack season indicates that the era of a labour shortage is started in rural areas especially in developed states like Tamil Nadu, Haryana, Punjab and Andhra Pradesh, which needs to be tackled through labour saving technology and wide scale farm mechanisation. On the other hand, it appears that the underdeveloped states like Madhya Pradesh, Uttar Pradesh and Bihar are not reached the LTP and needs to develop policies to increase productivity of rural labour in these backward states

Venkatesh (2013) examined the shift in rural employment pattern, trends in rural wages and agricultural growth, and relationships between agricultural wages, productivity and rural non-farm employment (RNFE) in India. The study observed that although the wages were lower for farm labours than non-farm labour, the growth rate of agricultural wages has been higher than of non-farm wages. The wage determinant analysis has revealed that agricultural productivity and RNFE have a positive influence on agricultural wages while labour availability (labour-land ratio) and high dependency on agriculture pull down the wage rates. The study confirmed that the growths of agriculture and RNFE have trickled down to the agricultural labour, indicating an inclusive growth. The study concluded that policies directed towards improving agricultural productivity and promoting RNFE would provide better agricultural wage rates and assure rural livelihood security.

Berg, et al. (2015) estimated the impact of Mahatma Gandhi National Rural Employment Guarantee Act (MNREGA) on agricultural wages. The rollout of MNREGA in three phases is used to identify difference-in-difference estimates of the programme effect. Using monthly wage data for the period 2000-2011 from 209 districts across 18 Indian states, study finds that, on average, MNREGA boosts the growth rate of real daily agricultural wages by 4.3% per year. The effect is concentrated in some states and in the agricultural peak season. The effect appears to be gender-neutral and biased towards unskilled labour. The study concluded that rural public employment programmes constitute a potentially important anti-poverty policy tool.

4. Research methodology:

Descriptive cum analytical research methodology is used in present study, which is based on secondary sources, CSO data, Agricultural Wages in India (AWI), compiled and published by the Directorate of Economics and Statistics, Census Report, Rural Labour Enquiry Reports on Wages and Earnings, Labour Bureau, Ministry of Labour

Chandigarh/Shimla, Ministry of Agricultural, Employment and Unemployment Situation in India (NSSO) and other publications, books, journals, reports and government publications.

5. Technical terms used:

Labour force refers to the population which supplies or offers to supply labour for pursuing economic activities for the production of goods and services

Labour force participation rate (LFPR) is defined as the number of persons in the labour force per 1000 persons.

Worker-population ratio (WPR) is defined as the number of persons employed per 1000 persons.

Earnings refer to the wage/salary income receivable for the wage! salaried work was done during the reference week by the wage/salaried employees and casual labourers. The wage/ salary receivable may be in cash or in kind or partly in cash and partly in kind. The kind wages are evaluated at current retail prices. Bonus and perquisites evaluated at retail prices and duly apportioned for the reference week are also included in earnings. Amount receivable as 'overtime' for the additional work done beyond normal working time is also included.

An agricultural labourer is a person who follows one or more of the following agricultural operations in the capacity of labourer on hire or in exchange, whether paid wholly in cash or kind or partly in cash and partly in kind:

- farming including cultivation and tillage of the soil, dairy farming, etc.,

- production, cultivation, growing and harvesting of any horticultural commodity,

- the raising of livestock, bee-keeping or poultry farming, and

- any practice performed on a farm as incidental to or in conjunction with farm operations (including any forestry or timbering operations) and the preparation for market and delivery to storage or to market or to the carriage for transportation to market of farm

55

produce.

Manual work in fisheries is excluded from the coverage of agricultural labour. Further, 'carriage for transportation' refers only to the first stage of the transport from farm to the first place of disposal.

6. Trends in Cultivated Area, Production and Yield of Major Crops

The cropping pattern in India has undergone significant

Table 1 : Area, Production and Yield of Major Crops
(Area in Lakh hectare, Production in Million Tonnes, Yield in kg/hectare)

Crops	Area			Production			Yield		
	11-12	12-13	13-14	11-12	12-13	13-14	11-12	12-13	13-14
Rice	440.06	427.54	439.49	105.30	105.24	106.54	2393	2462	2424
Wheat	298.65	300.03	311.88	94.88	93.51	95.91	3177	3117	3075
Cereals	264.22	247.62	256.73	42.01	40.04	43.05	1590	1617	1677
Pulses	244.62	232.57	252.27	17.09	18.34	19.27	699	789	764
Foodgrains	1247.55	1207.76	1260.37	259.29	257.13	264.77	2078	2129	2101
Oilseeds	263.08	264.84	285.25	29.80	30.94	32.88	1133	1168	1153
Sugarcane	50.38	49.99	50.12	361.04	341.20	350.02	71668	68254	69839
Cotton@	121.78	119.77	117.27	35.20	34.22	36.59	491	486	532
Jute #	9.05	8.63	8.51	11.40	10.93	11.58	2268	2281	2449

@ *Production in million bales of 170 kg each*
# *Production in million bales 180 Kg. each*
Source : GOI (2015), Annual Report 2014-15, Department of Agriculture & Cooperation, Ministry of Agriculture, Government of India, New Delhi, p. 2.

changes over time. As the cultivated area remains more or less constant, the increased demand for food because of increase in population and urbanisation puts agricultural land under stress resulting in crop intensification.

As per the land use statistics 2011-12, the total geographical area of the country is 328.7 million hectares, of which 140.8 million hectares is the reported net sown area and 195.2 million hectares is the gross cropped area with a cropping intensity of 138.7%. The cropping intensity was 124.23% in 1983-84 which has continuously increased to 129.96% in 1993-94, further to 137.78% in 2008-09. It clearly indicates that the increased demand for food puts agricultural land under stress resulting in crop intensification.

7. Trends in Gross Capital Formation (GCF) in Agriculture and Allied Sector

Items included in the estimates of GCF in agriculture are; improvement of land and Irrigation works, laying of new orchards and plantations, purchase of agricultural machinery and implements agriculture construction works, additions to livestock, fishing boats and nets, etc.

Table 2 : Gross Capital Formation (GCF) in Agriculture and Allied Sector relative to Gross Domestic Product (GDP) at 2004-05 prices

(Rs in Crore)

Year	GCF in Agriculture	GDP	GCF as % of GDP
2006-07	92057	619190	14.9
2007-08	105741	655080	16.1
2008-09	127127	655689	19.4
2009-10	133162	660987	20.1
2010-11	132734	717814	18.5
2011-12	157172	753832	20.8
2012-13	162084	764510	21.2

Source: Central Statistics Office

GCF in Agriculture and Allied Sector relative to GDP in this sector has been showing a steadily increasing trend from 14.9% in 2006-07 to 21.2% in 2012-13.

8. Trends in Structure of Workforce

Agriculture provides employment to not only the adult males of a household but also to women in the households. Women work extensively in the production of major grains and millets, in land preparation, seed selection and seedling

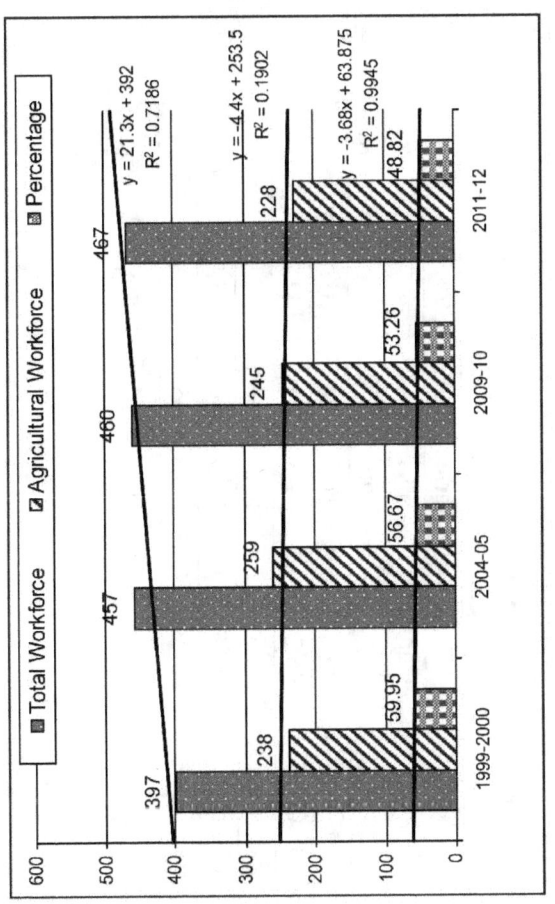

Fig 1 : Trends in Structure of Workforce

production, sowing, applying manure, weeding, transplanting, threshing, winnowing and harvesting.

It has been observed that over time that as economies progress and move towards development, workforce tends to move away from agriculture sector as a percentage of people employed in agriculture has been consistently declining, from 59.95% in 1999-00 to 48.82% in 2011-12.

9. Trends in Agricultural Workers in India

The population of India has increased from 43.92 crores in

Table 3 : Population and Agricultural Workers (India)

(in Millions)

Year	Total Pop.	Rural Population		Agricultural Workers					
				Cultivators		Agri. Labour		Total	
		Pop.	%	Pop.	%	Pop.	%	Pop.	% to RP
1961	439.2	360.3	82.0	99.6	76.0	31.5	24.0	131.1	36.4
1971	548.2	439.0	80.1	96.2	66.9	47.5	33.1	143.7	32.7
1981	683.3	525.6	76.9	92.5	62.5	55.5	37.5	148.0	28.2
1991	846.4	630.6	74.5	110.7	59.7	74.6	40.3	185.3	29.4
2001	1028.7	742.6	72.2	127.3	54.4	106.8	45.6	234.1	31.5
2011	1210.6	833.5	68.8	118.7	45.1	144.3	54.9	263.0	31.6

Source : Computed from various Census Reports of India

1961 to 121.06 crore in 2011, but its decadal growth rate is having a continuous decreasing trend. In the same period rural population has increased from 36.03 crores to 83.35 crores with a sharp decrease in decadal growth from 21.84% to 12.24%.

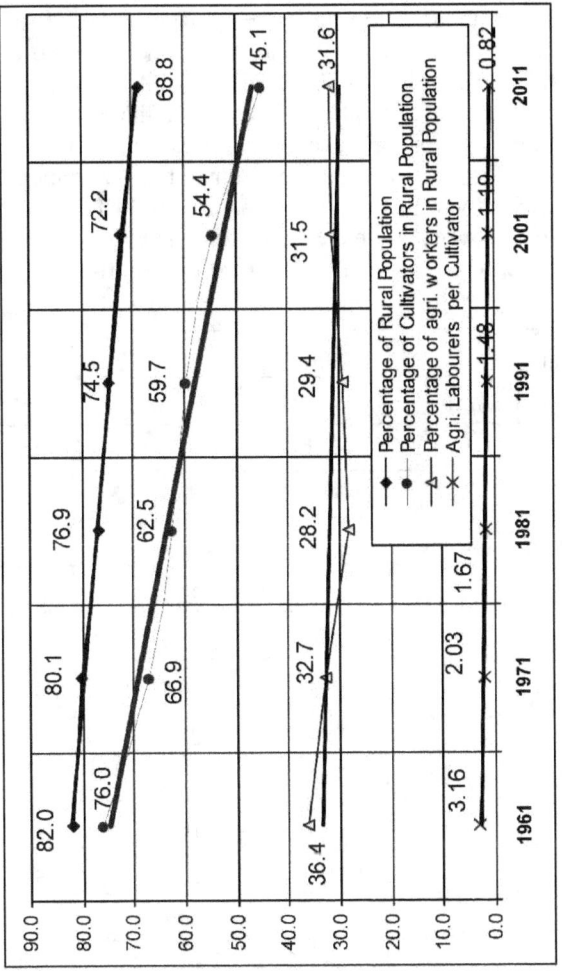

Fig 2 : Population and Agricultural Workers in India

Fig. 2 shows that there is a continuous decrease in the percentage of cultivators in rural population. Although the percentage of the agricultural labourer is having a mixed trend but agricultural labourer per cultivator is continuously decreasing, indicating the scarcity in agricultural labourer.

10. Trends in Agricultural Wages:

A comparison of remunerations for farmers across crops shows that a farmer only earns Rs. 2,400 per month for each hectare of paddy and Rs. 2,600 per month for a hectare of wheat. Farm labourers, on the other hand, earn less than Rs. 5,000 per month. An average industrial worker, on the other hand, earns close to Rs. 7,000 per month while a construction worker earns over Rs. 8,000 per month. Additionally, jobs in the non-farm sector are available round the year, unlike agriculture jobs which are seasonal in nature. For women, the agricultural daily wages are between 15% to 30% lower than those of men depending on the agricultural activity.

Table 4 : Wages for Different Occupation

(In ₹)

Occupation	2007-08	2011-12	2014-15
INDUSTRIAL WORKS			
Manufacturing	204	287	549
Industries	167	230	448
NON-FARM WORKS			
Mason	143	278	385
Carpenter	130	250	349
Blacksmith	99	196	287
Tractor drivers	99	214	298
AGRICULTURAL WORKS			
Ploughing	91	165	270
Sowing	79	145	235
Harvesting	75	142	239
Picking	72	142	202
Transplanting	74	135	222
General	70	127	227

Source : Various Reports on Wages and Earnings, Labour Bureau, Chandigarh

Comparison of wages in farm and nonfarm employment reveals that many simple jobs in non-farm sectors offer higher wages. The daily wage of a mason in construction is more than double the average wage for weeding and close to double that of ploughing. Wages for nonfarm professions like carpentry, drivers, blacksmith etc are at least 15-20% higher than agricultural wages. Manufacturing wages when compared to agricultural professions are more than 2 times which clearly explains the preference for these sectors.

Table 5 : Difference in wages (In terms of ratio)

Occupation	2007-08	2011-12	2014-15
Manufacturing to Nonfarm works	1.73	1.22	1.66
Industrial to Nonfarm works	1.42	0.98	1.36
Manufacturing to Agricultural works	2.66	2.01	2.36
Industrial to Agricultural works	2.17	1.61	1.93

Source : Computed from various Reports on Wages and Earnings, Labour Bureau, Chandigarh

11. Conclusion:

Analysis of trends in Employment, Wages and Productivity in Indian Agriculture clearly indicate that the increased demand for food puts agricultural land under stress resulting in crop intensification. Gross Capital Formation in Agriculture and Allied Sector has also been showing a steadily increasing trend. It is observed that with the progress and development of Indian economy, the workforce is moving away from the agriculture sector.

There is a continuous decrease in the percentage of cultivators in rural population. Agricultural labourer per cultivator is also continuously decreasing, indicating the scarcity in agricultural labourer. There are many reasons for this, e.g. jobs in the nonfarm sector are available round the year whereas agriculture jobs are seasonal in nature. Many simple jobs in non-farm sectors offer higher wages. Wages in manufacturing and industrial sector are more than 2 times to agricultural workers.

Agriculture plays a significant role in overall socio-economic development. Therefore, fostering rapid, sustained and broad-based growth in agriculture remains key priority for the country. With the decreasing labour force in agriculture, increasing yield or productivity is the key to growth, which has to be accelerated. Shortage of labour and finding solutions thereof should become a major focus.

REFERENCES

Berg, E., S. Bhattacharyya, D. Rajasekhar & R. Manjula (2015), Can Public Works Increase Equilibrium Wages? Evidence from India's National Rural Employment Guarantee, Policy Paper on Improving Institutions for Pro-Poor Growth, Department for International Development, Government of U.K., London, 2 December.

Bhalla, G.S. (2008), "Globalization and Employment trends in India" Indian Journal of Labour Economics, 51(1): 1-23, The Indian Society of Labour Economics, New Delhi.

Bhalla, S. (1993), The dynamics of wage determination and employment generation in Indian agriculture. *Indian J. Agric. Econ.,* 48(3): 448-470.

Chand, Ramesh & A.K. Chauhan 1999. Liberalization Of Agricultural Trade And Net Social Welfare : A Study Of Selected Crops, EPW, Dec.1999.

Ghose, Ajit K., Chandrasekhar (2008), *The Global Employment Challenge,* Geneva, ILO.

Habber, B.G. & S. Bisaliah (1987), Stability in Seasonal Labour Absorption Under Dryland Farming. Artha Vijnana, Vol. 29, No. 3, pp. 262-285.

Jha, Brajesh (2006), Employment, Wages and Productivity in Indian Agriculture, Working paper Serries, Institute of Economic Growth, University

Kannan, Elumalai & Sujata Sundaram (2011) Analysis of Trends in India's Agricultural Growth ISBN 978-81-7791-

132-9

Narang, R.S. & S.M. Virmani (2001). Rice-Wheat Cropping System of Indo-Gangetic Plain of India.

Nithyashree, M.L. & Suresh Pal (2013), Regional Pattern of Agricultural Growth and Rural Employment in India : Have Small Farmers Benefitted? *Agricultural Economics Research Review*, vol. 26, issue 2.

Padhi, Kulamani (2007), Agricultural Labour in India - A Close Look, Orissa Review, February-March, 2007: 23-25

Reddy, A.A. (2013), Trends in Rural Wage Rates : Whether India Reached Lewis Turning Point, Indian Agricultural Research Institute (IARI), New Delhi, September 5.

Reddy, D.N. & M. Venkatanarayana (2013), Declining Labour Use in Agriculture : A Case of Rice Cultivation in Andhra Pradesh, MPRA Paper No. 49204, pp. 1-38.

Sharma, & Kumar (2003), functioning of agricultural labour market: Micro evidence from an agricultural developed region of Himachal Pradesh. *Indian J. Agric. Econ.*, 58(4): 695 -714.

Sharma, H.R.(2001), "Employment and Wage Earnings of Agriculture Labourers : A State Wise Analysis." *Indian Journal of Labour Economics*, Vol. 44, No.l.

Shiyani, R.L. & Vekariya, S.B. (1999), Role of women in groundnut and wheat production in south Saurashtra zone of Gujarat. *Indian J. Agric. Econ.*, 54(3): 318.

Sreedharan; N. & I. Narendra Kumar (2012), Gender Discrimination In Agriculture Sector - A Study In Andhra Pradesh, *Z.I.J.B.E.M.R.*, Vol. 2 Issue1, January. P. 245.

Thomas, J.J. (2014), The Demographic Challenge and Employment Growth in India. *Economic and Political Weekly*, Vol. XLIX, No. 6.

Tomer, B.S., Singh, V.K. & Khatkar, R.K. (2000), Pattern of land lease and labour use in Haryana agriculture. *Indian J. Agric. Econ.*, 55(3): 348.

Venkatesh, P. (2013), Recent Trends in Rural Employment and Wages in India: Has the Growth Benefitted the Agricultural Labours?, Agricultural Economics Research Review, Vol. 26, pp 13-20

Vyas, V.S. (2003), *"India's Agrarian Structure, Economic Policies and Sustainable Development: Variations on a Theme"*, Academic Foundation, New Delhi.

REPORTS

Annual Report 2014-15, Department of Agriculture & Cooperation, Ministry of Agriculture, Government of India, New Delhi.

Census of India (2011), Office of the Registrar General & Census *Commissioner,* India, Ministry of Home Affairs, Government of India.

CSO (2011), *"Revised Estimates of Annual National Income 2010-11: A Quarterly Estimates of Gross Domestic Product, 2010-11"*, Central Statistics Office (CSO), Ministry of Statistics and Programme Implementation, Govt. of India, New Delhi.

GOI (1989), Employment and Rehabilitation, Report of National the Commission on Labour, Ministry of Labour, Govt. of India, New Delhi.

GOI (2011), *"Faster, Sustainable and More Inclusive Growth: An Approach to the 12th Five Year Plan (Draft)"*, Planning Commission, Government of India, New Delhi.

GOI (2012), *"Economic Survey 2011-12"*, Economic Division, Department of Economic Affairs, Ministry of Finance, Govt. of India, Oxford University Press, New Delhi.

Wages Rates in Rural India (2015), Ministry of Labour & Employment, Government of India, Labour Bureau, Chandigarh.

7 GROWTH WITH JUSTICE – TECHNOLOGICAL ASPECTS

(By: Mr. M. V. Rangacharyulu)*

Abstract

Growth is a natural process when it comes to living organisms. For non-living beings like countries, structures, sculptures, landscapes etc. growth is a result of conscious efforts of mankind. In the present context, growth is a mix of both health and wealth. Past and present history is a testimony to the fact that very often than not, this growth takes place in an unjust manner. Precisely for this reason, revolutions take place across the world.

There has to be a paradigm shift in our approach to nation building. The performance of any social benefits scheme should be appraised on the basis of wealth that it has been able to create. This helps us in focusing on prosperity building rather than thinking on poverty management. It should bring about a drastic change in the mindset of the people who are supposed to be benefited by such schemes so that they will be

Senior Faculty at Regional Staff College, Punjab National Bank, Panchkula, Haryana. In his own words he is " Brahmin (Brahmin is one who truly and firmly believes in well being of all) by birth. Farmer by heart. Banker by profession. Faculty by passion to learn. Indian by soul. Human being by God's will. In short, Spec in Space. Growing young at 55. Graduation in Agricultural Sciences, Diploma in Management, Certified in Banking and Computer Applications".

prompted to think in terms of maximizing their wealth, properly utilizing the support extended by the state.

Growth with justice can take place only if transparency exists and prevails. Technology can support and maintain transparency. Technology empowers people, improves efficiency and sharpens effectiveness. It can also make it difficult to tamper with the systems and easy to identify the aberrations and fix them up. Technology can be a pivot to balance growth and justice.

There has always been an issue of lopsided growth that divided society into segments; rich and the poor. It is just natural that in any society, there will be some variation in the wealth, prosperity, incomes and well-being of different people. The society revolts and reacts if the inequality becomes significantly unbearable. Public perception gathers unpredictable momentum to bulldoze the walls of empires that erected and promoted the barriers of disparity.

When Gandhi broke the salt laws at 6:30 am on 6 April 1930, the immediate reasons are economic. But it laid a foundation for a massive political movement.

After independence, the country witnessed development in various sectors. However, the disparity between poor and the rich has not been bridged. In fact, it has widened. The agriculture sector which was once the main driving force of the economy has now been reduced to shambles. The manufacturing sector which had shown progress immediately after independence could not keep the momentum in the long run. Due to powerful emergence of the IT sector overseas, the services started contributing more to the Indian GDP.

Although agriculture is likely to register low growth for the second year in a row on account of weak monsoons, it has performed better than last year. The industry has shown significant improvement primarily on account of the surprising acceleration in manufacturing (9.5 per cent vis-à-vis 5.5 percent in 2014-15). Meanwhile, services continue to expand rapidly[1]

During the last decade, the governments had lost focus on the development of agriculture and resultantly the farming community suffered extensive damage. Consequently, unfortunate suicide deaths have taken place and continue to take place across the country in an alarming manner.

Indian agriculture, is in a way, a victim of its own success, which over time is posing to be a major threat.[1]

During the last three decades, the country had suffered because of the regionalism and lost many global opportunities that could have come its way on account of various technological breakthroughs .

Though the country has been blessed by nature with vast natural resources and wonderful human talent, the political leadership could not take the country forward because of its own internal skirmishes and indulgence in corrupt activities. The infographic reflects India's growth. It does also reflect India's lost opportunities when its growth rate had steeply come down while the world average was managing to hold on to its own.

The education system has deteriorated to churning out youth that has degrees and qualifications but not basic skills. Consequently, despite spending years in acquiring qualifications, the youth is not able to find itself suitable for openings that can offer a respectable career .

According to Annual Status of Education Report (ASER) 2014, there is sharp decline between 2007 to 2014 in the number of children in Standard V who can read a textbook of Standard II, in both government and private schools. [1]

The political leadership in the country has vitiated the atmosphere so much that certain communities have lost hope in getting employment in the government sector. The state governments have also failed in catering to the requirements of the people in respective states, resulting in unwarranted migrations.

When a person is enumerated in the census at a different place than his / her place of birth, she / he is considered a migrant. This may be due to marriage, which is the most common reason for migration among females or for work, what is the case as generally among males, etc. It also happens that many return to their place of birth after staying out. To capture such movements of population census collect information on migration by last helps to understand the current migration scenario better. In India, as per census 2001, about 307 million people have been reported as migration by place of birth. Out of them about 259 million (84.2%), migrated from one part of the state to another, i.e., from one village or town to another village or town. 42 million (2%) from outside the country. The data on migration by the last residence in India as per Census 2001 shows that the total number of migrants has been 314 million. Out of these migrants by the last residence, 268 million (85%) has been intra-state migrants, those who migrated from one are of the state to another. 41 million (13%) were interstate migrants and 5.1 million (1.6%) migrated from outside of the country.[3]

'Natural increase' does not then account for the growth in urban numbers — certainly not for the 30 percent rise in urban population in the States. Thousands of towns today have far larger populations than they used to have — but not due to natural increase. The reason is migrations on a massive scale. Rural folk still outnumber urban people by more than two to one. In the 2001 Census, rural family size (5.4) remained bigger than urban family size (5.1). Also striking, States like Uttar Pradesh and Bihar show massive falls in growth rates in 2011. In 2001 Census, Uttar Pradesh and Bihar were "the two States with the largest number of net migrants migrating out of the state."[4]

The widening disparity between the rich and the poor calls for paying immediate attention to various aspects of development so that the growth takes place with justice being delivered.

The land is very critical for undertaking agriculture, manufacturing or any other vocation. Unfortunately, the ownership of a substantial chunk of land is with those people who are not actually using it. The state should consider the acquisition of such land and make it available to the needy persons through proper process for using it to pursue their profession.

Though the government is undertaking land distribution to farmers, it is not adding prosperity to them or to the nation because this resource is not being optimally utilized. Therefore, the concept of limited period lease system should be introduced so that the benefit is passed on to other people on completion of the tenure . The same holds good for the other natural resources such as water bodies.

The concept of providing government accommodation on rental basis to all the citizens on carefully structured terms should be considered. It will facilitate easy availability of the accommodation to the people who would need it. Affordable, easy accommodation availability could change the mindset of the people to such an extent that they may not find it necessary to own a property or land, to live.

It is unfortunate that the rich, who can afford, acquire many properties for speculation purposes leading to national wastage of resources.

Unbridled growth without discipline is not beneficial. Discipline definitely calls for subtle sacrifices. Therefore, to grow as a nation, the country needs to plan for the future of each and every common as well as private land use. The lopsided development that has taken place in towns and cities left them polluted to the brim, and the peripherals chocked in an inadequate infrastructural quagmire. Had there been extensive planning, traffic jams, water loggings and unpredictable floods would not be there.

Transport is an essential requirement for growth with justice. Again, the land acquisition being a major issue, the strategy in this respect should call for advanced planning for a sufficiently longer future. The planning adopted so far has left us with road structures that would not take care of our requirements in the next decade.

Growth with justice requires providing all citizens with a given facility to live in comfort. While the rich enjoy a lot of benefits and subsidies from the government, the same goes without publicity and public knowledge. Media has apparently downplayed this aspect over the decades for its own obvious reasons. The poor have been doled out cash subsidies that never really reached them as admitted by none other than the prime ministers in the past.

In contrast, the rich people got the land allotted for setting up of industries and have prospered to such a position where from they can now command the government, dictate about even political appointments.

The other important requirement would be power. The power distribution system adopted by the respective state governments has also discriminated against the poor people. To correct this injustice, it immediately calls for the extensive establishment of solar power systems across the rural India so that its domestic power requirements could be taken care.

The farmers' power requirements should be given utmost priority because without agricultural production the manufacturing and other segments of the economy will not be able to deliver optimally.

Strategically, uninterrupted quality power will facilitate improvement in the medical facilities of the areas, and will help in improving the education standards in the rural hinterland. Providing uninterrupted power to rural areas should also help reduce the criminal activities. The contemplated solar power structures can be effectively integrated with regional grids so that the local power shortages can be better managed and efficiently minimized.

The power usage by commercial establishments needs to be controlled. While industrial sector uses the power after due prioritization, there is rampant power wastage by the commercial sector.

Growth with justice requirement set up should have a robust social security mechanism to fall upon for people who have become senior citizens. While it is true that India has a mechanism, it is not adequate. The insufficient and inadequate pension made available to a vast majority of the population does not add any respect to the living of these poor people. The cash subsidies should be supplemented with focused and positively discriminating public services. There should be exclusive cells or counters in each and every government department to cater to senior citizens.

The concept of good governance requires that the well-being of the population in the country has to be ensured by the rulers. It is not necessary for governance to differentiate the subjects on the basis of numbers, like the majority and minority. It will be just to identify and support the needy persons on the scale of their wealth and well being.

In retrospect, all Indian governments have been dealing

with the people on the basis of poverty. It is time for us to sit up and start thinking in terms of handling the public benefits schemes on the basis of wealth. The objective and motive of the schemes should be to build up wealth rather than reducing poverty. There has to be a paradigm shift in our approach to nation building. The performance of any social benefits scheme should be appraised on the basis of wealth that it has been able to create. This helps us in focusing on prosperity building rather than thinking on poverty management. It should bring about a drastic change in the mindset of the people who are supposed to be benefited by such schemes so that they will be prompted to think in terms of maximizing their wealth, properly utilizing the support extended by the state.

The present concept of providing subsidies to the people who are remaining below the poverty line should be dispensed with a new concept whereby people who have prospered out of poverty line should be given more support to become rich and wealthy.

This helps the poor people to think in terms of becoming rich rather than to exert their minds in managing and pretending to be below the poverty line.

Technology has to be used extensively as well as intensively to collate the data on the benefits passed on to the individuals and a very strict monitoring coupled with provisions for penalizing in case of misappropriation of the funds provided by the government under various schemes has to be put in place. This can be effectively put in place synchronizing the adhaar data of not only the beneficiaries but also that of the persons responsible for delivering the benefits.

The information technology domain is witnessing a series of explosions in terms of various innovations. The people across all the segments of the society are flooded with a plethora of information both positive and negative.

The sheer size of the country and the magnitude of the population makes it very difficult for the state to keep a watchful eye on the criminal elements bent upon to spoil the minds of the young and the vulnerable.

As a sequel to this, the country witnessed different communities taking up, sometimes very violent agitations seeking various kinds of reservations rather than campaigning for equal opportunities in various activities including politics.

The political leadership in the country drifted in a wrong and patently dangerous direction where the people have divided themselves into caste and other segments.

This kind of thinking is creating further cracks in the fabric of the society and nation as a whole is becoming more and more vulnerable to the manipulation of the antisocial and unscrupulous political elements.

While the constitution envisages equal opportunities, the approach of various political parties and the intellectuals across the country has been to divide the society into minute fragments seeking to get political mileage from such approaches.

Growth with justice is not feasible unless the state is able to guarantee equal opportunities to all citizens irrespective of caste, creed and religion. However, it is a fact that there is predominant gender-based disparity against women socially, politically, economically, religiously and sexually. Growth with justice is meaningless and mockery if half the population is discriminated against.

The country is witnessing very disturbing incidents whereby the national and federal structure is being challenged.

This is happening primarily because of the ability of anti-national elements to reach out to the vulnerable segments of the population. It is also owing to the inability of the political setup and the intelligence mechanisms to assess the mood prevailing among the various segments and the approaches and tactics being adopted by the anti-national elements. These developments at a deeper level, are indications of the disintegrating faith in the system of governance and the inability of the state to protect the subjects.

While there may not be an immediate panacea to all the ailments engulfing the nation, there is a clear hope across the tunnel. Technology is evolving very fast and rapid, and the growing population is equally eagerly lapping it up. It, however, poses a great challenge to the policy makers and administrators to leverage these emerging technologies to provide transparent and just governance. Technology can be used as a very effective tool to tackle many of the bottlenecks that have crept into the system, crippling the few and far efforts of the administrators.

It is essential to understand the depth and scope of the capability of the technology to deliver justice to the poor, downtrodden and the hapless.

Despite global headwinds and a truant monsoon, India registered robust growth of 7.2 percent in 2014-15 and 7.6 percent in 2015-16, thus becoming the fastest growing major economy in the world.[1]

Adhaar is an excellent and reliable process whereby the identity of a citizen can be established. It forms the foundation to deal with many corrupt modus operandi that has stifled the economy. It can be used to eliminate wastages in terms of subsidies may be related to cooking gas or even bank credit.

Adhaar helps in evolving seamless processes so that false caste certificates, unscrupulous claims for scholarships, pension disbursals and the like can be identified and resolved.

Adhaar also enables banks, state governments, local bodies, gram panchayats and the central government to administer education, health and other benefits to the public at large in a very efficient and professional manner.

Online Registration System (ORS) is a framework to link various hospitals across the country for Aadhaar based online registration and appointment system, where counter based OPD registration and appointment system through Hospital Management Information System (HMIS) has been digitalized.[5]

The JAM (Jandhan Adhaar and Mobile) trinity espoused by India is something for the world to emulate.

The info- graphic data in the economic survey 2015-16 reflects positive outlook, which the state (all government bodies) has to leverage to reach to the people.

The computerization of the land records and the use of satellite prowess support the state in managing both public and private land. It could be put to optimum use for the land is a very scarce resource.

Technology benefits the humanity by helping prediction of weather data to face the disasters more boldly and act informed. This capability, however, is yet to be drilled down to come up with one to one solutions for individual farmers.

India is a nation of farmers. Technology has been used to improve the farming. However, unfortunately, the production of the farm could be increased, but not the income of the farming community. If the state set up really wants, technology has the capability to deal with the information dissemination, inefficiencies, wastages and corruption to some extent. These concerns, even if partially addressed would substantially change the income levels of the farming community.

According to NSS data, the average annual income of the median[*] farmer net of production costs from cultivation is less than R20,000 in 17 states[1]

Irrigation is the life line of any agricultural activity. Technology can help the nation in clearing up the mess that has been created in the areas of life and canal irrigation systems. Improving groundwater level across the geographies ought to be our immediate concern, that can happen by satellite mapping of the ponds, lakes and water bodies and take steps for better management of them.

"As per the latest available data on irrigation, the all India percentage distribution of net irrigated are to the total cropped area during 2012-13 was 33.9 percent. There is a regional disparity in irrigated farming, with net irrigated area to Total cropped area at more than 50 percent in the states of Punjab, Tamil Nadu and Uttar Pradesh, while it is at less than 50 percent in the remaining States. There is a need to scope for increasing the coverage of irrigated area across the country to increase productivity in agriculture."[1]

"The overall irrigation efficiency of the major and medium irrigation projects in India is estimated at around 38 percent. The efficiency of the surface irrigation system can be improved from about 35-40 per cent to around 60 per cent and that of groundwater from about 65-70 per cent to 75 per cent."[1]

---

[*] *Median refers to the median farmer of each state by net income.*

Although water is one of India's most scarce natural resources, India uses 2 to 4 times more water to produce a unit of major food crop than does China and Brazil (Hoekstra and Chapagain [2008]). Hence, it is imperative that the country focuses on improving the efficiency of water use in agriculture.[1]

Produce storage and warehousing are one area where the nation failed miserably. If our system is able to better manage the agricultural produce storage processes, the country need not have to increase the production for a decade. Technology can offer solutions to achieve it, provided the intent is not missing.

Poor marketing facilities, inefficient distribution channels and nonexisting market intelligence are the trinities of epidemics that are sucking out the life out of the farming community. Technology has highly cost effective solutions to address these maladies, provided those in power wake up from slumber and look around.

Power and energy are the twin forces that drive lives of our farmers. Technology has innumerable options and solutions to deal with these issues so that integrated development can happen across the rural landscape.

There is no need to discuss what the technology can do to the other sectors of economy or society for the simple reason that if the farming community of the nation can grow and develop, the rest of the society would automatically get endowed with greater and better opportunities.

For instance, the betterment of the farming community and rural economy should result in reverse migration and have an immediate impact on and reduction in the urban slums and the consequent improvement in the facilities for the urban dwellers.

Growth with justice can take place only if transparency exists and prevails. Technology can support and maintain transparency. Technology empowers people, improves efficiency and sharpens effectiveness. It can also make it difficult to tamper with the systems and easy to identify the aberrations and fix them up. Technology can be a pivot to balance growth and justice.

Before concluding, it is necessary to flag that the media

plays a very important role in harnessing growth with justice. Technology made the media very powerful. But the contemporary media has digressed from the very purpose of its existence and playing its role more in harping on the negative aberrations in the society rather than highlighting positive aspects of governance and promoting constructive criticism. The media should also grow, but with justice to its professional ethics.

Bibliography:

1   Economic Survey 2015-16, Press Information Bureau , Ministry of Finance, Government of India World Economic outlook – January 2016 update

2   Ensusindia.gov.in/Census_And_You/migrations.aspx

3   Census findings point to decade of rural distress. P. Sainath, The Hindu, September 25,2011

4   www.ors.gov.in – Government of India, Ministry of Communications & IT, Department of Electronics and Information Technology

8 GROWTH WITH JUSTICE AND THE PETROLEUM SECTOR, A GLOBAL PERSPECTIVE

(By: Mr. Syed Ghulam Murtuza Rizvi*, Advocate)

Abstract

*T*he use of petroleum is not of recent origin. The Petroleum in the form of Asphalt was used, in the construction of the walls and towers of Babylon; More than four thousand years ago, by which we may infer that there were oil pits near Babylon. The current status of Petroleum as the key component of politics, society, economy and technology has its roots in the early 20th century. The invention of the internal combustion engine was the major influence on the rise and the importance of petroleum.

One of the most striking trends in the beginning of this century is the clear drive towards global integration. With the increasing importance of the international exchange of goods, services and other factors, and the seemingly limitless possibilities offered by new communication technologies, the degree of interdependence of countries and the influence beyond national borders are reaching to the new level of heights. The government's freedom is being reduced and there is a trend of dilution of sovereignty, and the governments are

---

Retired Additional Chief Legal Adviser, ONGC.

forced to consider the conditions imposed on their decisions by the international framework. National spaces, previously fragmented, are being integrated on a global scale. There is an increased prevalence of interdependencies in the international arena. International and National Legal, regulatory and Justice Frameworks, are essential for organizing and running the business and its existence.

1   Petroleum Industry in India

Perhaps no other sector of Indian economy was so much neglected during the British regime as Petroleum. At that time, it was widely believed that except Digboi in Assam, there was no Petroleum elsewhere in India. Though the exploration of hydrocarbon in India commenced in 1866 when Mr. Goodenough of McKillop Stewart Co. drilled a well near Jaypore in Upper Assam and struck oil, but failed to establish satisfactory production. In 1882, the Assam Railway and Trading Company (ARTC), a company registered in London in 1881, with an objective to explore the rich natural resources of Upper Assam, acquired rights for exploration over about 30 sq miles in the same area. The Sub-surface oil exploration activities started in the dense jungles of Assam in North-East India. The first commercial discovery of crude oil in the country was, however, made in 1889 at Digboi. A new company, known as Assam Oil Company (AOC) was formed in 1899 with a capital of £ 310,000 headquartered at Digboi to take over the petroleum interests, including the Makum and Digboi. UK based Burmah Oil Company (BOC) which had a successful oil exploration record in Burma, bought all the shares from ARTC and was appointed a commercial and technical manager of AOC. By 1931, crude oil production has gone up to about 250,000 tonnes per annum and exploration activities were spread all over the Assam-Arakan region. After independence, the Government of India (GoI) realized the importance of oil and gas for rapid industrial development and its strategic role in the defence. Consequently, while framing the Industrial Policy Statement of 1948, the development of petroleum industry in the country was given top priority. In 1955, GoI decided to develop the oil and natural gas resources in the various regions of the country as a part of the sdevelopment of the Public Sector. With this objective, Oil and Natural Gas Directorate (ONGD) was set up towards the end of 1955, as a subordinate office under the then Ministry of Natural Resources and Scientific Research. The department was constituted with a nucleus of geoscientists from the Geological Survey of India (GSI). In April 1956, the GoI adopted the Industrial Policy Resolution, which placed mineral oil industry among the schedule 'A' industries, the future development of which was to be the sole and exclusive responsibility of the state.

Soon, after the formation of ONGD, it became apparent that it would not be possible for the Directorate with its limited financial and administrative powers as a subordinate office of the Government, to function efficiently. So in August 1959, the Directorate was raised to the status of a commission by an act of Parliament with enhanced powers, although it continued to be under the government. The main functions of ONGC subject to the provisions of the Act were "to plan, promote, organize and implement programmes for development of Petroleum Resources and the production and sale of petroleum and petroleum products produced by it, and to perform such other functions as the Central Government may, from time to time, assign to it". ONGC Videsh Limited (OVL) is a company, fully owned by the ONGC, was incorporated with a view to undertaking the overseas exploration and production activities on behalf of ONGC.

Oil India Private Ltd. was incorporated on February 18, 1959. AOC/BOC-owned two-thirds of the shares and the GoI, one-third. On July 27th, 1961, the Government of India and BOC transformed OIL into a Joint Venture Company (JVC) with equal partnership. In October 14th, 1981, OIL became a wholly-owned GoI enterprise by taking over BOC's 50 percent equity and the management of Digboi oil fields changed hands from the erstwhile AOC to OIL.

Offshore exploration was initiated in 1962 through experimental seismic surveys in the Gulf of Cambay. Detailed seismic surveys carried out in the western offshore in 1972-73 resulted in the identification of a large structure in Bombay Offshore which was taken up for drilling in 1974 leading to India's biggest commercial discovery, thereby establishing a new hydrocarbon province. Encouraged by the success at Bombay Offshore, exploratory efforts were expended systematically, and Mumbai High discovery, along with subsequent discoveries of huge oil and gas fields in Western and Eastern offshore has changed the oil scenario of the country.

The liberalized economic policy was adopted by the Government of India in July 1991. Following this, ONGC was re-organized in February 1994 as a limited company under the Companies Act. Directorate General of Hydrocarbon was set up by a Government Resolution in April 1993 through which certain advisory regulatory roles were entrusted but no development role was assigned. In 1997, the GoI, in order to accelerate the pace of exploration efforts in the country, approved the New Exploration Licensing Policy (NELP) by providing a number of attractive fiscal and contractual terms. Till now, nine rounds of NELP have been concluded.

2   Global Petroleum Industry

Most of the world's oil supplies are being controlled by state agencies. The oil industry can be divided into two major categories:

- International Oil Companies (IOCs)
- National Oil Companies (NOCs)

2.1 International Oil Companies (IOCs)

International Oil Companies include familiar names like ExxonMobil and Royal Dutch Shell. These are publicly traded corporations that function like any other corporation except that the product they deal is petroleum. Some information of major IOCs is given below for reference:

Name	Location	Revenue (Billions of Dollars)	Reserve Size in Billions of Barrels
ExxonMobil	Texas – United States	383	72
Royal Dutch Shell	The Hague – Netherlands	368	20
BP/Amoco	London – United Kingdom	308	18
Total SA	Paris – France	229	10.5
Chevron	California – United States	204	10.5
ConocoPhillips	Texas – United States	198	8.3

The American Petroleum Institute divides the industry into five categories based on function.

The industry segments are:

Category	Function
Upstream	Exploration and development of crude
Downstream	Tankers, refineries, and consumers
Pipeline	Any hazardous pipeline, including petroleum, liquid CO2, etc.
Marine	For transport by water of petroleum
Service and Supply (General)	Equipment manufacturers, consulting firms, etc.

Most major companies are referred as "vertically integrated." This means that divisions of the company specialize in various segments of the industry like upstream, downstream, and marine. While all majors participate in upstream and downstream operations, some do not get involved in the pipeline or marine segments. Most have some involvement in service and supply. The upstream segments of most majors are their primary income divisions. Most of the major companies do the majority of the upstream work in the industry and thus derive most of their income from providing these services both for their own oil reserves and to others.

2.2 National Oil Companies

State agencies are called National Oil Companies (NOC) and are set up much like any International Oil Company (IOC). The major difference is that IOCs release earnings reports and have stockholders. In the early history of oil, IOCs were the major producers. In recent decades, NOCs have been organized in most countries with large oil reserves. This trend has occurred mainly for two reasons:

- Political change,
- Industrial progress.

The top ten largest NOCs in the world, in terms of reserve size, are given in the following table. It is important to note that the numbers in the table below are for liquid petroleum and do not include such things as extra heavy petroleum, oil shale, etc.

Name	Location	Reserve Size in Billions of Barrels
Saudi Armaco	Saudi Arabia – Middle East	303
National Iranian Oil Company	Iran – Middle East	300
Quatar Petroleum	Quatar – Middle East	170
Iraq National Oil Company	Iraq – Middle East	134
Petroleos de Venezuela	Venezuela – South America	129
Abu Dhabi National Oil Company	Abu Dhabi – Middle East	126
Kuwait Petroleum Corporation	Kuwait – Middle East	111
Nigerian National Petroleum Corporation	Nigeria – Africa	68
Libya NOC	Libya – Africa	50
Sonatrach	Algeria - Africa	39

3   World Requirement of Petroleum

According to Mr. Pierce Riemer, Director General, World Petroleum Council (https://www.ief.org/news/challenges-and-opportunities-in-the-petroleum-industry-and-   the-role-of-the-wpc) the 'Global oil reserves and production, currently respectively at 1.4 trillion barrels and 87 million b/d, have been growing steadily over the last decades. The main challenge going forward will be not only to meet the increasing demand, which according to most estimates will reach about 110 million b/d by 2030 but, most importantly, to offset the natural decline of the current reservoir productivity. Even if a moderate decline rate of 3.5 percent per year is assumed, by 2030 the production of the reservoirs currently on stream will decrease to about half of today's rate. In summary, the production gap to be met with a new field and reservoir developments is of around 65 million b/d, a daunting task.

Natural gas demand will also steadily increase, particularly in the developing countries, with the current global consumption of approximately 112 tcf per year expected to reach 160 tcf per year by 2030. While the world's natural gas resources are plentiful, at about 6,600 tcf total reserves plus, at least, the same amount of resources from unconventional sources in the United States only, delivering these to the consuming markets will require innovative solutions in production, processing and transportation, and stable geopolitical relations between producing and consuming countries.

To continue meeting the world's demand for oil and natural

gas, the industry will have to invest massive amounts of capital and venture into ever more challenging and costlier production provinces, such as the ultra-deep waters, ultra-deep reservoirs, unconventional resources, and inhospitable environments like the Arctic, remote deserts, jungles, mountain ranges and conflicted areas. It is estimated that the exploration and production activity alone will require a total capital deployment of more than $20 trillion in the next 30 years.

One of the main challenges that the industry is already facing is to continue attracting skilled human resources, both in the technical and managerial areas, to successfully implement such massive projects. In order to attract these talented professionals, the industry will need to improve its overall image, tarnished by the lingering memory of past poor records, some recent highly visible accidents, and reach out to all pools of professionals, particularly the youth and women.

And all of the above will have to be accomplished in a sustainable way, which implies ensuring attractive returns to investors, operating with increasingly higher standards of safety and care with the environment, returning a fair share of the wealth to society and local communities, and doing business in an ethical and regulatory compliant manner.

4   Oil and Gas Industry in India

The oil and gas industry is part of India's six core industries. India was the fourth largest consumer of crude oil and petroleum products in the world. In 2013, it was behind the US, China, and Japan. It's a net importer of crude oil. India's import dependency is ~80%. For domestic consumption, it requires imports of ~77% of demand.

The petroleum sector contributed 1.53 trillion rupees to the Indian Exchequer from April 2013 to March 2014. At 63 rupees to one US dollar, it works out to be $24.3 billion. In the same period, the sector contributed 1.52 trillion rupees to the states. Its total contribution was 3.05 trillion rupees.

5   Subsidies

Subsidies have been an important aspect of India's spending. However, subsidies are debilitating. They're like double-edged swords. When a country is growing, they're necessary to help certain sections of society and the industry. They pressure government finances. Consumers also get used to unrealistically low prices. That's what low gasoline and diesel prices did to Indians.

The pressing need for fiscal consolidation led the government to deregulate gas and diesel. Through a notification on June 25, 2010, gas prices were determined by the market. However, diesel prices were only partially set free. From that period, due to a surge in gasoline prices, a huge difference was created between gasoline and diesel prices. During that time, diesel passenger vehicle sales surged.

However, subsidies on all petroleum products haven't ended. Kerosene and domestic LPG (liquefied petroleum gas) are still subsidized by the government. Kerosene and domestic LPG are used for cooking and other uses.

6   Role of Law and Justice in Growth

One of the most striking trends in the beginning of this century is the clear drive towards global integration. With the increasing importance of the international exchange of goods, services and other factors, and the seemingly limitless possibilities offered by new communication technologies, the degree of interdependence of countries and the influence beyond national borders are reaching to the new level of heights. The government's freedom is being reduced and there is a trend of dilution of sovereignty, and the governments are forced to consider the conditions imposed on their decisions by the international framework. National spaces, previously fragmented, are being integrated on a global scale. There is an increased prevalence of interdependencies in the international arena. International and National Legal, regulatory and Justice Frameworks, are essential for organizing and running the business and its existence.

The Law plays a major role in growth and development. It provides stability and clarity to the society and business. The distribution of wealth, methods of distributive justice, sustainable development and check to corruption can be achieved only through a clearly defined system of Law and Justice. Oil and Gas Law or Petroleum Law is a branch of law which pertains to the acquisition and ownership rights in oil and gas both under the soil before discovery and after its capture, and adjudication regarding those rights.

In most of the European and Asian countries, oil and gas are owned by the national government. In U.S., extraction of oil and gas is by and large regulated by the individual states through statutes and common law. Federal and the constitutional law do apply as well.

6.1 **Rule of Law**

The rule of law has been viewed as an important factor for growth and development. For instance, according to the World Bank, 'a lack of access to justice is itself a central dimension of poverty'. It is an enabling condition for development and growth. It is also a process through which other development outcomes are achieved, that determines which decisions are made, rules are adopted and enforced, and grievances and disputes are resolved.

The UN Secretary General (UNSG) defines it as a "principle of governance in which all persons, institutions and entities, public and private, including the State itself, are accountable to laws that are publicly promulgated, equally enforced and independently adjudicated, and which are consistent with international human rights norms and standards. It requires, as well, measures to ensure adherence to the principles of supremacy of law, equality before the law, accountability to the law, fairness in the application of the law, separation of powers, participation in decision- making, legal certainty, avoidance of arbitrariness and procedural and legal transparency." In any region where the principle of Rule of Law is followed, it gives confidence to the Oil and Gas Companies in doing business in that region.

6.2 **Political Stability**

There is one thing which business leaders and entrepreneurs hate that is the Political instability. Businesses operate according to forecasts and scenarios about the future that comprise surprises as well as certainties, but the one thing that business leaders and entrepreneurs want to avoid at

all costs is the political instability, which results from political gridlock, extremism, and political dysfunction. This is the reason many emerging markets in Asia and Africa either attract or repel foreign investors. Business and industry, including transnational corporations, play a crucial role in the social and economic development of a country. A stable political regime enables and encourages business and industry to operate responsibly and efficiently and to implement longer-term business policies. The growth of the Business and Industry largely depends upon the Stability of Government, the Economic and trade policy of the Government, and the Diplomatic events in surrounding countries. The Political instability can affect the core of any business and industry, in its Decision-making process and the strategic financial decisions, Inconsistencies in the supply chain, sales, and distribution, Business continuing strategies and plans, Safety of human and material resources in an organization, Reputation in the global market, and Expansion vision.

6.3 Legal Stability

Legal stability in the country where the business is going to be run is very essential. It helps in resolution of problems, getting a full assessment of the possible legal and financial risks and to take a better-informed decision. It helps in fully understanding all of the obligations, potential strengths, weaknesses, opportunities and threats to the business. For example, it can help to evaluate environmental liabilities, determining compliances, Tax Liabilities, Labor Laws etc. for a long time. According to economic historian Douglass North countries that protect property rights and establish predictable rules for resolving contract disputes provide a better environment for economic growth than those that do not. He is of the view that the legal system's protection of property rights and enforcement of contracts lowers transaction costs for exchange and allows resources to be transferred to those who can use them in the most productive fashion. Thus, the Legal stability is very crucial and important for the growth of business and industry.

6.4 Corporate Governance

The World Bank's corporate governance assessments have revealed that there is a growing concern around the world regarding corporate governance's importance. The majority of the countries are upgrading their legal and regulatory structures under the Organization for Economic Co-operation and Development's (OECD) principles of corporate governance. Companies heavily depend on external funds to finance their activities, investment and most importantly, growth. Thus, it is a very important concern to assure the financers that their money is being used efficiently and that the management is utilizing it for the best interests of the company. Healthy Corporate Governance as established by law creates wealth, jobs and financially sound enterprises; which ultimately results in growth. It also helps in the growth of society in following areas:

- To raise capital in easier way;
- To lower the cost of capital;
- Improvement in business and economic performance;
- Good impact on share price.

All these factors ultimately help in the growth of business and industry.

6.5 Corruption

The corruption is futile and frustrates the society. A society with corruption cannot possibly enjoy leaps and bounds of sustainable economic growth and development. Corruption is now recognized to be one of the world's greatest challenges. It is a major hindrance to sustainable development, with a disproportionate impact on poor communities and is corrosive on the very fabric of society. It impedes the economic growth, distorts competition and causes serious legal and reputational risks. Corruption is also very costly for business, with the extra financial burden estimated to add 10 % or more to the costs of doing business in many parts of the world.

The rapid development of Law and justice around the world is also prompting the governments and business companies to focus on anti-corruption measures as part of their mechanisms to protect their reputations and interests. The internal controls are increasingly being extended to a range of ethics and integrity issues.

The international legal fight against corruption has gained momentum in more recent times through the Organization for Economic Cooperation and Development (OECD) 1997 Convention on Combating Bribery of Foreign Public Officials in International Business Transactions and through the entering into force of the first globally agreed instrument; the United Nations Convention Against Corruption (UNCAC) – adopted in Merida, Mexico in December 2003- on the 14th of December 2005. The Arab Convention against Corruption was signed by both the ministers of interior affairs and ministers of justice of all state members of the Arab League (save for Somalia) on the 21st of December 2010.

On the 24th of June 2004 during the United Nations Global Compact Leaders Summit, it was announced that the UN Global Compact henceforth includes a tenth principle against corruption. The Principle reads as follows: "businesses should work against corruption in all its forms, including extortion and bribery." The adoption of the 10th Principle commits UN Global Compact participants not only to avoid bribery, extortion and other forms of corruption but also to develop policies and concrete programs to address corruption.

6.6 Dispute resolution

Litigation, arbitration, and expert determination are the most common methods of dispute resolution into oil and gas industry. These mechanisms have their own set of pros and cons.

6.6.1 Litigation

6.6.1.1 PROS

- The process is formal with both sides given the opportunity to plead and lead their evidence in support of their pleading.
- The verdict is final and binding, subject to appeal.
- The process is open to the public.
- It creates precedent for future disputes.

6.6.1.2 CONS

- The process is formal and involves lawyers and judges, who are in fact a foreign party to the dispute and usually lack awareness of oil and gas contract technicalities.

- The decision is final, but appealable which could result in another round of litigation.

- It's open to the public, oil and gas industry is a closely knit fraternity and requires confidentiality.

- The decision is enforceable but difficult to enforce in a foreign jurisdiction unless an agreement exists between the two countries.

- It's costly and time-consuming.

- Litigation may end up in a business divorce between the contesting parties.

6.6.2 Arbitration

6.6.2.1 PROS

- Parties have the right to choose the arbitrator or institution

- Process is done in private, confidentiality is maintained, which is crucial in the oil and gas sector.

- More flexible than litigation and can be customized according to disputant needs.

- The award of arbitrator or institution is easily enforced in countries that have ratified the 1958 New York Convention and Geneva Protocol.

- Cost element may be lesser than that of litigation and may consume lesser time.

- The disputants are free to choose the venue and platform for arbitration.

6.6.2.2 CONS

- It may become much expensive and time consuming if

any party decides to prolong the proceedings.

- Arbitration has the potential to become as formal as litigation in case of adverse parties.

- Limited scope of appeal.

- The decision may not be enforceable in countries that are signatories of 1958 New York Convention or Geneva Protocol.

6.6.3 Expert determination

6.6.3.1 PROS

- Matters can proceed behind closed doors and confidentiality is maintained.

- If parties have agreed to bind with expert determination then the dispute outcome is final.

- It is much faster and cheaper than litigation and arbitration, and less formal.

- The business relations usually remain intact.

- Gives flexibility to choose their own set of rules and regulations.

6.6.3.2 CONS

- Narrow margin of it being appealed other than fraud and manifest error.

- This method is usually used to determine the technical and financial side of dispute.

- The expert or umpire concludes the outcome based on his own findings and there are no rules for natural justice or due process to be followed.

- Not easily enforceable until there is a bilateral agreement between Parties.

7 Laws of Oil Extraction

1- In United States of America subsurface rights to oil and gas go with the surface title, unless specifically separated.

However, in most other areas of the world subsurface rights are not owned by the surface rights owner; instead they are owned by the national government.

2- In Mexico all ownership rights to oil, in the state, is to the government. Mexico undertook important reforms to its oil industry. The country opened some oil, gas, and electricity industries to foreign and private companies. The state owned oil companies will still have the opportunity to set aside some fields for themselves. With the reforms, the government hopes to increase output to 3 million barrels by 2018 and 3.5 million by 2025, by attracting private companies with the expertise and technology to exploit the country's vast shale and deep water reserves.

3- In Canada, mineral rights are owned by the state. But this was not always the case. Prior to 1887, settlers were given subsurface rights to their land and retain them, selling them with their above ground rights over time. These freeholds still make up about 10% of the Canadian oil market. Additionally, lands owned by the federal instead of provincial governments, make up about another 10%of the market. Under the Canadian system, where mineral rights are vested in the government, the private energy sector pays about $26 billion in taxes and royalties to the government to exploit these resources. This revenue is raised in three different stages. First, exploration rights are sold to private oil and gas companies. Second, royalties are paid by the oil companies based on the amount of oil and gas produced. And finally, corporate taxes are collected on oil company income.

4- In Great Britain, the Petroleum Act of 1934 provides that ownership of oil and gas reserves automatically vest in the Crown, regardless of where they are found. Interestingly enough, in Great Britain only the subsurface rights to hydrocarbons, gold and silver vest in the Crown, not other minerals. Private exploration and development, including for offshore oil under the Continental Shelf Act, requires a license from the government.

5- Middle East Oil Concessions: The law governing oil exploration and extraction in the Middle East has been of particular interest to oil companies and the global marketplace. Many of the states in the region are monarchies and some are even dictatorships, and oil and gas rights are controlled by the government, not landowners. After the initial discovery of oil, but before such nations had the technological know-how, Middle Eastern leaders (as well as governments in Latin America) invited private oil companies to explore and produce oil reserves located in their lands. These arrangements took the form of concession agreements.

Concessions agreements are arrangements whereby oil-rich countries contract with international oil companies to develop their reserves. Typically, a concession agreement will include provisions that provide for stock ownership in the local company undertaking the exploration, a bonus upon signing the agreement, an obligation on the part of the oil company to pay a royalty percentage to the government based upon oil produced and the exclusivity / duration of the rights to develop the reserves. In 1933, the King of Saudi Arabia granted Standard Oil a 60 year concession to develop reserves in an area almost 500,000 square miles for only £50,000 a minimal sum. The United States did not obligate the oil company in this way. The company has to release the land if they were not developing it. Often times, international oil companies would also negotiate to not incur tax liabilities in the host countries. In United States, individuals who leased their land to oil companies to develop reserves, typically enjoyed standard clauses, which called for a fixed royalty of one eighth of the amount of oil produced, as well as a fixed primary term during which the lease would terminate, if no oil was produced. Characteristics of International Petroleum Agreements At present, international petroleum agreements used by host governments to grant operating rights to private oil companies typically take one of the following three forms:

1. Form contracts. These agreements between the host government and an oil company are governed by detailed and rigid legal codes which may prescribe not only the conditions under which rights will be granted, but also the forms of such rights. In such a system, the government does not have much latitude to customize individual contracts. Rigid agreements such as these are commonly used in the United States, Canada, and Australia and between international oil companies and the governments in Latin America and Western

European nations. This structure allows for the achievement of general policy objectives while imposing a standardized system that makes oversight and enforcement easier and more effective. However, as a disadvantage, it lacks flexibility and does not allow the host government to adjust the terms of its agreements over time.

2. Ad hoc contracts This type of system authorizes a state commission or national oil company to negotiate and execute ad hoc agreements with individual foreign oil companies. For example, a national oil company may negotiate contracts with foreign companies for exploration and development and customize each individual contract to allow, for example, differences in duration, exclusivity and royalty rates. An ad hoc mechanism gives a state agency considerable latitude in negotiations, allowing the country to structure more attractive proposals than they otherwise might be offered. On the other hand, it creates uncertainty among investors and results in highly complex agreements that may be hard to monitor, leaving open the possibility of corruption.

3. Hybrid contracts These contracts are a combination of the hybrid approach that permits a degree of flexibility in formulating each transaction and form of contracts. This method is beginning to be used in an increasing number of countries. A hybrid mechanism allows for flexibility and assures adherence to public policies through non-negotiable minimum conditions. But it would still contain some of the complexity of ad hoc contracts that can lead to enforcement difficulties.

8. Process for awarding international petroleum contracts

A host government will follow one of three types of procedure in awarding a private international oil company the right to develop oil reserves:

Complete government discretion Under such a system, the host government retains complete discretion over the selection of a licensee or contractor to develop oil reserves. This procedure allows the government to select the best investor and adjust license term.

Public auctions A host government may also hold a public auction for the purpose of selecting the licensee. This procedure allows for competitive pricing and a pre-screening of bidders. This system also requires all terms other than those being bid on to be determined in advance.

Open competition Finally, a host government may hold an open competition based on an announcement of general terms by the government. This procedure provides assurance that the winning bid maximizes the financial benefit that can be extracted by the government for a license under the circumstances. However, this system is inherently inflexible except for the few terms being bid upon. It favors big firms that can make large bonus payments and, like public auctions, it requires state licensing boards to be experts on developing offers.

9. Structure of international petroleum investment contracts

Such contracts take one of three forms:

1. Concession or license A concession is much like the system of federal land leases utilized in the United States. Such an agreement provides the oil company with an exclusive right to explore and produce and is further governed by work commitments that require government approval. The revenues flow to the host government in the traditional forms, which includes royalties, bonuses, rentals and taxes. In the concession or license agreement, the government does not bear any of the production or exploration risks.

2. Production Sharing Agreement (PSA). A PSA gives the oil company a specified area and uses a portion of the oil produced to pay for the oil company's investment and operational costs. The remaining oil produced is shared between the host government and the foreign firm. Alternatively, the host government could require that the firms compensate them in cash. This can be accomplished through entering into a risk service agreement, which is effectively the same as a

PSA, only that the payments are in cash as opposed to oil. Under a PSA arrangement, both the host country and the private oil company may bear the risk of exploration and production if agreed.

3. Technical service contract (TSC). In a TSC the host country pays for an oil company to come in and provide services or technical assistance, paying them a flat fee for their help. The host country can pay them a portion of production, such as two dollars a barrel produced, but the oil company must also be paid for exploratory wells regardless of whether they produce oil. In this arrangement the host country bears the risk in exploration and shifts in market prices. However, once oil producing nation has in place the infrastructure and gains the knowledge to produce oil on their own, without the assistance of independent oil companies, host governments often no longer wish to be restrained by agreements such as TSCs. In such a circumstance, a host government could move to nationalization the oil production process.

10. Legal Due Diligence

The aim and purpose of Legal Due Diligence to verify the information provided about the business and the place of business is correct; and to discover any undisclosed problems, getting full assessment of the possible legal risks and to take a better informed decision. For any person or business entity doing business in any field or area, an intensive legal investigation is the first steps. It would include fully understanding all of the obligations, potential strengths, weaknesses, opportunities and threats. For example, to evaluate environmental liabilities, determining compliances, Tax Liabilities, Labour Laws etc are some of the important factors which should be examined. A systematic research to gather the critical facts and descriptive information are most relevant to making an informed decision in the matter.

Bibliography:

1. https://users.wfu.edu/palmitar/Courses/Energy%20La w/Wiki%20Book/Chapters/04%20-%20Int'l%20Petroleum.pdf.

2. http://marketrealist.com/2014/12/indias-oil-industry-stand/

3. http://home.uchicago.edu/~tginsburg/pdf/articles/Does LawMatterForEco nomicDevelopment.pdf

9 ISLAMIC BANKING ENTERING THE INDIAN MARKETS WITH SPECIAL REFERENCE TO GROWTH WITH JUSTICE

(By: Dr. Syed Mohammad Ali Rizvi[*], Prof. Somesh Kumar Shukla[**] and Ms. Guncha Fatima[***])

Abstract

The Reserve Bank of India (RBI) is in correspondence with the government of India to look into ways to bring in new rules to accommodate the concept of Islamic banking, informed RBI Governor D Subbarao, speaking at the Jawaharlal Institute of Postgraduate Medical Education & Research, Puducherry. On the other hand in January 2010 a division bench of the Kerala High Court had stayed all further move by the state-owned Kerala State Industrial Development Corp (KSIDC) to set up an Islamic bank but in Feb 2011 the division bench of the Kerala High Court dismissed the writ petitions filed against the government sanction for starting a non-banking finance company by the KSIDC, based on Islamic principles.

Interest free banking or Islamic banking has experienced global growth rates of 10-15 percent per annum, and has been

[*] Assistant Professor, Department of Business Administration, Unity Degree College, Lucknow, Uttar Pradesh, India. E-mail: mohdali_rizvi@yahoo.co.in
[**] Professor and Head, Department of Commerce, University of Lucknow, Uttar Pradesh, India
[***] Researcher, Lucknow, Uttar Pradesh, India

moving in number of Muslim countries at such a rapid pace that Islamic financial institutions are present today in over 51 countries. Despite this consistent growth, many other Countries like India Bangladesh remain unfamiliar with the process of Islamic banks. The countries based on conventional banking are trying to adopt Interest free banking (Conventional Banking vs. Interest-free Banking) to achieve socio-economic and financial goal. This paper attempts to shed some light in this area by describing the main pillars or principles' of Interest free banking. The study explores the differences in conventional and interest free institutions. The major thrust to acknowledge about the beginning of interest free banking in India with the aim to remove the two main crisis- interests on loan to rural population and inflationary pressure in the economy.

Keywords: *Islamic Banking, Planning Commission, Inflation, Zakat, Shariah.*

1 The Banking Business, as we know it:

In India the Banking Regulation Act, 1949 defines banking as "accepting for the purpose of lending or investment, of deposit of money from the public, repayable on demand or otherwise......". Thus a banking company must perform both the actions, (i) accepting of deposits and (ii) lending or investing the same. The explanation to Section 5 (c) makes it clear that any company which is engaged in the manufacture of goods or carries on any trade and which accepts deposit of money from the public merely for the purpose of financing its business as such manufacturer or trader shall not be deemed to transact the business of banking.

Thus in nutshell bankers are traders in debt as they borrow money from the public by accepting funds deposited on current accounts, by accepting term deposits, and by issuing debt securities such as banknotes and bonds and lend money by making advances to customers on current accounts, by making installment loans, and by investing in marketable debt securities and other forms of money lending and profit from the difference between the level of interest paid for deposits and other sources of funds, and the level of interest charged in lending activities which is generally called The Spread.

2 Islamic Banking:

India is probably the birth place of modern Islamic Banking as far as the ideology is concerned. Maulana Maududi (1961), Muhammad Hamidullah (1944, 1955, 1957 and 1962) and Mohammad Nejatullah Siddiqi (1969) are among the first authors to propound the idea. However, much of the basis for modern Islamic Banking is provided by Iqtisaduna (English: "Our Economics"), written between 1960 and 1961, by prominent Shia cleric Muhammad Baqir al-Sadr. A O Abudu (1996) and Muhammad Taqi Usmani (1998) may be quoted as two of the recent authors in the series, who have written on the subject post facto i.e., after Islamic banking system has become established in many places.

Although all major religions and ancient philosophers and thinkers did not like interest, and although interest of any kind was completely forbidden by Islam, a modern society cannot exist without its banking system. The banking system, provides the capital for our enterprises, collecting funds from those who do not wish to claim their full share of consumption goods at present (the savers) and making them available to those who wish to spend more funds than they have at present (the borrowers). Some of the borrowers are of course mere consumers, who are borrowing to buy consumer goods and services, but the more significant group are those borrowing to set up or expand business, and thus create wealth for the nation.

3 Islamic Banks and Shariah Boards:

Most of the Islamic banks are working under the supervision of their Shariah Boards. They bring their day to day problems before the Shariah scholars, who examine them in the light of Islamic rules and principles and give specific rulings about them. Thus, if a practice is held to be un-Islamic by them, a suitable alternative is also sought by the joint efforts of the Shariah scholars and the management of Islamic banks.

Islamic Banks and India:

The Report of Working Group to Examine Financial

Instruments used in Islamic Banking (2006) elucidated that the mode of working of Islamic Banks (as we have seen above) does not permit them to be called "Banks" in India by the Banking Regulation Act, 1949 because of their involvement in equity participation in their borrowers' business and their involvement in sale purchase. The Raghuram Rajan Committee Report (2008), however recommended interest-free banking to be allowed to run side by side with main stream banking. While in the mutual fund space, we already have many Shariah compliant funds.

According to the Financial Express (Nov 04, 2010):

Tata Group's investment unit is seeking to attract about $100 million within three years to India's first Shariah-compliant fund aimed at global investors, targeting equities in a country that lacks regulations for establishing an Islamic debt market.

Interest free banking is based on Islamic law *(Shariah)*. It is known as Islamic banking. An Islamic bank is based on the Islamic faith and must stay within the limits of Islamic Law or the *Shariah* called *fiqh muamalat* (Islamic rules on transactions). The original meaning of the Arabic word *sharia* was 'the way to the source of life' and it is now used to refer to legal system in keeping with the code of behavior called for by the Holly Qur'an.

During the Islamic Golden Age, early forms of proto-capitalism in Caliphate, where an early market economy and an early form of mercantilism were developed between the 8th-12th centuries, which refer to as Islamic capitalism. The monetary economy of the period was based on widely circulated currency Dinar. A number of economic concepts were applied in early Islamic banking counting bills of exchange, partnership (mufawada) such as limited partnerships (mudaraba), and forms of capital (al-mal), capital accumulation (nama al-mal), cheques, promissory note, trust (Waqf), loaning, ledgers and assignments. Many of these early capitalist concepts were adopted and further advanced in medieval Europe from the 13th century onwards.

Interest free banking has been defined as banking in agreement with the culture and value system of Islam and governed, in addition to the conventional good governance and risk management rules, by the principles laid down by Islamic Shariah. Interest free banking is a narrow concept denoting a number of banking instruments or operations, which avoid interest. It prohibits the charging of interest because Islam considers interest an unjustified increase of capital, with no effort made to earn it, it is considered of false value therefore it is prohibited. It is also avoid unethical practices and participate actively in achieving the goals and objectives of an Islamic economy.

4   Four pillars for foundation of interest-free banking:

Owing to the growing demand by the Muslim population in Western countries and also to the increasing interest of Islamic investors mostly from the Gulf region to diversify geographically their portfolios, conventional banks are increasingly becoming interested in entering the market of Islamic financial products. Unfortunately, it is often the case that these institutions in many countries are not entirely familiar with the range of principles governing Interest free or Islamic banking. The basic four principles are very helpful in making balanced economy.

a)   The absence of Riba or interest based transactions:

Riba refers to the addition in the amount of the principal of a loan according to the time for which it is loaned and the amount of the loan. In banning *riba,* Islamic seeks to establish a society based upon fairness and justice (Qur'an 2.239). A loan provides the lender with a fixed return irrespective of the outcome of the borrower's business enterprise. It is much fairer to have a sharing of the profits and losses. Fairness in this context has two dimensions: the supplier of capital possesses a right to reward, but this reward should be equal with the risk and effort involved and thus be governed by the return on the individual project for which funds are supplied. Hence, fixed return is forbidden in Islam. The sharing of profit is legal and that practice has provided the foundation for Islamic banking.

b) The avoidance of economic activities Gharar involving speculation:

Gharar mean buying goods or shares at low and selling them for higher price in the future is considered to be unlawful. Similarly an immediate sale in order to avoid a loss in the future is condemned. The reason is that speculators generate their private gains at the expense of society at large. By avoiding the speculations leads to equitable distribution of income and wealth. The poor people would get the share of Income.

c) The introduction of an Islamic tax, zakat:

A mechanism for the redistribution of income and wealth is basic in Islam, so that every Muslim is guaranteed a fair standard of living, *(nisab)*. An Islamic tax, *Zakat* (a term derived from the Arabic *zaka,* meaning "pure") is the most important instrument for the redistribution of wealth. This tax is a compulsory levy, one of the five basic tenets of Islam and the generally accepted amount of the *zakat* is one fortieth (2.5 per cent) of Muslim's annual income in cash or kind from all forms of assessed wealth exceeding *nisab*. Every Islamic bank has to establish a *zakat* fund for collecting the tax and distributing it exclusively to the poor directly or through other religious institutions. This tax is imposed on the initial capital of the bank, on the reserves, and on the profits as described in the Handbook of Islamic Banking.

d) The discouragement of the production of goods & services which contradict the value pattern of Islamic; haram:

It is forbidden for Islamic banks to finance activities or items forbidden in Islam, *haram*, such as trade of alcoholic beverage and pork meat. While the production and marketing of luxury activities (*israf-wa-traf*) is considered as unacceptable from a religious viewpoint. A strict code of 'ethical investment' operates in *haram*.

5 Conventional *vs.* Islamic banking

The main difference between Islamic and conventional banks lies in the fact that conventional banks charge and pay interest, whereas Islamic banks do not consider interest as *riba*. Even with such, Islamic law does not require that the seller of a product be Muslim, or that its services also be Islamic.

An Islamic bank is similar to a modern western bank in almost all functions which empower it to mediate any shortcomings or surpluses that may exist in a monetary exchange economy. The Islamic bank requires a careful management team to balance the different levels of credit (personal credit, secured credit, letters of credit), and also functions as a specialist in estimating projects risks and estimated returns. Many gulf countries have the Islamic banking system and they follow the principles due to their affirmative system. The difference among two has shown in table-a. The concept of Islamic banking is the base of their business. The list of Islamic bank in Middle East is given in table-b. The trend of Islamic Banking has been followed by other countries too. It is expanding not only in nations with majority Muslim populations, but also in other countries where Muslims are a minority, such as the United Kingdom or Japan. Similarly, countries like **India,** the Kyrgyz Republic, and Syria have recently granted, or are considering granting, licenses for Islamic banking activities. In fact, there are currently more than 300 Islamic financial institutions spread over 51 countries, plus well over 250 mutual funds that comply with Islamic principles. Over the last decade, this industry has experienced growth rates of 10-15 percent per annum a trend that is expected to continue.

6 Movement of interest-free banking or Islamic banking in India:

6.1 Planning Commission Recommendation

In August 2007, Govt. of India under the Planning Commission constituted a high level committee on Financial Sector reforms (CFSR) under the chairmanship of Dr. Raghuram Rajan, former chief economist; IMF along with other eleven members CFSR submitted its final report in Sept. 2008 to Prime Minister with the specific recommendation of interest free banking in the country

6.2 Kerala entering into Interest-free Banking

Another significant development has taken place in the state of Kerala. Govt. of Kerala under KSIDC (Kerala State Industrial Development Corporation) has taken a courageous and commendable step to form an Islamic Investment company named Al Barakah Financial Services Company, Non-Banking financial Companies (NBFC) after a thorough reasonable report undertaken by a reputed international consulting firm Ernst & Young. This NBFC will be turned into a global Islamic bank as soon as the RBI accommodates it after an amendment in the Banking regulations.

The court order petition had been filed by a Janata Party leader and others. According to "The Economic Times" Feb 04, 2011, the bench observed that when KSIDC proposed to carry on NBFC business in accordance with Shariah law in addition to complying with the laws of the country. The company, Al Barakh Financial Services, has welcomed the green signal for its venture. "It is a very favourable development and the board of directors will meet to decide on the plan of action," said by Al Barakh director.

If we study the concepts and practices associated with Islamic banking or Interest free banking and contrast them with those of conventional banking we shall find that Islamic banking can better serve the latest socio-economic goals which are professed by most of the developed and developing countries. Therefore like India, In Bangladesh too, Islamic banking is being started very shortly both in public and private sectors. As in India 70 percent of rural population working on high interest paid on loan and Inflation is the main cause of economic crunch. The Interest free Banking will be the best to control inflation and also beneficial to the rural sector. In this article we shall examine some superior features of Interest free banking with two major factors in India.

7 Special effects of interest-free banking on india:

Rural Sector:

The interest-based conventional banks have remained traditionally urban oriented and have left an institutional vacuum in the rural areas. This vacuum has facilitated the money lenders to a great extent. The private money lenders operating in the informal sector charge excessive interest, encourage default, manipulate accounts and find excuse to remove the securities. The money lenders are rich through these exploitative means, i.e. high rate of interest and liquidation of the income-earning securities. It is rising, richer and the poor borrower, still poorer. Recently in India, these conventional banks are required to move to the rural areas, but their way of financing and recovery forces the borrower to off load their crop immediately on harvesting. This reduces their money income and increases the fluctuation of crop prices to the disadvantage of the growers and borrowers. While if one country which is having a total approach to the issue has introduced mechanisms of Islamic banking i.e. *Bai-muajjal, Bai-salam* and interest-free loan. Through the process of *Bai-Muajjal* which means sale on deffered payment basis, agricultural inputs are being supplied to the farmers. This process combines credit and input supply and works as a safeguard against diversion of funds. Needless to mention, diversion of funds generally reduces the productivity of loans, causes inflation. Thus this Islamic mechanic is a definite improvement over traditional loaning. Similarly, through the mechanics of *Bai-salam*, a bank makes advance purchase of future crop at a reasonable price. This mechanism solves the marketing problem of the client farmers and works as or safeguard against price fall during harvesting period. Simultaneously it ensures recovery of bank's money advanced through *bai-muajjal* or interest-free loan. The marginal farmers who cannot be served through either *bai-muajjal* or *bai-salam* are being provided with interest-free loan.

Inflation:

Islamic banking by abolishing interest creates an anti-inflatioary effect in the economy. Let us analyze the contribution of interest to inflation. In an interest-based framework as followed by India, the depositors receive interest as to their money income despite their functioning. On the other hand, the interest paid by the borrowers' entrepreneur is added to the cost of production. The later rate (lending rate) is always 5 to 6% higher than the former (deposit rate). Thus, increased money in come and inflated cost of production both caused by interest are two built-in causes of inflation in an interest-based-economy. Moreover they do not remain static. The deposit rate, which is always lower than the lending rate and inflation to the extent of cost of intermediation, has a tendency to catch up with the inflation rate which pushes the cost further up. Moreover, the higher the rate of interest, the higher will be the opportunity cost of capital and expectation about the future remaining the same the lower will be the incentive for real investment. The lower real investment will result in lower production and lower supply of goods and services. This will add to the inflationary pressure further. Thus in our interest based economy there is a secular rise of prices. Abolition of interest removes these three basic built-in-causes of inflation in India.

8   Concluding thoughts:

Interest-free Banking can be main tool with accordance to Islamic principles and laws; it is based on the principle of sharing risk, and profit/loss between financial institutions and individuals. One major difference between Islamic banks and conventional banks is the prohibition of interest on loans, given the fact that Islam does not allow unjustified capital increases, and also it emphasizes on deriving capital increase through investment and going through full economical cycle. The number of Muslim countries adopted the Interest free Banking, followed by the favorable impacts the other Nations like India, Bangladesh also trying to adopt the same banking pattern. As India has two major factors of financial and economic crisis i.e. major of population in rural India has been suffering from interest on loan taken and inflationary pressures. In India, Islam is the second-most practiced religion after Hinduism, with more than 13.4% of the country's population i.e. over 138 million as per 2001 census. Thus, Interest free banking would be the apt decision to the economy. We can say with the adoption of Interest free Banking in India - "Banking is now about cooperating in the morning so that you can compete in the afternoon"

Conventional Bank vs. Islamic Banking
Table-a

Difference	Conventional Banking	Interest free or Islamic Banking
Principles	Manmade	Islamic sharia
Rate of Interest	Predetermined RoI	Risk sharing between investors & entrepreneur
Profit	Profit maximizing without any restrictions	Profit maximizing subject to sharia restrictions
Zakat	It does not deal with zakat	Zakat collection centres are available and they also payout their zakat
Key function	Lending money and getting it back with compounding interest	Participation in partnership business
Penalty	Penalty & Compound interest in case of defaulters	No provision to charge any extra money from the defaulters. Rebates are given for early settlement at the Bank's discretion.
Growth	Own interest becoming prominent, no efforts to ensure growth with equity	It gives due importance to the public interest. Its ultimate aim is to ensure growth with equity.
Relations to clients	Creditors & debtors	of partners, investors and trader, buyer and seller
Emphasis	on credit-worthiness of the	On the viability of the projects.

	clients	
Guarantees	All its deposits	can only guarantee deposits for deposit account, which is based on the principle of al-wadiah, thus the depositors are guaranteed repayment of their funds, however if the account is based on the mudarabah concept, client have to share in a loss position

Major Islamic Banks in the Middle East Table-b

BAHRAIN	UAE	IRAN
Bahrain Islamic Bank	Dubai Islamic Bank	Bank Melli Iran
ABC Islamic Bank (E.C.)	Abu Dhabi Islamic Bank	Bank Sederat Iran
Shamil Bank	National Bank of Sharjah	Bank Mellat
Noriba Bank	QATAR	Bank Tejarat
Gulf Finance House	Qatar Islamic Bank	Bank Sepah
Albaraka Bank Bahrain	Qatar International Islamic Bank	Bank Refah
Citi Islamic Investment Bank E.C.	Qatar Islamic Insurance Company	Export Development Bank of Iran
First Islamic Investment Bank	KUWAIT	Bank Sanaat o Maadan
Al-Amin Bank , Bahrain	Kuwait International Bank (K.S.C.)	Bank Keshavarzi

JORDAN	Kuwait Finance House	Bank Maskan
Jordan Islamic Bank	Boubyan Bank (K.S.C.)	Karafarin Bank
Islamic International Arab Bank	LEBANON	Saman Bank
SAUDI ARABIA	Al-Baraka Bank Lebanon	Bank Eghtesad-e-Novin
Islamic Development Bank		Bank Parisian
Al Baraka Investment & Development Co.		

9   Conclusions:

It seems very probable that Islamic Banking is going to start in India in a few years and the economists, CAs, financial managers and lawyers will have to deal with this new concept in the country soon. They must get themselves ready with the necessary expertise in the field.

Bibliography:

1. Muhammad Bāqir as-Sadr, Iqtisaduna, Our Economics, Volume One — Part One , wofis , world organization for Islamic services Tehran – Iran

2. S M Masood Azhar Rezvi, "Implications of Islamic Banking and Finance Entering the Indian Markets" *Commerce and Business Studies*; Faizabad, India (July 2013).

3. Michael Silva, "Islamic Banking Remarks" *Law and Business Review of the Americas*; (Spring 2006).

4. Literature," *Finance India* (April/May 2004).

5. Ibid.

6. Farhad F. Ghannadian and Gautam Goswami, "Developing economy banking: the case of Islamic banks," *International*

7. *Journal of Social Economics* (2004).

8. Silva, "Islamic Banking Remarks."

9. Abdul Gafoor, A.L.M., 1995. Interest-free Commercial Banking. Groninigen, The Netherlands: Apptec Publications.

10. Ahmed, Z., Iqbal, M., and Khan, M. f., 1983. Money and Banking in Islam. Jaddah: international Centre for Research in Islamic Economics, King Abdul Aziz University.

11. Algaoud, L. M. and Lewis, M. k., 1997. Bahrain as an International Centre for Islamic Baking, Proceedings of international Conference on Accounting, Commerce & Finance. The Islamic Perspective, University of West Sydney, Macarthur.

12. Arif M. (ed), 1982. monetary policy in an interest free Islamic economy: nature and scope in Arif, M. (ed), Monetary and Fiscal Economic of Islam, Jaddah: International Centre for Research in Islamic Economics.

13. Handbook of Islamic Banking, 1977-86. Published in

Arabic by the International Association of Islamic Banks, 6 Vols., Cairo.

14. Islamic finance: Turning the Prophet's profits. Economist, 8/24/96, Vol. 340 Issue 7980, p58, 2p.

15. Janahi, A. L., 1995. Islamic Banking, Concept, Practice and Future, 2nd edition. Manama: Bahrain Islamic Bank.

16. Khalaf, Roula: Banking the Islamic way. World Press Review, Jan. 95, Vol. 42 Issue 1, p35, 5/6p.

17. Khan, M S., 1986. Islamic interest-free banking: A Theoretical Analysis, IMF Staff Papers, Vol. 33, No. 1, pp. 1-25.

Website:

1. www.imf.org/external/pubs/ft/wp/2007/wp07175.pdf

2. www.ibtra.com/pdf/journal/v4_n2_article1.pdf

3. http://en.wikipedia.org/wiki/Islamic_banking

4. www.finance-trading-times.com/.../2208-shariah-compliant-islamic-banking. html

5. www.shariabanking.info/

6. http://en.wikipedia.org/wiki/Islam_in_India

10 HIGHER EDUCATION AND THE SOCIO-ECONOMIC DEVELOPMENT OF INDIAN MINORITIES

(By: Mr. Mohammad Allam)*

Abstract

*A*s per the census 2011, the total population of Indian minorities is about 19 percent. Among the minorities, the percentage of the population of Muslims is about 14.2 percent, Christian 2.3 percent, Sikhs 1.7 percent, Buddhists 0.7 percent, Jain 0.4 percent etc. The largest minority community is Muslims which constitute more than 70 percent of the total population of the minorities.*

In term of higher education, Muslims whose percentage is about 13 percent (2012-13AISHE), is the most backward community among the minorities communities. The present paper has comparatively studied the relationship between higher education and socio-economic development among minorities of India. The paper has taken higher education as a focal point of socio-economic development. The minority community which is much advanced in higher education has achieved much higher social development too.

This paper is important for the point of view of understanding

PG Teacher, Minto Circle, AMU Aligarh.
E-mail: *mohammad_allam@rediffmail.com*

A compendium of papers presented for the national seminar of April 10, 2016 organised by the LEAD Trust and Unity Degree College, Lucknow, India

the role of higher education in the socio-economic development of minorities of the country.

The present paper has adopted a descriptive analytical method based on secondary data derived from various sources like Sachar committee, Ministry of minority Affairs, MHRD, NSSO etc.

Key Words: Minority; Higher education; Census survey; Socio-economic development; GER; Make in India

1   Introduction

India is the second largest country in the world after China in term of population. According to Census 2011, the total population of India is 1.21 billion[1].The total populations of minorities (here in term of religion) is about 19 percent. There are six minority communities in India. The last community which declared as minority community is Jain.[2]At present, there is six government declared minority communities in India.[3]   Among all the minority communities, Muslim is in a dominant position with the largest numbers while the numbers of Parsis is merely 69000(2001); very negligible to the total population of the country and minority communities. So, the data related to Parsi uses to be omitted by the various studies.

There is a strong relationship between socio-economic development and higher education which the UNESCO acknowledges in its World Declaration on Higher Education for the Twenty- First Century: Vision and Action. As per the UNESCO "Higher education has given ample proof of its viability over the centuries and of its ability to change and to induce change and progress in society. Owing to the scope and pace of change, society has become increasingly knowledge-based so that higher learning and research now act as essential components of cultural, socio-economic and environmentally sustainable development of individuals, communities and nations"[4]   Due to emergence of knowledge-based society, higher education has assumed the importance among the people, nations and world community. The speedy emergence of the Global world in the 21th century has put the importance of higher education beyond the boundaries of the nations. The research oriented development models of the societies around

116

the world and ongoing market-driven regions in the world have put higher education as a catalyst for economic, social, human development etc. of the world.

In the context of a nation like India, the socio-economic development of minority communities is important for the advancement of the nation. The socio-economic development means the improvement in the standard of living due to changes in education, employment, income, skill development etc. In this paper, the socio-economic development has been used to see the overall improvement in the standard of living of the community due to changes in the higher education. The socio-economic development is referred "to the ability to produce an adequate and growing supply of goods and services productively and efficiently, to accumulate capital, and to distribute the fruits of production in relatively equitable manner"[5]

There are many indicators of the improvement in the standard of the living of a community. These are employment, income, skill development, life expectancy; education etc. This paper has used some important indicators to find the impact of higher education on the socio-economic development of the communities.

There is a wider difference at the socio-economic, educational, cultural, political etc. levels among the minority communities of India. The most backward community among the minorities is Muslims. In spite of being the largest community among the minorities, constituting about 72.[6] percent of all minority population, Muslims are behind than other minority communities of India. There are many reasons for the backwardness of Indian Muslims. These may be the low educational attainment, weak economic condition, low level of access to modern technology, poor health care system, lack of employment, political marginalization etc. This paper has taken higher education as one of the reasons for the study of the socio-economic conditions of Indian minorities comparatively.

2   Objectives of Study

There are following objectives of the paper.

I.   To study the population of Indian minority communities

II.   To study the higher education of minority communities

III.   To study the role of higher education in socio-economic development of minority communities

IV.   To compare the socio-economic condition of Indian minority communities

3   Question and Importance of Study

In the light of the objectives, there are following questions which have been raised by the present paper whose answers are essential to understanding the central points of study the relationship of higher education with the socio-economic condition of minorities. These questions are:

a)   What is the population of Indian minority communities?

b)   What is the status of higher education among Indian minorities?

c)   What is the role of higher education in the socio-economic development of minorities?

d)   Is any community ahead in higher education, also ahead in socio-economic development?

This study is important to understand the role of higher education in the socio-economic development of minority communities. In many studies much emphasis has been put on just education particularly on primary education. There is no doubt that primary education is important but without converting that primary education attainment into higher education, no community could advance in socio-economic matters. Higher education provides skills for employment, for business, for the job, for innovation, for research, for vision, and for political empowerment. This paper has studied the socio-economic advancement of the minorities due to attainment in higher education. This paper would give insight to the policy maker, planner, community developer, NGOs, international communities and international organizations into the socio-economic development of the minority communities of India. So, in future, they could consider on the attainment of the higher education and its impact on the socio-economic development of a community. They could allocate more resources on the expansion of higher education among minority communities particularly Muslims.

The present government under Honorable Prime Minister Mr. Narendra Modi has started numerous campaigns like "Make in India[7]", "Start-Up India[8]" to make India as leading economic powers of the world by encouraging manufacturing in India. This study would help to understand the potentialities of minority communities and their contribution to the economic development of the country. The 'Make in India' campaign could be realized through higher education and human development as many leading economies of the world have achieved in the past. The more a community would attain higher education, the more that community would be higher in human development and the socio-economic development.

4   Methodology and Data

The present study is based on the secondary data derived from various sources and has used Descriptive Analytical Method. The data have been derived from the following sources.

A.   Census Survey

B.   Ministry of Human Resource Development (MHRD)

C.   Ministry of Minority Affairs (MOMA)

D.   All India Survey on Higher Education (AISHE)

E.   University Grants commission (UGC)

F.   National Assessment And Accreditation Council (NAAC)

G.   UNESCO

H.   National Sample Survey (NSSO)

I.   Make In India website

J.   Sachar Committee Report

K.   Planning Commission

L.   Documents of Five Year Plans

M.   Journals

N.   Magazines

O.   Paper

P.   Theses

Q.   News Papers etc.

The data have been taken directly from the sources while in somewhere the data have been taken from the sources and re-arranged as per the requirement of the paper. Much care has been taken to use the reliable data derived from the authentic sources and concerned special agencies. So, the study would be more valid and reliable.

5   Minority Communities and their Numbers

Among all the six declared minority communities of India, Muslim is the largest and dominant community. As per the Census 2011, the numbers of the various minority communities are given in Table-1

Table-1 Population of Minority Communities in India

SN	Name of the Minority Community	Total Population (in Crores)	Percentage of the Total population of Country(2011-1.21 billion)	Percentage of Increase in the population
1	Muslim	17.22	14.2	24.6%
2	Christian	2.78	2.3	15.5%
3	Sikh	2.08	1.7	8.4%
4	Buddhist	0.84	0.7	6.1%
5	Jain	0.45	0.4	5.4%
6	Parsi	69000(2001)	-0.007(2001)	12% decadal decline

Source(s): a-Census-2011 b-The Hindu [9]

The Table-1 shows that in term of numbers, among all the minority communities, Muslim is the largest community. This community is about sixth times bigger than the second-largest minority community of India. Among other minority communities, Sikhs are 2.08 crores, Buddhists are 0.84 crores; Jains are 0.45 crores and Parsi below one lakh.

In term of the rate of growth, Muslim community growth rate is 24.6 percent which is the lowest growth rate in six decades. The other minority communities like Christian, Sikh, Buddhist and Jain are 15.5 percent, 8.4 percent, 6.1 percent and 5.4 percent respectively. The growth rate of Parsis is on the decline and their numbers have negligible impact in comparing to the total population of the country and minority communities.

6 Minority Communities and their level of literacy

There is a need to see the literacy ratio to understand the socio-economic condition of minority communities. The more the literacy ratio of a community, the more that community is advanced in numerous areas. The Table-2 gives the literacy ratio of major minority communities of India.

Table-2 Literacy Ratio of Minority Communities of India

SN	Name of the community	2001			2015		
		Male	Female	Total	Male	Female	Total
1	Muslim	67.6	50.1	59.1	72.9	63.9	68.4
2	Christian	84.4	76.2	80.3	91.4	85.3	88.3
3	Sikh	75.2	63.1	69.4	87.6	81.2	84.4
4	Buddhist	83.1	61.7	72.7	89.2	76.5	82.8
5	Jain	97.4	90.6	94.1	98.3	94.6	96.4
6	Parsi	---	----	97.9	----	---	---

Source(s): a-Census survey b-ClickPune.com[10]

The Table-2 shows the data of literacy of Census 2001 and 2015(calculated on the basis of Census 2011).As per the Table-2, the community which lags behind in the literacy is 2011 and 2015 are Muslim while the highest literacy rate is of Parsi and Jain. The Jain has been declared as a minority community in 2014.The other communities which follow Jain in literacy are Sikh, Christian Buddhist etc.

7 How near a community is to Higher education?

There is a need to see the status of minority communities

from just literacy to senior secondary levels to understand the performance in higher education. The question is; are those communities which higher in literacy ration, ahead in senior secondary-the near to higher education, too? The Table-3 gives the status of minority communities from primary level to senior secondary level.

Table-3 Status of Minority community from Primary to Senior Secondary levels

SN	Name of Community	Up to Primary Level*	Middle	Secondary	Senior Secondary
1	All Religion	55.57	16.09	14.13	6.74
2	Hindu	54.91	16.18	14.25	6.92
3	Muslim	65.31	15.14	10.96	4.53
4	Christian	45.79	17.13	17.48	8.7
5	Sikh	46.70	16.93	20.94	7.57
6	Buddhist	54.69	17.52	14.09	7.65
7	Jain	29.51	12.27	21.87	13.84
8	Others	62.12	17.48	11.24	4.55

Source: Census 2001

- Includes Literacy without education level, below primary level and Primary level

The Table-3 shows that the status of all minority communities is not equal at every level. The status of Muslims is better at Primary level with 65.31 than other communities but reaching to senior secondary level, the community lags behind than other communities while other communities somehow are reaching to senior secondary level in better position. On the whole, the minority communities could not sustain the momentum till senior secondary level. There may be many reasons which are right now beyond the scope of the present paper.

8   Minority Communities in Higher Education

The purpose of this paper is to see the relationship between higher education and socio-economic development. The advancement in higher education is mostly seen in term of Gross Enrolment Ratio (GER).GER is defined as "the ratio of students enrolled in a particular level of education (regardless of age) to the population of official school age for that level of education"[11]There is a wider gap in the condition of minority communities in Higher education in India. The Table- 4 gives the clear picture of the minority community for the last 25 years. The data have been derived from NSSO gives a constant growth in higher education among all minority communities. The data about the Jain has been given as religious group as this community has been declared as a minority community in 2014 only. The Table-4 is about the Gross Enrollment Ration (GER) of the minority communities taking both rural and urban status.

The Table- 4 shows the GER of the minority communities of India. The GER in higher education is highest in Jain community; followed by Christian, Buddhist and Hindu communities. The lowest GER in higher education is of the Muslim community; Starting from 5.59 GER in 1983 to 9.56 in 2007-08.

The main features of GER of minority communities are; the lower growth of GER in rural areas as compared to the urban areas and less GER of females against males. There is also a difference between a male of urban and rural areas and female in an urban area to the rural female of rural area.

There is a constant increase in all communities' higher education with the passage of time. The advancement in higher education for those communities is higher whose economic condition is better than other communities. This relation shows that higher education promotes socio-economic development and socio-economic development promotes higher education.

Table-4 GER by religious groups: Rural + Urban

Gender/Religious Groups	1983 M	1983 F	1983 Total	1993-94 M	1993-94 F	1993-94 Total	2004-05 M	2004-05 F	2004-05 Total	2007-08 M	2007-08 F	2007-08 Total	2009-10 Total
Hindu	14.82	7.12	12.15	16.45	8.01	12.38	19.86	14.04	17.08	20.50	16.08	18.40	20
Muslim	7.35	2.80	5.59	8.30	4.36	6.39	11.15	7.44	9.38	11.31	7.68	9.56	11.3
Christian	15.14	23.05	17.20	23.00	19.27	21.14	30.07	25.68	27.83	25.30	31.39	28.45	31.3
Sikh	12.13	8.87	11.28	9.90	11.01	10.48	15.64	19.16	17.24	14.57	19.50	16.90	23.1
Jain	36.69	27.21	33.04	30.81	24.83	28.19	56.88	27.11	43.68	47.33	60.02	53.44	54.6
Buddhist	13.36	4.41	10.77	17.54	7.72	12.44	20.74	21.50	21.10	16.27	22.94	19.57	17.9
Others	14.54	10.31	13.34	15.61	7.98	11.92	17.66	8.70	13.32	7.40	5.19	6.24	---
Total	13.91	7.01	11.52	15.61	7.98	11.92	18.84	13.53	16.31	19.12	15.32	17.31	18.8

Source(s): a-National Sample Survey b- Dalit Studies[12]

9   What Role the Higher Education plays in the Socio-economic Development of Minority Communities?

Higher education plays an important role in the socio-economic development. A community which is higher in higher education is also ahead in socio-economic development. Here, only a few parameters of socio-economic development have been taken to the advancement of the minority communities'. These are Income of the community, Level of poverty, Work participation, employment, life expectancy etc. The Table-5 gives the status of the various parameters of the in the socio-economic development of the communities.

Table-5 Status of Minority Communities in Socio-economic Development

SN	Name of minority community	Living standard	Level of Poverty	
		Exp-2009-10 (Monthly Per Capita Consumption Expenditure (MPCE)/Per Day)	2004-05	2011-12
1	All India	1,128/37.51	37.7	22.0
2	Muslim	980.00/32.66	43.6	25.4
3	Christian	1,543/51.43	24.5	16.4
4	Sikh	1,659/55.30	18.9	5.9
5	Buddhist	------	-----	------
6	Jain	-----	4.6	3.3
7	Parsi	------	-------	-------

Source(s): a-NSSO Data 2009-10 b- The Hindu[13] c- Panagaria A.[14] d-Sunita Sanghi, A Srija [15]

The Table-5 shows due to better in higher education, there is also found the difference in the living standard of the communities. In term of living standard, the Muslims are lowest both at rural (Rs. 833) and Urban (Rs 1,272) areas. The condition of other communities is better than Muslims in rural areas. The MPCE of Hindu is Rs 888, Sikhs Rs 1,498 and Christian Rs 1,296 respectively.

In term of urban areas, the other communities are also better than Muslims. The MPCE of Sikh community is Rs 2, 180, Christian Rs 2,053 and Hindu Rs 1,797 respectively.

If one sees in term of per day MPCE, Muslims are behind than other communities with 32.66.The other communities like Christian and Sikh etc. have Rs 51.43 and Rs55.30 per day respectively.

Due to better higher education, the other minority communities also have less incidence of poverty. If one compares the level of the poverty of 2004-05 data with 2011-12, he finds that the level of poverty has declined. The level of poverty is highest in Muslim community. According to the calculation of Panagaria A. (Columbia University), [16] the incidence of poverty is the least among the higher educated people. It is about 2.8 for 2011-12(on Tendulkar Line) as compared to other levels of education and illiterate. The incidence of poverty for Secondary or higher secondary is 9.9, Middle is 18.3, Primary or less is 24.5.5 and illiterate is 33.5 for the year 2011-12.This shows the more the higher education the less level of incidence of poverty in a community.

Another parameter of socio-economic development is employment. The more and higher education a community attains the more and higher employment it gets. The Table-6 gives the employment status of the minority communities. The categories of employments e.g. Self-Employment (SE), Regular(R) and Casual(C) have been taken into consideration.

Table-6 Per 1,000 Distribution of Usually Employed by Status during 2009-10

Community	Rural Male			Rural Female			Urban Male			Urban Female		
	SE	R	C	SE	R	C	SE	R	C	SE	R	C
Hinduism	537	83	379	547	41	411	397	441	161	393	404	203
Islam (Muslims)	528	79	393	649	39	312	496	298	205	597	216	187
Christianity	500	168	332	554	114	332	294	450	256	284	607	109
Sikhism	545	123	333	789	86	125	444	352	204	515	367	118
All India	535	85	380	557	44	399	411	419	170	411	393	96

SE=Self Employed   R=Regular C=Casual

Source(s):a- NSSO Data 2009-10 Sunita Sanghi, A Srija [17]

The Table-6 Shows that the self-employment is higher among Muslims than other minority communities. While in the case of Regular Employment(R) the number of Muslims is less than other communities. Most of the Regular employment is based on the education. Here the number of employment (for males rural) in1000 for Muslim, Christians, Sikhs is 79,168 and 123 respectively. In rural for female in 1000 is least among Muslims which is 39. In Urban (males) and Urban (Females), Muslim's numbers are 298 and 216 respectively which are less than other communities. Even, both at Rural and Urban levels, Muslim's numbers are less than All India levels.

10 Conclusion

There are many reasons for the socio-economic advancement of minority communities in India. The present paper has studied the relationship between Higher education and socio-economic development of minority communities of India. The role of the higher education in the socio-economic development has been studied and reached on this conclusion that those minority communities of India which have a higher level of higher education they are ahead in socio-economic development too. The Muslim community is behind in higher education than other minority communities; as a result, this community is also behind in socio-economic development. The highest number in higher education is of Jain, so this community is higher in socio-economic development too. The study proves that higher education plays an important role in the socio-economic development.

11 Suggestions

In the light of the study about the relationship between higher education and socio-economic development, the following suggestions could be put forwarded.

1.   There is a need to enhance the Gross Enrolment Ratio at All India level to advance the higher education among all the minority communities.

2.   There is a need to promote higher education among the members of Muslim, Sikh, and Buddhist communities.

3.   There should be an increase in the expenditure on higher education. The present spending of 1.2 percent of GDP on higher education is not sufficient as compared to world's leading economies.

4.   The Human development of India could not meet the world standard without the high expenditure on higher

education. The performance of the country could not improve at international level until and unless there would be no advancement of higher education accessible to all communities equally in India.

5.   Socio-economic development and higher education are interlinked. So, there is a need to promote the development of both.

6.   There is a need to emphasis on the higher education for women. In the study, it has been found that women of rural and urban areas are behind than their male counterpart at every level. No improvement can be done without the advancement of higher education among women.

7.   There is need to release complete data on various aspects of the higher education of minority communities.

8.   There is need to release data on higher education of minority communities at an equal interval. The government should direct the concerned departments/agencies to release data yearly community wise for higher education.

9.   There is a need to direct to Ministry of Minority Affairs to the commission or assign the duty to the organizations/agencies to collect data on socio-economic development and higher education of minority communities and release regularly.

10.   There is a need to promote higher education among minorities, particularly among Muslims by granting financial help or scholarship or loan or waiving fees at an institutional level to admitted students.

References:

1 http://censusindia.gov.in/

2 http://www.minorityaffairs.gov.in/sites/upload_files/moma/files/ notification_jain.pdf

3 http://www.minorityaffairs.gov.in/sites/upload_files/moma/files/ notification_jain.pdf

4 http://www.unesco.org/education/educprog/wche/declaration_en g.htm

5 J. David (1998).Levels of Socio-economic Development Theory; West port, Connectient.London.2nd ed. Introduction: The Meaning of Development and the Levels of Theory; pp-03

6 http://censusindia.gov.in/Census_Data_2001/India_at_glance/reli gion.aspx

7 http://www.makeinindia.com/home

8 http://www.startup-india.org/

9 (http://www.thehindu.com/news/national/census-2011-data-on-population-by-religious-communities/article7579161.ece

10 http://clickpune.com/literacy-rate-in-india-2015-religion-wise-literacy-rate-india.html

11 http://hdr.undp.org/sites/default/files/reports/271/hdr_2011_en_c omplete.pdf

12 http://www.dalitstudies.org.in/wp/wp604.pdf

13 http://www.thehindu.com/news/national/muslims-poorest-among-religious-groups-says-nsso-survey/article5042032.ece

14 http://indianeconomy.columbia.edu/sites/default/files/working_p apers/working_paper_2013-02-final.pdf

15 http://www.ies.gov.in/pdfs/Employment_Trends_among_Religio us_Communities_of_India.pdf

16 http://indianeconomy.columbia.edu/sites/default/files/working_p apers/working_paper_2013-02-final.pdf

17 http://www.ies.gov.in/pdfs/Employment_Trends_among_Religio us_Communities_of_India.pdf

11 THE ENVIRONMENTAL PROTECTION IN ARMED CONFLICT: NEED OF A FIFTH GENEVA CONVENTION

(By: Dr. Jaishree Jaiswal[*])

Introduction

*T*hroughout the human history the environment has been one of war's many victims. Thucydides records the Greek tactic of scorching the earth during the Peloponnesian Wars. The Romans salted the soils of Carthage after winning the Punic Wars. The Dutch breached their dykes in 1792 to prevent a French invasion. In World War I, the British set afire Romanian oilfields to prevent the Central Powers from capturing them: in World War II, Germany and the Soviet Union engaged in "Scorched Earth" tactics: and in the Korean War, the United States bombed North Korean dams. During the Vietnam War, the United States destroyed nearly 20% of Vietnam's forests. Including, 54% of its mangrove forests, through chemical defoliants, bulldozers and bombings. Towards the end of the First Gulf War, Iraq burned hundreds of oil wells and dumped massive amounts of oil into the Persian Gulf. The United States and its allies dropped more than 47,500 cluster bombs, containing 13,167,500 bomb blasts. NATO forces destroyed major oil refineries, pharmaceutical and petrochemical plants in Kosovo, causing significant damage to the environment. The civil war in the Congo has

---

[*] Assistant Professor Unity Law College, Lucknow, India

decimated the country's wildlife - killing thousands of elephants, gorillas and okapis.

During the most recent fighting - between 27 December 2008 and 18 January 2009- Israeli Defence Forces (IDF) conducted a major combined military operation in the Gaza Strip. The operation comprised bombardment by land, sea and air, and incursions into the Gaza Strip by Israeli troop[s, causing serious environmental damage. The ongoing conflicts in Afghanistan and Iraq have had serious repercussions both on the nation's survival and the environment. More than two decades of war have played havoc with the physical environment-besides the loss of more than two million people and crippling of an additional half a million, the natural resources of these countries have suffered a tremendous loss. Landmines have had a devastating effect on the environment, compounding the already existing problems, such as deforestation and overuse of marginal wildlife species.

1 Effect of Military Activities on Environment

Military activities have a significant impact on the environment. Nuclear as well as conventional weapons pose serious threat to environmental. The preparation, including the testing, development, production and maintenance of conventional, and nuclear weapons, has generated large quantities of hazardous, toxic and radioactive substances, These, together with their wastes have contributed on a large scale to the depletion of natural resources and degradation of the environment.

Today, the world's eight-nuclear weapon states have 36,000 nuclear bombs, containing 5,000 megatons of destructive energy - More than sufficient to destroy the world. The scientific dimension of nuclear weapons in understandably difficult to comprehend. A single large nuclear weapon could releases explosive power comparable to all the energy released from the conventional weapons used in all past wars. Nuclear weapons have the potential to destroy the entire ecosystem of the plant. Those already in the world's arsenals have the potential of destroying life on the planet several times over.

During the Gulf War, American and British forces introduced armors piercing ammunition made of depleted uranium (Du), a radioactive and toxic waste. By war's end, more than 2,90,000 kilograms of depleted uranium contaminated equipment and the soil on the battle fields of Saudi Arabia, Kuwait, and southern Iraq. DU is chemically toxic like other heavy metals such as lead, but it is also primarily an alpha particle emitter with a radioactive half-life of 4.5 billion years. DU weapons contaminate impact areas with extremely fine radioactive and toxic dust. In addition to the fine uranium dust created by impacts, depleted uranium fragments and intact DU penetrators also pose a hazard. DU is acknowledged to cause kidney damage cancers of the lung and borne Non-malignant respiratory disease, skin disorders. Neaurocognitive disorders, Chromosomal damage, and birth defects. Depleted uranium contamination is unlikely to be cleaned up by victor or vanquished because of the extreme cost and the prospect of further environmental damages.

The cleanup of DU effects involves removing the "the top layer of soil." which could be potentially devastating to an environment, especially if depleted uranium contaminates arable land or wetlands. Further, the cost involved in removing the topsoil from contaminated areas could be astronomical. For example the cost of cleaning up 290.000kg of depleted uranium on thousands of hectares in Saudi Arabia. Kuwait and Iraq would be tens of billions of US dollars.

Landmines and unexploded military ordnance (UXO) also pose serious threat to environment, livelihood and process of sustainable development, affecting not only present but also future generations. They prejudice economic development by disrupting the biosphere's life support systems and diminishing the capacity of the environment to supply the raw materials and natural resources. Mines deny access to natural resources; promote the rapid and unsustainable exploitation of marginal and ecologically fragile environments. Deplete biological diversity by destroying flora and fauna contaminate the surrounding soil and water with highly toxic substances, and destroy the ecosystem itself by disrupting soil and water processes.

Landmines kill livestock as well as wildlife. In Libya, between 1940 and 1980 mines and other UXO have killed more than 125.000 camels, sheep, goats, and cattle. There were about 264.000 goats and sheep killed in Afghanistan, at a value of about $31.6 million dollars. The same holds for cows, horses, camels, and vehicles. In Libya, gazelles have disappeared from sites that were mined during World War II. In Croatia brown bears are regular victims, In India, landmines have killed barking deer, clouded leopard, snow leopards, and Royal Bengal tigers.

Warfare today uses explosives and machinery to subdue enemies and territories. The intensity of environmental damage resulting from wars has been remarkably parallel to the technological advancement in warfare. Use of more advanced arms and ammunition means more damage to environment. There are currently some 40 armed conflicts going on in the world involving tens of millions of people. Many of these are taking place in locations that are critical to maintain biodiversity, such as, Africa, South Asia and Latin America, Because these are often in highly populated, lower income nations, they also tend to be regions that are already suffering severe environmental stresses.

A simple alternative, non-scientific non-legal clarification is provided by Lanier-Graham (1993): (1) Intentional incidental direct destruction of the environment during war; (2) incidental direct destruction; and (3) indirect or induced destruction as a medium - or long-term consequence of war but still attributable to war, "Intentional direct destruction" refers to deliberate attacks on cultivated and uncultivated lands and resources, where the objective is indeed environmental destruction for its own sake. The burning of oil wells during the Persian Gulf War is an example of this. An example of "incidental direct destruction" is soil disturbance caused by the movement of battle tanks from one location to another: environmental damage is collateral but not the primary objective of the action undertaken. Finally, "indirect or induced destruction" may occur as a result of the shifting of human populations on account of war that, in turn, may cause undue environmental stresses.

2 Protection of Environment: Treaties under International humanitarian Low (IHL)

The existing rules of IHL for the protection of the

environment aim not to prevent damage altogether, but rather, to limit it to a level deemed tolerable, Unfortunately, there is reason to fear that the use of particularly devastating means of warfare (whose effects are often still unknown) could wreak such large-scale destruction as to render illusory the protection afforded to civilian under IHL Indeed. Severe environmental damage could seriously hamper or even prevent the implementation of the provisions to protect the victims of armed conflict. Two treaties under IHL have provisions relating to the protection of the environment.

2.1 The Convention on the Prohibition of Military or Any Other Hostile Use of Environmental Modification Techniques (ENMOD), 1976.

The ENMOD was convened in response to the severe damage suffered by Vietnam's environment as a result of the United States use of chemicals and defoliants. It was intended to prohibit the military use of climate modification techniques that are intended or could be expected to cause "widespread, long-lasting, or severe" destruction or damage to the enemy environment. These three terms are defined as follows: *Widespread:* encompassing an area on the scale of several hundred square kilometers: *Long-lasting:* lasting for a period of months, or approximately a season; and *Severe:* involving serious or significant disruption or harm to human life, natural and economic resource, or other assets.

While the ENMOD does not pre-empt the customary principle of military necessity, it does refine the balancing or environmental damage with military necessity by providing an upper limit on the acceptable level or environmental damage. The ENMOD prohibits "military or any other hostile use of environmental modification techniques having widespread, long-lasting or severe effect as the means of destruction, damage, or injury to any other State Party."

2.2 Protocol 1 of 1997 Additional to the Geneva Conventions of 1949.

Articles 35 and 55 of Protocol 1 specifically address the protection of the environment during periods of armed conflict. Article 35 begins by restating two principles developed in St. Petersburg and The Hague: the right to choose means of warfare "is not unlimited" and it is prohibited to employ "methods of warfare of a nature to cause superfluous injury or unnecessary suffering." Article 35 (3) Further strengthens the protection of the environment by stating that "it is prohibited to employ methods of warfare which are intended, or may be expected, to cause widespread, long-term, and severe damage to the natural environment".

While Article 35 (1) mentions the protection of the environment as a basic rule, Article 55 is entirely devoted to the environment and thus represents the only truly "environmental" provision in Protocol I. Article 55 states: "Care shall be taken in warfare to protect the natural environment against widespread long-term and severe damage. This protection includes prohibition of the use of methods or means of warfare, which are intended or may be expected to cause such damage to the natural environment and thereby prejudice the health or survival of the population. "

The purpose of Protocol I and the ENMOD was to reaffirm the earlier 1949 Geneva Conventions, and to address the widespread awareness of the environmental destructiveness of war that grew out of the Vietnam era. Previously, the international community had paid little attention to the consequences of war on the environment, as illustrated by the failure to mention the environment in the four Geneva Conventions following the Second World War. Media coverage during the Vietnam War, coupled with an increasing worldwide awareness of the environment, led to the adoption of Protocol I and the ENMOD. These two treaties prohibit different types of environmental damage. While Protocol I prohibits recourse to environmental warfare, i.e., the use of methods of warfare likely to upset the vital balance of nature, the ENMOD prohibits what is known as geophysical warfare, which implies the deliberate manipulation of natural process and may trigger "hurricanes, tidal waves, earthquakes, and rain or snow". Despite growing international concern about the effect of war on the environment, neither of these agreements has been universally adopted. There is also a danger that discrepancies in these laws might hamper their effective implementation in the future.

The rules of IHL treaty law that can be considered to indirectly protect the environment during armed conflict can be clustered into five categories: (i) rules limiting or prohibiting certain weapons and methods of warfare like the Chemical weapons Convention, 1993 (CWC), the Hague Convention IV of 1907 regulating the means and methods of warfare: (ii) clauses protecting civilian objects and properties; (iii) clauses protecting cultural hostage sites; (iv) rules concerning installations containing dangerous forces; and (v) Imitations on certain specifically defined areas. The CWC specifically prohibits destroying chemical weapons by "dumping in any body of water, land burial and open pit burning", thereby ensuring that the human and environmental costs of disposal minimal.

3 Protection of Environment: International Environmental Law

The 1972 Stockholm Declaration focuses exclusively on nuclear weapons. Principle 26 Provides; "Man and his environment must be spared the effect of nuclear weapons and all other means of mass destruction. Sates must strive to reach prompt agreement, in the relevant international organs, on the elimination and complete destruction of such weapons."

The 1982 World Charter for Nature adopts a more general approach, stating the "general principle" that "nature shall be secured against degradation caused by warfare or other hostile activities", and declaring that "military activities damaging to nature shall be avoided". The wording of the 1992 Rio declaration gets closer to the point, but is still ambiguous. Although not legally binding, the wording of Principle 24 could be interpreted either as requiring states to respect those rules of international Law which provide protection for the environment in times of armed conflict or as requiring states to respect international law by protecting the environment in times of armed conflict.

Most environmental treaties, including those on civil liability for damage, are silent on the issue of their applicability following the outbreak of military conflict. Most of them have provisions excluding their applicability when damage occurs as a result of armed conflict. Despite containing no provision expressly protecting the marine environment against the consequences of an armed conflict, it can be assumed that under the Convention on the Law of the Sea. 1982, such protection exists in the context of the provisions with regard to pollution of the sea.

Concern for the environment also emerged at the national level. A few countries made provisions for the protection and preservation of the environment in their constitutions, and also adopted a large number of legislative measures for the protection of the environment as such, or of its various components (such as water, air and forests).

4   Protection of Environment: Human Rights Law

Human rights law may provide additional guidance about the conduct of State and central government affecting the environment and natural resources during armed conflict. Both treaty law and customary international law contain rules that ensure that the basic social and political rights of individuals are respected including several that have been linked to environmental protection without pure environment human being is this world cannot exist. No country is this world can develop without pure environment as it is necessary for the welfare of human being. It precautions would not taken for the protection of environment then the flora and fauna will not exist. The existence of human being would be vanished if the possible precaution would not take to restrain the pollution in order to protect the environment.

5   Protection of Environment: Customary International Law

The fundamental principles of customary international law applicable to the protection of the environment are those of humanity, discrimination, proportionality, and military necessary. The principle of humanity, also known as the "principle of unnecessary suffering and destruction", prescribes the use of means of warfare which cause unnecessary suffering not justified by legitimate military objectives. The principle of discrimination provided that the means and methods of warfare must distinguish between military and civilian targets. The principle of proportionality is a fact-specific concept requiring that the force employed by the attacker not be disproportionate to the military advantage sought. The principle of military necessity for military advantage states that a combatant may use only the level of force required for the partial or complete submission of the enemy" that incurs the least loss of time, life, and physical resource" in the attainment of a legitimate military objective. While at first glance, it might appear that the military necessity exception tramps all restrictions on the conduct of war, it is still subject to the limits of humanity, discrimination and proportionality.

These rules of customary law were developed to protect humans and their property, and may only indirectly protective of an environment which is not intended to be the direct beneficiary of these principles.

6   The ICRC Guidelines

In 2004, the International Committee of the Red Cross has drawn "guidelines" concerning the protection of the environment against the effects of armed conflict. It provides that the general principles of international law such as the principle of distinction and the principle of proportionality provide protection to the environment. The guidelines state that care should be taken in warfare to protect and preserve the natural environment. The military or any other hostile use of environmental modification techniques having widespread, long-lasting or severe effects as the means of destruction, damage or injury to any other State party is prohibited. Attacks against the natural environment by way of reprisals are providing. Under the guidance, the States are urged to enter into further agreements providing additional protection to the natural environment in times of armed conflict. The guidelines provide the the states must take all measures required by international law to avoid:

(a) Making forests or other kinds of plant cover the object of attack by incendiary weapons except when such natural elements are used to cover, conceal or camouflage combatants or other military objectives, or are themselves military objectives.

(b) Attacks on objects indispensable to the survival of the civilian population. Such as foodstuffs, agricultural areas or drinking water installations, if carried out for the purpose of denying such objects to the civilian population:

(c) Attacks on works or installations containing dangerous forces. Namely dams dykes and nuclear electrical generating stations, even where they are military objectives, if such attack may cause the release of dangerous forces and consequent severe losses among the civilian population and as long as such works or installations are entitled to special protection under Protocol I additional to the Geneva Conventions;

(d) Attacks on historic monument works of art or places of worship which constitute the cultural or spiritual heritage of people.

The existing international legal framework contains the cultural or spiritual heritage of people.

The existing international legal framework contains many provisions that either directly or indirectly project the environment or govern the use of natural resources during armed conflict. In practice however these provisions have not always been effectively implemented or enforced. Except in case of Iraq which was held accountable for damages coursed during the 1990-1991 Gulf War, so far no other States or individual has been held responsible for environmental harm caused during armed conflict and the environment continues to be the silent victim of armed conflicts worldwide.

It is now widely recognized that the planet faces a diverse and growing range of environmental challenges which can only be addressed through international cooperation. To protect the natural environment as one of our fundamental security needs. We have to recognize that all species have a right to exist, that humans should only take what the natural environment can sustainably contribute to our life support system, and that nations should not assume that warfare and preparation for warfare justify environmental destruction. There are no ultimate winners in war-nighters people, or nations, or the planet's ecosystem. War is indiscriminate and can bring harm or destruction to life anywhere. Damaging national and global ecosystems also damages the people living within them.

7   Recommendations

In order to ensure that environmental violations committed during warfare are prosecuted, the provisions of international law that protect the environment in times of conflict should be fully reflected at the national level. States should adopt and reflect the ICRC Guidelines on the Protection of the Environment during Armed Conflict (1994) in national legislation and military manuals, as well as integrate them into the training of their armed force. The international Law Commission (ILC), as an UN body, should examine the effectiveness of the legal framework, to identify the gaps and barriers to enforcement, and to explore possibilities for clarifying and codifying this body of law. A new legal instrument granting place-based protection for critical natural resources and areas of ecological importance during international and non-international armed conflicts should be developed. This could include protection for watersheds, groundwater aquifers, agricultural and grazing lands, parks, national forest, and the habitat of endangered species. At the outset of any conflict, critical natural resources and areas of ecological importance would be delineated and designated as "demilitarized zones." and parties to the conflict would be prohibited from conduction military operations within their boundaries.

8   Conclusion

The issue of destruction of the environment in one of the most disturbing aspects of armed conflicts today, Destruction of the environment through the excessive human demands placed on it and due to the harmful effects of the production, testing, stockpiling and use of military weapons is the major concern of the international community, Following the 1991 Gulf War, concern was reawakened about the environment effects of war. As for the ENMOD and Protocol I, several major belligerent countries were not parties to, Besides, the specific environmental provision of these agreements, which only prohibit destruction that is widespread, long-lasting, and/or severe, raise difficult questions of legal interpretation and scientific valuation.

In its 1996 Advisory Opinion on the Legality of the Thereat or Use of Nuclear Weapons. The International Court of Justice stressed the "the obligations of State to respect and protect the natural environment," applied equally "to the actual use of nuclear weapons in armed conflict." We have to decide whether the human need for aggression to settle local, national or international disputes should be allowed to outweigh environment integrity, This would involve a reinterpretation of the interaction between international environmental law and international humanitarian by the international community to the extent they can never be undertaken, even if essential to defend national sovereignty, Why should international environmental desecration not be similarly proscribed? As the existing international legal regime is inadequate, we need a Fifth Geneva Convention for environmental protection during the armed conflict.

Notes and References:

1. Nuclear-Weapon State: China, France, Russia, United Kingdom, United State, Each of these five states originally declared it nuclear-weapons program and was recognized under the 1968 Nuclear No-Proliferation Treaty (NPT) as a nuclear weapon state because it had tested a nuclear weapon prior to January I, 1967. Estimated total nuclear warhead stockpiles: United State, 12.070; Russia, 22,500; United Kingdom, 260; France, 452; Non-NPT Nuclear - Weapons States; India, Israel, Pakistan.

2. Akin, William, Damian Durant, and Marianne Cheri 1991. on Impact; Modern Warfare and the Environment. A Case Study of the Gulf War, London; Greenpeace.

3. Austin JE and Carl E Bruch. 2000. The Environmental Consequences of War, Cambridge: Cambridge University Press.

4. Glen Plant (ed.) 1992. Environmental Protection and the Law of War, London: Behaves Press.

12 GROWTH AND JUSTICE IN INDIA: A HISTORICAL PERSPECTIVE

(By: Dr. Sadaf Khan*)

Abstract

" Growth can best be described as a process of transformation whether one examines an economy that is already modern and industrialized or an economy at an earlier stage of development, one finds that process of growth is uneven and unbalanced."[1]

The concept of Growth with Justice is founded on the basic ideal of socio-economic equality and removal of socio-economic disparities and inequalities, the concept related with fairness. Justice is one of the Central virtues of any social order, it matters enormously how we distribute the burdens required to maintain social organization and the benefits that occur from it.[2]

From the past we have been recording 'growth'. But the benefits of that growth were not equally distributed giving rise to the question as to why some are rich and some are poor? Is growth equally distributed among the people? Growth is only a measurement of short term economic performance. That never measures opportunities and social and economic problems of the weaker sections of the society.

* Assistant Professor (History) Unity Degree College, Lucknow, India

This paper examines Indian Growth from Ancient to Modern era in its historical perspective.

In India particularly, past persists in the present. The economic and social problems which confront us today are either those which existed in the past or have resulted from them. Hence a thorough knowledge of the past economic institutions provides better insights into the understanding of the present structure of economy.[3]

1 Ancient Indian Era:-

The history of India begins with the dawn of Indus valley civilization which flourished between 3500 BC and 1800 BC. The Indus civilization's economy appears to have depended significantly on trade which was facilitated by advances in transport. But the right of people and exact system of administration is not traced due to lack of sources. Due to the fact that the small amount of epigraphic evidence is yet to be deciphered. But available sources indicate that division in the society existed. All were not having equal rights.

The second phase of the process of society formation was started with the Vedic age. After that process, people began to feel the necessity of an organised administration of justice by the state, for peaceful life and to secure the rights of individual.

Around 600 B.C. the *Mahajan-padas* minted punch marked silver coins. The period was marked by intensive trade activity and Urban development.[4] By 300 BC, when middle east was under the Greek Seleucid and Ptolemaic empires, the *Maurya* empire united most of the Indian sub continent. The political unity and military security allowed for a common economic system and enhanced trade and commerce, with increased agricultural productivity. The empire spent considerable resources building roads and maintained them throughout India. The improved infrastructure combined with increased security, greater uniformity in measurements, and increasing usage of coins as a currency enhanced trade. For the next 1500 years India produced its classical civilisation which generated wealth in huge amount.[5]

Along with this progress, judicial system also developed. The beginnings of civil and criminal laws have to be assigned to this period. From the beginning the society was divided into four classes, and all were not equal in the eyes of law. The rules of punishments were based on class considerations and while an offence committed by a *Shudra* invited capital punishment for the same offence, a *Brahmana* went scot-free. At best, he washed off his sins by performing penance.[6] *Brahmana* were considered to be the highest in society, their duty according to the *Dharma Shastras* was to read and teach the Vedic literature and to perform various sacrifices.

The *Kshatriyas* were primarily concerned with administration of the country especially defence. Both classes were regarded as upper class and were exempted from taxes. They were having special rights and privileges in the society.

The *Vaishyas* were connected with the economic life of the country. They were responsible for the production of wealth[7]. The fourth class was the strongest creation of the Indo-Aryan system. They were denied the study of the Vedic literature and the wearing of sacred thread[8]. They were having very few rights in the society. Both these sections payed taxes and performed services to the upper classes.

Slavery was also a recognised institution of Indian society. The '*Smriti*' law of the Gupta age developed rules in respect of slavery. Slaves suffered from certain disabilities According to Manu a slave could not be a judicial witness except in the last resort[9].

On one side economy grew rapidly while on the other side discrimination among the people became so rigid. Under the *Kushana* India reached to the highest peak of urbanisation, trade, commerce, and monetary economy. A new section of society took birth, known as '*setthis*', (artisans and traders) accounted for a large proportion of city population and were engaged in trade and commerce[10].

All these progresses increased the gap between the poor and the rich. But the rulers, ruled with the principle of welfare of state and the protection of the people was thought to be the divine duty of the kings. The taxes collected and wealth of the country were invested in development of her own land.

Thus, the Indian economy was a prosperous and well

developed economy.

2   Medieval Indian Era:

The country ushered into the new era marked with some changing events. In the year 1206 Qutub-ud-din Aibak laid the foundations of the Delhi Sultanate which ruled for over three centuries. Under the Sultanate rule Muslim theology was derived. The Muslim theology had its roots in the Quran, the tradition of the Prophet and the precedent. The Quran which has a divine origin and possesses a sacred character contains injunctions for the regulation of social life and political organisation[11].

With the beginning of new era "Urbanisation" was marked. A number of new towns and urban centres also came up in the thirteenth and fourteenth centuries[12]. The ruling class, which came from different cultural milieus, had need of leisure and comforts of a different type[13]. They motivated craftsmen, artisans, physicians, singers, musicians, dancers, poets, etc. Trade and commerce were also increased.

Apart from this agriculture was the main occupation and land revenue was the main source of income. The sultanate period belongs to the various new techniques introduced by the Turks in the field of textiles. Cotton cultivation is also part of agriculture technology. Under the ruling of sultan a number of reforms were introduced, like Alauddin Khajli measured the land and then fixed tax in kind on each unit of area. He demanded land revenue at the rate of one-half of the production to be levied separately on the holding of each individual cultivator[14]. The taxation principles, followed by the Delhi Sultan, were to some extent based on the *Hanafi* school of Muslim Law. The revenue was broadly categorised into the *fay* and the *zakat* by Muslims. *Jizya* was imposed on non Muslims in return for which they received protection of life and property and exemption from military services[15]. Under the Sultanate rule prosperity of country was marked.

Administration according to *shariyat* and Muslim legal system prevailed. The condition of society was still like previous period. King, *Ulema*, Nobles and *Iqtadars* having previlages and rights.

Under the Mughals economic growth and prosperity raised on his heights's. The Mughals welcomed the foreign traders, provided them security and protection for his transaction and levied a very low custom duty[16]. Thus the foreign trade flourished under the Mughal rulers. The manufacture of cotton goods had assumed such extensive proportions that in addition to satisfying her own need, India sent clothes to almost half of the world. The textile industry was well established in Akbar's days, continued to flourish under his successors' and soon the operations of Dutch and English traders brought India into direct touch with western markets. Silk industries were also on flourishing condition. Other industries were shawl, carpet, weaving, woollen goods, pottery, leather goods and articles made of wood. The emperor controlled a large number of royal workshops.[17]

All foreign travellers speak of the wealth and prosperity of Mughal cities and large towns. The efficient system of city government under the Mughals encouraged trade. Most of this flourishing commerce was in the hands of the traditional Hindu merchant classes. If Muslims enjoyed advantages in higher administrative posts and in the army, Hindu merchants maintained the monopoly in trade and finance that they had during the Sultanate. Socio-economical condition during the Mughal period was excellent.[18]

During the Mughals India experienced unprecedented prosperity in history. The GDP of India in the 16th century was estimated at about 25.1% of the world economy[19]. The first notable result of the political denomination of the Muslim was that the Brahmanas lost their privileged position and now they found it difficult to earn with their hereditary occupation. 'Smritis' had to redraft their regulation to permit the Brahmans to adopt occupation other than their own. It was also permissible to eat the food of certain *sudra* castes under some special circumstances[20]. Thus we say the rigidity of the caste system kept the lower castes practically out of the Hindu fold. Social equality which the conversion conferred on the lower castes now enabled them to out their shoulders with high caste Hindus who had despaired them before, and enjoy civil rights so long denied to them. These benefits led the Hindus to embrace Islam in increasing number[21].

The society was transformed under the Muslim ruler, caste rigidity almost diminished. But the class differences between ruling and ruled continued to exist. Aristocrats and Nobles were exempted from paying taxes; legally they had many rights and privileges, but still the divine duty of the kings was to protect their people and welfare of the state. Ala-uddin Khalji, Muhammad bin Tughlaq, Feroz Tughlaq and Akbar introduced series of administrative reforms to strengthen the fabric of the state. The monarchical form of government existed during medieval period. But rulers had followed tolerance policies. They established uniform system of administration and peace that encourage economical growth. The growth rate of Indian economy was highest during the Mughals.

3   Modern Indian Era:-

The British came to India primarily as traders but ultimately succeeded in carving out a strong empire in India. During their rule of over two centuries, they brought about far reaching changes in the economic system of India. They completely destroyed the isolationist and self sufficing character of the village, they contributed to the growth of new urban centres by opening up opportunities for trade and evolving credit instruments, they also contributed to the establishment of large scale industries, destruction of handicrafts, concentration of workers in certain areas and thus, contributing to the growth of slums.[22]

The main objective of British rulers, in India was concerned more with protecting and promoting British interests than with advancing the welfare of the Indian population.

With the British rule new era of exploitation, sadness, deterioration and injustice were started in India. Firstly from Battle of Plasy to 1858 the policy of expansion was followed by East India Company. Under that policy they established extended empire in India. Gradually Indian economy started the process of transformation from feudal to a capitalist economy. The history is a witness to the progressive transformation of the feudal economy, of pre-British India into a capitalist economy, however imperfect or distorted.[23]

First of all they commercialised Indian agriculture. As a result of the process, the agriculture was no more devoted to the production of food. More and more land was brought under cultivation for the purpose of exportation, and then they systematically destroyed the Indian handicrafts and replaced them with British manufactured goods.[24]

The above policy accelerated the process of subdivision of land that created further pressure on agriculture. This can be seen in the following census records.

Percentage of population dependent on agriculture

Years	Percentage
1891	61.1
1901	65.5
1911	72.2
1921	73.0
1931	75.0[25]

The revenue policy of the British resulted into the growth of landless labourers. The British Government continued to give every possible encouragement to the English manufacturers in exploiting the Indian markets. With this protection they succeeded in completely eliminating the Indian handicraft industries out of competition.[26]

The exploitation of the peasants by the moneylenders generated lots of social tension and gave a rule stock to the traditional peace and harmony of village life. This growing tension often found outlet in the shape of incidents of looting tension often found outlet in the shape of incidents of looting and murder of moneylenders.[27]

Apart from this, the process of draining of wealth was the major cause of poverty of the Indians. In fact the British from the very beginning followed a systematic policy of transferring the economic resources of India to Britain and carried away more and more of the Indian wealth to their country.

Under the rule of East India company and the Crown agricultural land expanded, Indian resources improved the living standard of the British people and encouraged the agricultural and industrial revolution in Britain. Thus we can say the policies of the British contributed to the economic prosperity of England and poverty of India. The worst of the maladies created by the policy was unjust growth. A historian writes "Under the British rule, Indian agriculture rose to the level of a national agriculture but it did not grow into a prosperous agriculture. The material condition of the agrarian population as a whole also did not rise. Nor did agriculture as a whole reach any high level of organization and productivity.[28]

In the mid nineteenth century a period of massive investment of British capital in India began. But this capital was not brought from England. The capital plundered from the people of India was invested as British Capital[29]. The Government supported and encouraged large investments in building the railway network. Though designed to facilitate the transport of raw materials from the hinterland to ports and to meet strategic requirements, the railways did stimulate development by providing easier and cheaper access to a wider market.[30]

4   Conclusion:

From the Ancient time to the Modern Era in the Indian history, class conflicts and discrimination did exist while rights and privileges were also secured. But the ruler always gave priority to the growth of the country. India used to be economically prosperous and developed. But under the rule of the British that condition was completely reversed. Indian resources contributed to development of Britain, meanwhile Indian economy deteriorated. The condition of Indian artisans, peasant, traders, needed a consideration, which it never received. On the one hand Britain flourished with developing and on the other Indian remained deprived from the new inventions, technology and industrialization. That unjust condition pushed India many decades back. That injustice of yesterday is affecting India's today.

References:

1. The new Encyclopaedia Britannica Inc, Vol 17, 2007, p 879, Ib.

2. Brighouse Harry, Justice, Polity Press, USA, 2004, (P. Preface vi).

3. Shrinivas Murthy H.V., History of India, Eastern Book Company, Lucknow, 2003, P-135.

4. History of Indian Economy, Cgijeddah.Mkcl.org/ web files/History of Indian Economy, pdf P-1

5. Ibid

6. Shrinivas Murthy H.V., History of India, Eastern Book Company, Lucknow, 2003, P-163.

7. Mahajan V.D. Ancient India, S. Chand & Company, New Delhi, 2004, P-166.

8. Ibid

9. Shrinivasa Murthy H.V., History of India, Eastern Book Company, Lucknow, 2003, P-108.

10. Ibid 149.

11. Ibid 219.

12. Kumar Vipul, Interpriting Medieval India : Vol-I, Macmillan, New Delhi, 2009, p-166.

13. Ibdi.

14. Habib Irfan, Essays in Indian History towards a Marxist perception. Anthem Press, London, 2002. P. 82-81.

15. Kumar Vipul, Interpreting Medieval India, Vol-I, Macmillan, New Delhi, 2009, P-168.

16. Economics and social development under the Mughals. http//www.calumbia.edu/itc/mealac/pritchett/oo islamlinks/ikram/part2_17 html.

17. Ibid.

18. Ibid.

19. Jayapalan N. Social and Cultural History of India, Atlantic Publishers, Delhi, 2000, P-4.

20. Shrinivasa Murthy H.V., History of India, Eastern Book Company, Lucknow, 2003, P-240.

21. Ibid, P-241.

22. Jayapalan N. Economic History of India Atlantic Publishers, Delhi, 2009, P-110.

23. Desai, A.R., Social Background of Indian Nationalism (6th ed), Popular Prakashan Pvt., Mumbai, 2010, P-27.

24. Jayapalan N, Ibid P-112.

25. Desai A.R., Ibid P-44

26. Jayapalan N, Ibid 132.

27. Ibid, 120.

28. Desai A.R. Ibid.

29. Rezvi Masood, Tightening Noose of Poverty, LEAD Trust, Lucknow-2015. P-118.

30. Raychaudhuri Tapan, Kumar Darma, Habib Irfan, The cmabridge, Economic History of India, Vol-2, Cambridge University Press, Great Britain, 1989, P-942.

Bibliography:

1. Brighoure Harry, Justice, Polity Press, USA, 2004.

2. Chandra Bipin, India's struggle for Independence, Penguin Books, New Delhi, 1989.

3. Chandra Satish Social changes and development in Medieval Indian History, Har Anand Publication, New Delhi - 2008.

4. Desai, A.R., Social Background of Indian Nationalism (6th Ed) popular Prakashan Pvt., Mumbai. 2010.

5. Habib Irfan, Eassays in Indian History towards a Marxiest perception, Anthem Press, London 2002.

6. Jayapalun N. Social and Cultural History of India, Atlantic Publishers, Delhi, 2000.

7. Jayapalan N. Economic History of India, Atlantic Publisher, Delhi, 2008.

8. Kumar Vipul, Interpreting Medieval India Vol-I, Macmillan, New Delhi, 2009.

9. Mahajan V.D., Ancient India, S. Chand & Company, New Delhi, 2004.

10. Ray Chaudhuri Tapan, Kumar Dharma, Habib Irfan, The Cambridge Economic History of India, Vol-2, Cambridge University Press, Britain, 1989.

11. Rezvi Masood, Tightening Noose of Poverty, LEAD Trust, Lucknow, 2015.

12. Shrinivasa Murthy H.V., History of India, FBC, Lucknow, 2003.

Internet -

1. Economics and social development under the Mughals. http//www.calumbia.edu/itc/mealac/pritchett/oo islamlinks/ikram/part2_17 html.

2. History of Indian Economy, Cgijeddah.Mkcl.org/ web files/History of Indian Economy, pdf P-1

13 ECONOMIC DEVELOPMENT WITH SOCIAL JUSTICE

(By: Dr. Nazia Naqvi *)

Abstract

*I*ndia is a vibrant democracy which is gaining strength day by day. If we consider the achievements made by India during the last few centuries, we at once become aware of the economic opportunities and entrepreneurial avenues that exploded in our country. Factors such as strong GDP growth along with the growth of service sector, and a well-defined financial system contribute to the backbone of the Indian Economy. The demographic dividend also plays an important role in shaping the economy of our country. In this paper we are going to analyse the Topic "Economic Development with Social Justice" under the broader terms such as*

1. *Definition of Economic Justice and Social Justice.*

2. *Is it possible to achieve economic development with social justice?*

3. *How can socio-economic equality, be achieved.*

In India, a number of steps have been taken to liquidate unjust privileges, institutions and practices, and fairly ambitious development plans have been implemented. But both from the stand point of Economic Growth and Social Justice, the results

---

* *Assistant Professor, Shia PG College Lucknow, India*

have been disappointing. Land reforms have not been fully carried out; the price situation causes dismay. Unemployment is increasing and income disparities are widening. The government has not able to deal successfully with anti-social practices. The economy of the country is influenced by black markets, smugglers, tax evaders, hoarders and corrupt bureaucracy. How can socio-economic equality be achieved? The government has taken a number of steps to remove the basic causes of inequality.

- *The abolition of princely order and the Zamindari and Jagirdari System.*

- *The feudal practice has no place in a democratic state.*

- *The government has enacted the Monopolies and Restrictive Trade practices Act to prevent concentration of Economic power to the common man.*

- *Licensing policy.*

- *Provide kind of assistance to the small producer and the co-operative sector.*

- *End regional imbalances and help backward areas.*

- *Huge funds are being plunged in agriculture to rationalise its product.*

- *Land reforms have been enacted to provide security to tenure to tenants.*

- *Ceilings on the urban property.*

- *The step towards equality will have been taken when full employment has been achieved.*

Thousands of engineers and scientists can find no job, our development projects are not sufficiently employment oriented. It is discriminating that a person who is working in the same post and performing the same duty is not getting legitimate rights, for example, PhD holders or in the banks. Government is doing nothing for social justice. If unemployment is to be substantially reduced our development plans must be far more ambitious in terms of investment it cannot be said that our capital resumes are to permit investment commensurate with our needs. The end of development ought to be not merely an increase in national income, but happiness of the masses. The list of economic growth must be more concrete happiness of the common man measured in terms of his primary need and other necessaries of life. The conviction of economic growth is one of the most prevalent and persistent guiding forces of the developed world. We must be quite clear in our minds as to what the democratic process involves. First and foremost, it involves, respect for "fundamental rights of citizenship." The degree of control exercised in the totalitarian states on the lives of the citizens is unthinkable in the open societies. Concentration of economic power is incompatible with democratic living. The constitution rightly directs the states to see that operation of the economic system does not result in the concentration of wealth and means of production to the common detriment what is not often realized is that concentration of wealth and means of production in the state is as inimical to the free way of life as that in private hands.

1 Introduction

Today, economic growth is everybody's concern and in such a milieu, growth theory has received particular attention of economists. Yet surprisingly, there is no consensus on the definition of the term. Different economists have used the term 'economic growth' to convey different meanings. In some cases the concepts differ in essence, whereas in others only in emphasis. Some of the economists are of the view that the term 'economic growth' is very much obvious and there is no need to frame a precise definition of it. Thus, quite often no distinction is made between 'economic growth' and 'economic development' and the two terms are used interchangeably. Others feel that clear and unambiguous definitions are a prerequisite to any precise analysis. Underlying the difficulties which most social scientists face in the absence of precise definitions, world A. Shearer stated: "The literature of social sciences is a testimony to the errors; unnecessary confusions and prolonged debates which can result from an ambiguity on the level of basic conceptualization[1]". We also feel that to avoid ambiguity, it is better to identify economic growth in terms of some measurable criteria, namely:

- The concept of economic growth

- The concept of economic development

- Growth and development

2 Definning social justice and economic justice

Social Justice encompasses economic justice. Social justice is the virtue which guides us in creating those organized human interactions we call institutions. In turn social institution when justly organized; provide us with access to what is good for the person both individually and in our association with others. Social justice also imposes on each of us a personal responsibility to work with others to design and continually perfect our institutions as tools for personal and social development this is also about keeping a balance between group of people in a society or a community. *Economic justice* is a component of social justice it is a set of moral principles for building economic institutions, the ultimate goal of which is to create an opportunity for each person to create a sufficient material foundation upon which to have a dignified, productive and creative life beyond economics.

3 Is it possible to achieve economic development with social justice?

Economic justice like every system, involves input, output and feedback for restoring harmony or balance between input and output. The system of economic justice is defined by Louis kelso and Mortimer Adler, there are three essential and inter dependent principles. Participative Justice – (The input principle), Distributive Justice (The out-take principle) and social Justice (The feedback principle). This principle of economic justice shows the relationship between economic development and social justice.

3.1 **Participative justice:**

It is about the 'Input' one makes to the economic process in order to make a living. It requires equal opportunity in gaining access to private property in production asset as well as equality of opportunity to engage in productive work.

3.2 **Distributive justice:**

It defines the output or outtake rights of an economic system matched to each person's labour and capital inputs. Through the distributional features of private property within a free and open market place, distributive justice becomes automatically linked to participative justice, and incomes become linked to productive contributions. The objective of distributive justice is to determine the just price, the just wage, and the just profit. The principle of participation does not guarantee equal results, but requires that every person be guaranteed by society's institution, the equal human right to make a productive contribution to the economy, both through one's labour (as a work) and through one's productive capital (as an owner). This principle rejects monopolies, special privileges, and other social barrier to economic self reliance.

3.3 **Social Justice:**

It is the feedback principle that detects flaws in distribution of the input and or outtake and guides the corrections needed to restore a just and balanced economic order for all. This principle is violated by unjust barriers to participation, by monopolies or by some using their property to harm or exploit others.

Economic harmony results when participative and distributive justice are operating fully for every person within a system or institution and social justice offers guidelines for controlling monopolies, building checks and balances with social institution, and resynchronizing distribution (outtake) with participation (input). Economic development can be measured in various ways, Ideology followed by a country, types of population residing in it, and the extent of foreign aid available to it for the economic development. In India we can point out various strong areas of economic growth, currently economic condition is not rosy in India Low productivity along with inflation, fiscal deficit, poverty and inequality. Democracy gives due preference to humanitarian concerns. People abiding by democracy are supposed to live within the framework of a free society and achieve economic growth by respecting the fundamental right and notice our contribution is designed in such a way that it envisages the functioning of an economic system that restricts the amassing of wealth and the means of production by a few people. It is in this context that the concept called social justice. War on poverty can be waged and unemployment can be successfully removed if all sections of the people particularly rich and middle classes make tremendous sacrifices in the interest of social justice. Is economic growth with social justice possible? In underdeveloped countries this possibility depends upon a number of factors 1. The government must be stable, resolute and with a progressive outlook. 2. The administration must be dynamic.

In India a number of steps have been taken to remove unjust privileges institutions and practices, and fairly ambitious development plans have been implemented but, both from the stand point of economic growth and social justice, the results have been disappointing. Development with social justices means that we should seek to achieve full employment, abolish poverty, disease and ignorance, wipe out all forms of exploitation produce more goods of common consumption food, textile goods, etc which the common man can buy with his small earning establish a network of schools and hospitals to eliminate ignorance and disease. Statistics of higher production and national income do not tell a whole story. The test of economic growth must be more concrete happiness of the common man measured in term of fulfillment of his primary needs employment, food, cloth, education and other necessaries of life. Economic growth with social justice demands huge public investment in industries, agricultural and social services. The investment of funds on such a large scale is possible only if all sections of the community practice rigid austerity and avoid all forms of ostentation.

4   How can socio economic equality be achieved?

The Government has taken a number of steps to remove the basic causes of inequality. According to the Planning Commission, the focus of the Ninth Plan could be described as "Growth with Social Justice and Equity" The specific objectives listed in the Plan were as follows:

a) Priority to agriculture and rural development with a view to generating adequate productive employment and eradication of poverty.

b) Accelerating the growth rate of the economy with stable prices.

c) Ensuring food and nutritional security for all, particularly the vulnerable sections of society.

d) Providing the basic minimum services of safe drinking water, primary health care facilities, universal primary education, shelter and connectivity to all in a time bound manner.

e) Containing the growth rate of population.

f) Ensuring environmental sustainability of the development process through social mobilization and participation of people at all levels.

g) Empowerment of women and socially disadvantaged groups such as Scheduled Castes, Scheduled Tribes and other Backward Classes and Minorities as agents of socio-economic change and development.

h) Promoting and developing people's participatory institutions like panchayati raj institutions, cooperatives and self-help groups.

i) Strengthening efforts to build self – reliance.

Economic growth must ultimately be judged by what it does to our lives – the quality of life we can enjoy and the liberties we can exercise. In general, economic growth cannot be dissociated from the 'end' of promoting human capabilities and of enhancing well-being and freedom. Governments are now becoming increasingly aware that unless they take corrective action, economic growth can become lopsided and flawed. 'Lopsided and flawed' economic growth would mean economic growth that is jobless, ruthless, voiceless, rootless and futureless[2]. Avoiding these pitfalls of growth requires fostering of strong links between economic growth and human development. This can be accomplished in the following ways:

a) Provision of remunerative employment to people as economic growth is translated into people's lives when they are offered productive and well-paid work. This would require the adoption of patterns of growth that are heavily labour-intensive.

b) More equitable distribution of income and economic opportunities as this is necessary for improving the general human well-being on the one hand, and to creating a close link between economic growth and human development on the other hand.

c) Access to productive assets – particularly physical infrastructure and financial credits – as the lack of access to such assets stifles the economic opportunity of many people, particularly those belonging to the category of poor.

d) Investment in the education, health and skills of the people and providing basic social services to the people. Experience of a number of countries like China, Hong Kong, Japan, Singapore, Thailand etc. shows that channeling of significant amounts of resources by the State in fields greatly enhances human development.

e) Taking steps to ensure gender equality as has been observed that fairer opportunities for women better access to education, child care, credit and employment contribute to their human development. They also contribute to the human development of other family members and to economic growth. HDR 1996 points out correctly "Investing in women's capabilities and empowering them to exercise their choices are the surest way to contribute to economic growth and overall development."

f) A population policy emphasizing the role of education, reproductive health and reduction in infant mortality in order to lowering fertility.

Strategies would contain at least the following distinct elements conspicuously lacking in most plans today.

Nutrition, education, health, housing etc. The basic needs targets, once identified in terms of national requirements, and specified in terms of the nation's resources, will then have to be built into detailed planning for production and consumption. "In other words, we must proceed from ends to means, not the other way around."

5   Equal   emphasis   on   production   and   distribution objectives:

The development plan should not only specify what is to be produced but also how national production is to be distributed equitably. This would require action, at least, on the following four fronts: (i) initiating action programmes and delivery mechanism to increase the productivity of the poor – particularly small farmers and small entrepreneurs; (ii) employment planning, as the only effective means of improving distribution in many societies is to create adequate employment opportunities; (iii) redistribution of productive assets particularly land, as the existing distribution in many developing countries is badly skewed; and (iv) creation of social safety nets for the poor. If human beings are to be declared the ultimate objective of economic planning, adequate steps are required to ensure their full participation in planning. Thus the human development strategy must be decentralized. The beneficiaries need to be involved fully in planning for themselves and then in implementing the plan that is finally drawn up. Annual assessments of the performance on human development front, changes in relative and absolute poverty levels etc., need to be carried out. The liberalization processes unleashed in 991 the Ninth Plan argued that "Our development strategy must be oriented to enabling our broad based and varied private sector to reach its full potential for raising production, creating jobs and raising income levels in society. A vigorous private sector, operating under the discipline of competition and free markets, will encourage efficient use of scarce resources and ensure rapid growth at least cost. Our policies must therefore create an environment which encourages this outcome." In this scenario, the Ninth Plan called for a 'reorientation' in the role of the State with the focus of its attention shifting from regulating and controlling the private sector to increasing its participation in social development especially in rural areas. Therefore the development strategy of the State in the Ninth Plan focused on creating the necessary economic and social infrastructure to enable the unhindered operations of the private sector.

6 Suggestions

1 Development program in the field of social services would open up immense scope for expansion of employment for the educated

2 People in village are to be assured of minimum medical facilities.

3 Doctors prefer to work in town.

4 Free and compulsory education is to be implemented.

5 Land reforms and redistribution of agricultural land.

6 Control over monopolies and restrictive trade.

7 Employment and wage policies.

8 Minimum needs programme.

9 Programmes for the uplift of the rural poor.

If the social services are liberally expanded, more employment greater production and better redistribution and better redistribution of the national income would follow all desirable goals. Development with social justice means that we should seek to achieve full employment, abolish poverty; disease and ignorance, wipeout all forms of exploitation produce more goods of common consumption food, shoes, textile etc., which the common man can buy with his small earnings, build cheap and durable house in millions for the poor and establish network of schools and hospitals to eliminate ignorance and disease, and wide disparities in the distribution of the national income and wealth have been progressively narrowed, we will be able to say that we have achieved economic development with social justice.

References:

(1) Renald A Shearer – The Concept of economic growth.

(2) UNDP, Human Development Report 1996.

(3) Depak Nayyar Economic Development and Political Democracy.

14 GROWTH, JUSTICE, DEMOCRACY AND DISSENT

(By: Mrs. Tahira Hasan [*])

Abstract

*D*emocracy is not only about votes it is also about dissent, difference of opinion, and criticism. Today we favour democracy as the most acceptable form of governance because a citizen has a right to dissent without fear of victimisation — as long as such dissent does not lead to inhuman or unconstitutional action. In fact, the history of progress of mankind is a history of informed dissent; much of creative activity of high quality in all areas of human endeavour at any given time has been a reflection of such dissent[1]. Dr. Donna Shalala, president of the University of Miami, who also has served as U.S. Secretary of Health and Human Services, viewed as the key value: the importance of individual thought and the right to dissent. According to her, dissent has served the United States well and has frequently evolved into orthodox wisdom in later years[2].

Justice is possible only in a vibrant democracy. And growth is possible only when justice prevails. What happens otherwise is evident from recapitulating, what happened to Hitler's Germany, to Mussolini's Italy, to Saddam's Iraq or to Taliban's Afghanistan. First, dissent was killed then died democracy then justice and then ultimately growth! This paper

---

[*] Secretary, All India Progressive Women Association (AIPWA), Lucknow, India

tries to briefly cast light on some disturbing developments back home and calls upon the academia to save the right to dissent at all cost in order to ensure that Justice as well as Growth remains intact for our posterity.

1. The Indian Democracy:

We, the people of India, under the guidance of the wisdom of our founding fathers have successfully managed to keep India the world's largest and one of the most vibrant democracies over the years since we won our independence from the British colonial rule. We faced challenges after challenges and passed tests after tests and survived under multiple and repeated external aggressions, sabotage, monetary crisis and all, and every time emerged victorious – thanks to our most cherished asset our value system, our tolerance and space for dissenting voices in our society.

2. Early Alarms:

For a little less than a couple of years or so, we have been witnessing a phenomenon of suppression of dissent at such an alarming frequency that it is becoming impossible for any person with a thinking mind to keep the eyes shut from them. I will quote only a few as example of the same.

2.1 Narendra Achyut Dabholkar (1 November 1945 – 20 August 2013):

He was a rationalist and author from Maharashtra, India. In 1989 he founded and became president of the *Maharashtra Andhashraddha Nirmoolan Samiti* (MANS), (the Committee to Eradicate superstition in Maharashtra). His voice was silenced by assassins, for the crime of his dissent against traditional superstitions. Interestingly enough he was not critical of any particular religion. He criticised one and all[3].

2.2 Govind Pansare (26 November 1933 – 20 February 2015):

Govind Pandharinath Pansare was born on 26 November 1933 in Kolhar village, Shrirampur taluka, Ahmednagar district, Maharashtra. He was the youngest of five siblings. His mother, Harnabai, was a farmhand and his father Pandharinath

166

worked odd jobs. They lost their land to the moneylenders and they lived in poverty.

Pansare used to run an organisation which encouraged inter-caste marriages. He had opposed the Putrakameshti yajna, a Hindu ritual that supposed results in a male child. He had protested toll taxes. He had also criticised the glorification of Nathuram Godse.

After the murder of Narendra Dabholkar, the anti-superstition activist, Pansare had asked the members of *Maharashtra Andhashraddha Nirmoolan Samiti* to continue his work. He had also supported the passing of the Anti-Superstition and Black Magic Act. Pansare said in his book that Shivaji in reality was a secular leader who appointed Muslims as his generals. He also pointed out that Shivaji respected women, abolished serfdom and also appointed them to prominent posts.

Like Dabholkar and Kalburgi he also was killed by gunmen. The modus operandi of the attackers was similar to that used by the criminals who killed activist Dabholkar and Kalburgi[4].

2.3 Malleshappa Madivalappa Kalburgi (28 November 1938 – 30 August 2015):

Kalburgi was shot dead in the morning of 30 August 2015 at his residence in Dharwad district of Karnataka by two unidentified men.

Kalburgi, was a progressive voice among Lingayat, a caste group dominating Karnataka state politics. Kalburgi's life work has been to provide insights and raise new perspectives into the Lingayat history and community, which have many times lead to controversy and opposition from other members of the powerful Lingayat community that he was member of. In 2014, he had also spoken against idolatry[5].

2.4 Dadri mob lynching:

A mob of fanatics attacked the family of Mohammad Akhlaq on the night of 28 September 2015 in Bisara village near Dadri. On 28 September 2015 evening, two boys used the local temple's public announcement system to spread an unsubstantiated rumour that the family had consumed beef. In the attack Akhlaq died and his son was badly injured[6].

Interestingly, Dadri is the same place where a few years back farmers – Hindus and Muslims alike had staged a demonstration against land acquisition – at allegedly a very low rate – for the power project of a private corporate house. Now they stand divided among themselves (The details of the case can be found at the website of National Human Rights Commission)[7].

Later the police also filed a charge sheet against one of the fiery political leaders – a member of the legislative assembly – at the forefront of the anti-beef protests for violating the prohibitory orders and ironically, as per the press reports, the same anti-beef crusader was found to have been a Director of Al-Dua, a meet producing company[9]!

So it reflects that there is a huge difference in what they preach and what they practice. It is an attempt to fracture the secular fabric in the name of pseudo nationalism. There is kind of strategic attack against all who have raised their voice against this hate politics and suppression of dissent.

In India the parties who come to power by public vote are sworn by the Indian Constitution and are supposed to uphold the Constitution, and not their agenda of *Hindutva* or *Islamitva*.

3   Silver lining in the darkness:

Every dark cloud has a silver lining, it is said. In India the intellectual class has fortunately proving to be that silver lining. Our intellectuals – writers, scientists, film makers and artists – chose not to remain silent and registered their protest by returning awards that they had won for their creative works. The distress they felt was reflected in their returning their awards which conveyed a message that we cannot let our democracy slip into the hands of fascist forces who are playing to the tunes of some greedy corporates, controlling infrastructure, natural resources, and the media. The poor people are fighting for their lands and their resources, and unfortunately the government appears to be siding with a few big corporates. Capitalist bank-defaulters of thousands of crores escape law easily while poor farmers are forced to commit suicide. Those who raise their voices in favour of the poor are being silenced by using draconian laws.

4 **Conclusion**:

Though it appears, that dissent will be perhaps suppressed more ruthlessly in the future, it is our true nationalistic duty to remain alive and awake and raise our voices of genuine dissent rather fearlessly in favour of the masses as and when necessary, lest we become guilty of *lokdhroh* (A treason against the true monarch in a democracy – the public at large).

If dissent will die, democracy will die. If democracy will die, justice will die and if justice dies, though in short run there may be an apparent spurt in growth, but ultimately growth will go and we will be sliding down a path of retrogression.

References:

1.Pushpa M. Bhargava (2014), The importance of dissent in democracy, The Hindu 18 June 2014

2.Wilson Center (2008), The Right to Dissent is Crucial to American Democracy,

https://www.wilsoncenter.org/article/the-right-to-dissent-crucial-to-american-democracy?gclid=COff77OL1MsCFRcfaAodZ6UP0g

3. Wikipedia, the free encyclopedia

4.ibid

5.ibid

6.ibid

7. National Human Rights Commission. (2006). NHRC Seeks report from the U.P. Government on its plan to relocate and rehabilitate persons affected due to land acquisition for Reliance Power Project. http://nhrc.nic.in/disparchi ve.asp?fno=1330

8.http://www.thehindu.com/todays-paper/tp-international/sangeet-singh-som-admits-he-was-director-of-aldua/article7744764.ece

15 ABUSE AND VIOLATION OF INTELLECTUAL PROPERTY RIGHTS
(By: Mr. Md. Wali Iftikhar *)

Abstract

*P*roperty has different dimensions and these dimensions have reconstructed and re-evolved in innovative discoveries which had never been into existence in the ancient times but for today the things have got completely changed; certain things have been identified by the name of property. The jurisprudential aspect of property also defines ownership and possession, which means hold on property. But for a hold on it the property must be in existence first. If there is no property on what basis a person may have his or her ownership or possession on it? Thus, existence is a must which should be real not unreal; otherwise the beauty of the commodity or thing will be lost, which is in itself a great issue, and needs to be properly rectified otherwise the situation is going to be different. Property is a legal concept created by the courts of justice not only in India but also in the continental and western countries. The owner or possessor has a right to alienate or transfer his property. If the property is movable it will be transferred without any problem but an immovable property has to be transferred with the help of legal documents.

The term 'property' includes movable, immovable, intangible

---

* Assistant Professor, Unity Law College, Lucknow, India

and tangible properties[1] including corporeal and incorporeal properties. Intellectual property rights have been properly defined as ideas, inventions, and creative expressions based on which there is a public willingness to give the status of the property. IPR also provide certain exclusive rights[2] to the inventors, authors or owners of that particular property, in order to enable them to enjoy the commercial benefits from their hard work. There are several types of intellectual property protection like patent, copyright, trademark, industrial designs, plant varieties (Breeders rights), etc. IPR is a prerequisite for better identification, planning, commercialization, rendering, and thereby protection of invention or creativity. Each industry should evolve its own IPR policies, management style, strategies, and so on depending on its area of specialty. Pharmaceutical industry currently has an evolving IPR strategy requiring a better focus and approach in the coming era. The important laws and administrative procedures relating to IPR have got their roots in Europe. The trend of granting patents for a discovery or a product was started in the fourteenth century. In comparison to other European countries, in some matters England was technologically very advanced and used to attract artisans from elsewhere, on special and specific contractual terms. The first known copyrights appeared in Italy. Venice can be considered the cradle of IP system as most legal thinking in this area was done right here. The laws and proper systems were made here for the first time in the world, and other countries followed in due course.

Patent act in India is more than 150 years old. The inaugural one is the 1856 Act, which is based on the British patent system and it has provided the patent term of 14 years followed by numerous acts and amendments like the Patent Act 1999, Design act 2000, The Information Technology Act 2000, The Copyright Act 1957 followed by Amendments of 1994 and 1999 and it was also evolved at the international level by the treaties like Berne convention for the Protection of Literacy and Artistic Works, Madrid Agreement for the Repression of False or Deceptive Indications of Source of Goods, Madrid Agreement Concerning the International Registration of

---

[1] *Textbook On The Transfer Of Property Act By Dr. Avtar Singh Page No.33*
[2] *http://www.ncbi.nlm.nih.gov/pmc/articles/PMC3217699/*

Marks, Hague Agreement concerning the International Deposit of Industrial Designs, Nice Agreement concerning the International Classification of Goods and Services for the Purpose of the Registration of Marks , Lisbon Agreement for the Protection of Appellations of Origin and their International Registration, Rome Convention for the Protection of Performers, Producers of Phonograms and Broadcasting Organisations etc. These national and International Acts and Agreements have given a new name to the subject of Intellectual Property and the gravity and scope of this study is on a new tide with the rampant increase of globalization and industrialization.

1 Introduction:

This era of technology is blessed with many things and there is a great scope in the present generation due to techno-savvy dimensions which have created a boom with a rapid expansion. The term intellectual property includes patents, trademarks, copyrights, geographical indications etc. It is also one of the most important reason in the development of industrial growth and trade and is expanding day by day due to its enormous importance in the present time. International character of IPR is also been recognized in various conventions like the Berne[3] convention universal copyright convention and most importantly India is also a member of Paris convention which is also called international convention for the protection of industrial property like patents copyrights etc. On the other hand international piracy of intellectual property rights has really emerged as one of the most important foreign policy issues for many industrialized countries, throughout the globe. The developing world is plagued by two problems with respect to intellectual property: a lack of formal laws providing an adequate scope of protection, and failure to enforce existing laws against violators[4]. Infringement of intellectual property is creating buzz throughout the globe and it is also increasing with the help of cyber technology specially the computer hacker use to manipulate their power by the easy access of

---

[3] .*Law For The Laymen Universal Law Publishing Co.Pvt.Ltd. 2012 Edition Page No 150*
[4] *http://www.pcworld.com/article/182333/article.html*

internet and use to infringe and violate the intellectual property of original owner by their name and it is not restricted to hackers multinationals and big business houses use to violate and abuse their dominant position in reference to specific intellectual property matters.

2   Methodology:

In the context of increasing number of infringements and violations of intellectual property all over the globe, this article is based on the study of the relevant acts and research papers by the notable writers.

3   What do you mean by Intellectual Property?

Intellectual property   rights (IP) means rights which are basically available on tangible properties and it results from industrial ,scientific and literary fields it includes patents ,trademarks ,copyrights etc. The scope of IPRs are increasing day by day IP system aims to foster an environment in which creativity and innovation can flourish.

3.1 Types of intellectual property:[5]

3.1.1   Copyright:

Copyright is a legal term used to describe the rights that creators have over their literary and artistic works. It is created under Copyright Act 1957.[6] It is a monopolistic right restraining other people to derive any commercial benefit. Works covered by copyright range from books, music, paintings, sculpture and films, to computer programs, databases, advertisements, maps and technical drawings.

3.1.2   Patents:

A patent is an exclusive right granted for an invention or a discovery . A patent provides the patent owner with the right to decide how - or whether - the invention can be used by others. Patents are of three kinds utility patent is one of them. In exchange for this right, the patent owner makes technical information about the invention publicly available in the

---

[5] *http://www.wipo.int/about-ip/en/*
[6] *Short Essays and Paragraphs on Law, by Manish Arora , P. 19, Edition sixth*

published patent document.

4   Trademarks:

A trademark is a is a recognizable sign, or design which is capable of distinguishing the goods or services of one enterprise from those of other enterprises.

5   Geographical indications:

"Geographical indications and appellations of origin are signs used on goods that have a specific geographical origin and possess qualities, a reputation or characteristics that are essentially attributable to that place of origin. Most commonly, a geographical indication includes the name of the place of origin of the goods."[7]

6   Principles, Nature, Role and Advantages of Intellectual Property

Intellectual Property is in itself the biggest gift to human kind because it is equipped with tremendous opportunities and is beneficial to the entire generation of this technological era. Besides this everything whether tangible, intangible, corporeal, incorporeal is assigned with principles which govern their essentials. In case of Intellectual Property the principles and rules are nearly the same in every country, and in the recent years it has played a very dominant role in the industrial development so it is the prime responsibility of every country to protect the rights from infringement and in case of violations it is the duty to take legal action against the violator whether civil or criminal according to the nature of the case and proper remedy is given to the author or inventor in case of damages.

Intellectual property includes trade secrets, industrial designs, geographical indications, patents, etc it includes the fundamental rights for the appropriate owner. In simple language the nature of Intellectual Property is intangible and incorporeal, means it cannot be seen and touched like corporeal and tangible properties.

---

[7] *http://www.wipo.int/about-ip/en/*

Laws in every country are recognized by the Acts specified by their respective parliaments and government agencies. Laws are meant for the development and protection of the countrymen. Patents, copyrights and trademarks have proved very helpful in the economic development of every country. For example patent is simply associated with the process of discovery if a product is discovered like a computer or a mobile it will be beneficial for the public at large on the other side copyright is related with literary and dramatic works, sound recordings, films etc. The entire film industry is dependent on copyrights and incase if a copyright use to get infringed it will affect the industries in a most negative manner. So if the infringement is controlled in respect to copyright, trademarks, patents and other sort of intellectual property the development process will increase day by day at a high level and economy will flourish at an immense high speed and it will shower impetus in the field of science and innovative technology as well in the field of business, culture, industry, literature etc.

IPRs are most advantageous to any country because they boost the economic development of the country and use to be productive in case of profit maximization and also in improving the living standards of the people by introducing several new regimes. IPR use to generate new opportunities in the open and international market by granting patents and copyrights on new products with the growth of technology the emergence of intellectual property has taken a new path altogether.

7   International treaties in respect of intellectual property rights:

Intellectual Property is a glowing international phenomenon all over and for its protection some of the important agreements and treaties are conducted for the development and protection of IPR which are given below.

7.1 List of International and Regional Agreements/Treaties in Intellectual Property Rights are as under:

"(1886) Berne convention for the Protection of Literacy and Artistic Works.

(1891) Madrid Agreement for the Repression of False or Deceptive Indications of Source of Goods.

(1891) Madrid Agreement Concerning the International Registration of Marks.

(1891)   Registration   of   Marks
(1925) Hague Agreement concerning the International Deposit of Industrial Designs.

(1957) Nice Agreement concerning the International Classification of Goods and Services for the Purpose of the Registration of Marks.

(1958) Lisbon Agreement for the Protection of Appellations of Origin and their International Registration.

(1961) Rome Convention for the Protection of Performers, Producers of Phonograms and Broadcasting Organisations.

(1968) Locarno Agreement Establishing an International Classification for Industrial Design.

(1970) Patent convention Treaty ("PCT").

(1971) Strasbourg Agreement Concerning the International Patent Classification.

(1971) Geneva Convention for the Protection of Producers of Phonograms Against Unauthorised Duplication of Their Phonograms.

(1973) Vienna Agreement Establishing an International Classification of the Figurative Elements of Marks.

(1974) Brussels Convention Relating to the Distribution of Programme-Carrying Signals Transmitted by Satellite.

(1977) Budapest Treaty on the International Recognition of the Deposit of Microorganisms for the purpose of Patent procedure.

(1981) Nairobi Treaty on the Protection of the Olympic Symbol.

(1989) Washington Treaty on Intellectual Property in Respect of Integrated Circuits.

(1989) Protocol Relating to the Madrid Agreement Concerning the International Registration of Marks.

(1994) Trademark Law Treaty ("TLT").

(1994) Trade Related Intellectual property Rights ("TRIPs").

(1996) Community Trademarks (1996)

(1996) Documents of the Diplomatic Conference on Certain Copyright and Neighbouring Rights Questions (Geneva, December 2-20,).

(1996) WIPO Copyright Treaty (WCT).

(1996) WIPO performance and phonograms Treaty (WPPT)"[8]

8 Abuse of intellectual property and its legal remedy:

An intellectual property infringement is the infringement or violation of an intellectual property right. There are several types of intellectual property rights, such as copyrights, patents, and trademarks. Therefore, an intellectual property infringement may for instance be a Copyright infringement Patent infringement, Trademark infringement. Techniques to deter intellectual property infringement include: Fictitious, such as: Fictitious dictionary entry. The legal term "intellectual property" ("IP")[9] refers to the broad variety of things created by the human imagination. Not only are such things as art and literature protected by IP laws, Other items protected by IP rights include. Moral rights, Utility model, Database right (which is protected by U.S. copyright laws). Industrial design right – Protection of the visual design of objects that aid in the actual production. Indigenous intellectual property, Plant breeders' rights.

8.1 Intellectual Property Theft:

Theft of intellectual property referred as "infringement" regarding copyright, patents, and trademarks, trade secrets etc and "misappropriation" regarding trade secrets, may be considered either a civil or a criminal matter, depending on the nature of the circumstances.[10]

In 2011, the issue of counterfeit trademarked and copyrighted works alone accounted for as much as 7 percent of

---

[8] *http://www.vigyanprasar.gov.in/dream/may2001/intelleactual.htm*
[9] *http://legaldictionary.net/intellectual-property*
[10] *ibid*

global trade, making it a $600 billion industry. In case of India the legal remedy which is sought in infringement of intellectual property is filing of a suit in form of injunction which may be a final or an interlocutory suit, and damages may be given and accounts of profits are also sought by the plaintiff in form of damages. Firstly in case of infringement of IPRs the suit is filed in the district or High Court on the basis of jurisdiction or depending upon the number of damages claimed. The limitation period of filing a suit is maximum 3 years.

8.2 Patent Infringement:

The use or sale of a patented invention without consent of the patent owner, patent infringement is a matter of civil law in the U.S. The scope of protection of patents under any patent issued often becomes an issue in civil litigation. In case of India patent infringement is punishable as an offence with a period of imprisonment of two years or with fine or both.

8.3 Trademark Infringement:

The use of a trademark that is either identical, or so similar as to be confusing, to that owned by someone else, especially in products or services that are similar to those offered by the other party, is considered trademark infringement.

8.4 Copyright Infringement:

The act of displaying, reproducing, or distributing copyrighted works without permission from the owner is considered copyright infringement, which includes unlawful publication, communication, reproduction of work without the permission of the owner. Other prohibited acts include unauthorized performing or making of derivative works of copyrighted materials. Many acts of copyright infringement, such as reproducing and selling movies or music, are referred to as "piracy."

9 Criminal Piracy, civil action and specific remedies:

9.1 Criminal offences (counterfeiting and piracy):

Infringement of trademarks and copyrights can be criminal offences, as well as being actionable in the civil law. A wide range of criminal provisions are set out in the relevant Acts, and other offences such as those under the Fraud Act 2006 may also be applied. These criminal offences are most often associated with organised crime groups who are dealing for illegal profit in   pirated products. There is also Bio Piracy which is an emerging topic of debate "Bio piracy" refers to the use of intellectual property systems to legitimize, manipulate the exclusive ownership and control over biological resources and products and processes that have been used over many centuries primarily in the non-industrialized culture[11].

Criminal IP offences are also referred as "counterfeiting" and "piracy". Counterfeiting can be simply defined as the manufacture, distribution and sale of products which illegally carry the trade mark of a genuine brand without permission and for gain or loss to another. Piracy, also means copying, distribution, importation etc of infringing works. For example possession of an infringing copy of a work protected by copyright in the course of your business may be classified as a criminal offence under section 107 (1)(c) of the Copyright, Designs and Patents Act 1988[12]. Not all cases that fall within the criminal law provisions will be dealt with as criminal offences and in many cases business to business type disputes are tackled by the civil law.

9.2 Civil Infringement and Avoidance:

The infringement or violation of IPRs is basically a civil matter in the case of patents, trademarks, designs and copyright. In the case of trademarks and copyright the act may also constitute a criminal offence. It is important that business men may take preventative steps to avoid infringing the IP rights of others by seeking permission, means obtaining a license for the activity. If it is stated IP rights are subject to infringement, the owner may wish to take action through the civil courts; other methods can also be used, such as mediation, the use of "cease and desist" letters or by seeking to use other services in resolving disputes.

---

[11] *http://www.countercurrents.org/bhargava140709.htm*
[12] *https://www.gov.uk/guidance/intellectual-property-crime-and-infringement*

10 The copyright tribunal:

"The Copyright Tribunal is an independent tribunal established by the Copyright, Designs and Patents Act 1988. Its main role is to adjudicate in commercial licensing disputes between collecting societies and users of copyright material in their business. It does not deal with copyright infringement cases or with criminal "piracy" of copyright works. Copyright infringement can be dealt with in the civil courts such as the High Court (Chancery Division), the Intellectual Property Enterprise Court and certain county courts where there is also a Chancery District Registry. Criminal matters are dealt with in the criminal courts. Where parties are unable to reach agreement in commercial licensing disputes they might also wish to consider, as an alternative to the Copyright Tribunal, mediation services[13]."

11 Important news related to intellectual property:

11.1 Intellectual property rights attorneys slam proposed amendments in patent rules: (By *A Subramani* | TNN | Dec 28, 2015, 07.58 PM IST)[14]

CHENNAI: A few key proposed amendments in the patent rules, such as limiting adjournments to just three and restricting the right to file patent applications only to patent attorneys and not all regular lawyers, have come in for criticism from an association of IPR attorneys.

In its objections to the Union ministry of commerce and industry, the Intellectual Property Rights (IPR) Attorneys Association has said the proposed conditions would hit advocates as well as applicants from rural or far-flung regions of the nation hard.

Taking exception to the proposed amendment rule that patent applications could be filed only by patent attorneys who clear the qualifying examinations, IPRAA president P Sanjai Gandhi cited an order of the Madras high court which held that patent applications filed by qualified advocates also should be

---

[13] *https://www.gov.uk/guidance/intellectual-property-crime-and-infringement*
[14] *http://timesofindia.indiatimes.com/india/Intellectual-property-rights-attorneys-slam-proposed-amendments-in-patent-rules/articleshow/50356598.cms*

processed.

"In S P Chockalingam vs Controller of Patent case, the high court of Madras said patent amendment Section 126 and 67(a) illegal and unconstitutional, and directed the government of India to process patent application by the advocate. As on date, the verdict is enforceable. In the circumstances, I request you to allow advocates to file the patent applications," he said.

According to the new draft rules, applicants can seek a maximum of only three adjournments. Fifteen extra days would be given if adjournment request is accompanied by acceptable reasons, Sanjai Gandhi said, adding: "This clause is not practical. Three-adjournment rule will affect the whole proceedings and will result in violation of natural justice and arbitrariness."

Objecting to the proposed rule that documents could be submitted only through electronic mode, the IPRAA president said since not everyone in the country had access to electronic media on daily basis, the condition could adversely affect the interest of the applicants from rural and far-flung regions.

Also, according to the draft amendment rules, in case of patent applications for biological resources, applicants must obtain no objection certificate (NOC) from the Biological Diversity Authority within three months.

Noting that the condition is impossible to fulfil, Sanjai Gandhi said: "Though the central government has ordered setting up of a biological diversity authority, many states have not set it up. Since the headquarters is in Chennai, applicants from other parts of the country cannot get the NOC, as it involved time lapse in travel and communication."

11.2 National policy suggests use of intellectual property rights as collateral to raise funds:(By *Ruchika Chitravanshi*, ET Bureau | Dec 16, 2015, 03.00 AM IST)[15]

NEW DELHI: In a potentially big boost to innovation, the country's first Intellectual Property Rights (IPR) policy has

---

15

http://economictimes.indiatimes.com/articleshow/50194124.cms?utm_source=contento finterest&utm_medium=text&utm_campaign=cpps

proposed securitisation of innovation rights, allowing them to be used as collateral to raise funds for their commercial development.

The policy also suggests financial support for developing intellectual property assets through banks, venture capital and angel funds and crowd funding mechanisms, a government official said. The national IPR policy, drafted by the Department of Industrial Policy & Promotion, is likely to be taken up for cabinet approval soon. Securitisation is a process by which various assets are consolidated into an instrument that can be issued to investors. "Countries such as the US and Japan do allow mortgaging of intellectual property assets," said R Saha, senior advisor with the Confederation of Indian Industry, backing the idea. A key objective of the policy is "to create public awareness about the economic, social and cultural benefits of IPRs."

11.3 Kwality mired in feud among founder families over intellectual property: (By *Divya Sathyanarayanan*, ET Bureau | Jan 04, 2016, 04.35 AM IST MUMBAI)[16]

MUMBAI: After Vadilal, another iconic ice-cream brand is seeing a meltdown in relations between the families of its founders. Ravi Ghai, son of Iqbal Ghai, who founded the `Kwality' brand, has dragged his father's former business partner, PL Lamba, to court, alleging the Lambas unlawfully transferred the intellectual property of brand `Kwality' to another company. This has come up at a time when the Vadilal Group, which sells the eponymous ice-cream products, is in the middle of a feud in the promoter family..

11.4 China Rules Microsoft Violated Intellectual Property Rights: (By *Owen Fletcher*, IDG News Service)[17]

A Beijing court has ruled that Microsoft violated a Chinese company's intellectual property rights in a case over fonts used in past Windows operating systems, state media said Tuesday. The Beijing Number One Intermediate People's Court this

---

16

http://economictimes.indiatimes.com/articleshow/50431890.cms?utm_source=contento finterest&utm_medium=text&utm_campaign=cppst
[17] http://www.pcworld.com/article/182333/article.html

week ordered Microsoft to stop selling versions of Windows that use the Chinese fonts, state broadcaster CCTV said. Microsoft plans to appeal the case, a company representative said in a statement. The ruling comes as Barack Obama visits China for his first time as U.S. president. The visit has brought renewed focus on tensions over piracy and the trade of high-tech products between the countries. A U.S. business association this week appealed to Obama for further efforts to protect intellectual property rights in China, where pirated copies of DVDs and computer software including Windows are widely sold on streets and in bazaars. Microsoft originally licensed Zhongyi's intellectual property more than a decade ago for use in the Chinese version of Windows 95, according to Zhongyi. Zhongyi argues that agreement applied only to Windows 95, but that Microsoft continued to use the intellectual property from Windows 98 to Windows XP.The court reportedly also ruled that Microsoft's use of a Chinese input system from Zhongyi did not violate any licensing agreements. Microsoft agrees with the court that the key in the two cases is a dispute over the scope of licensing agreements, the Microsoft representative said. But it disagrees with the ruling on the coverage of the agreements, which it believes also include its use of the fonts, the representative said. Windows XP is the most widely used OS in Chinese offices and homes, but countless users run pirated copies. Pirated versions of Windows 7 were on sale in one Beijing bazaar weeks before the software officially went on sale last month. Microsoft offers Windows 7 in China for a lower price than in developed markets, and often labels its software "legal" to differentiate it from the pirated versions common in the country. Windows 7 Home Premium costs 699 yuan (US$103) in China, compared to $199.99 in the U.S.

11.5 MNCs marrying into India Inc face patent test: (By *Gireesh Chandra Prasad* Jul 30, 2007, 04.32am IST)[18]

NEW DELHI: MNCs going in for mergers and acquisitions will soon be required to divest some of their patented technologies to a third-party rival if the intellectual property

---

[18] *http://articles.economictimes.indiatimes.com/2007-07-30/news/28435617_1_patents-ipr-mnc-pharma-companies*

rights (IPRs) of the combined entity undermine fair competition in the market.

While approving big mergers and acquisitions, the competition regulator will ensure the merged entity does not control the entire range of a particular product category through its combined intellectual property wealth. If the merging entities are the only two companies that have proprietary technology for a product category, they may have to agree to divest the knowhow to a third-party rival. The guidelines on how to balance competition law with IPR, which the Competition Commission of India (CCI) is evolving, aims to protect consumers from the ill effects of big firms gaining further in size and market share. This is particularly true for MNC pharma companies that want to consolidate to resist the storming generics competition. The move assumes significance as India recently started issuing patents on finished pharmaceutical products. Also, the merger of local arms of global majors would need CCI's blessings. In the 1990s, Swiss Pharma giants Ciba-Geigy and Sandoz - which merged to form Novartis AG - had to agree to such a condition to get the Federal Trade Commission's nod for the deal. Novartis has been rumoured to be in talks with its rival at home F Hoffmann La Roche for a possible merger that would result in the largest Pharma company in the world. Roche had bagged the first pharmaceutical product patent in India.

CCI will also work with the patents office and the government to ensure rigorous competition principles are followed in the grant of patents and, more importantly, their enforcement. It has identified nine areas where patents are globally abused by owners. Pooling of competing patents by rival companies through cross-licensing, insisting that any improvement in the patented innovation that a licensee makes should be exclusively granted back to the licenser and condition in the licensing agreement that the licensee will not challenge the validity of the patent are some of the possible abuses that the commission wants to check. Besides Pharma and biotech firms, the move has major implications for telecom companies that often fight in courtrooms over IPR issues. The maker of a leading brand, say a computer operating system, not disclosing how rival companies could make their application software, say for Internet browsing, compatible to the market leader's operating system is another form of abusing IPR rights. Broadening of patent claims to get monopoly for parts of the finished product other than the invention is yet another form of abuse that CCI would target."Competition authorities 1find problems not in IPR per se, but the way it is enforced by some owners. If conditions introduced in the exercise of rights go beyond the protection of IPR and result in throttling competition, then it defeats the purpose of IPR, that is, incentivising innovation," CCI member and acting chairman Vinod Dhall told ET. The harmonious enforcement of the two legal systems to complement and strengthen each other's purpose is needed, he said."IPR laws are meant to encourage innovation, not stifle it. Abusing IPR rights can defeat its very purpose and, therefore, competition principles should be kept in mind while exercising such rights," Mr Dhall said.

12 Harmful consequence in respect to economy:

The consequences are as under:-

i. The Counterfeit goods deprive companies of the fruit of their notoriety, positive image and their investments in research and development, innovation and marketing. This affects not only companies themselves but all of society.

ii. The loss of revenues from counterfeiting is estimated at hundreds of billions[19] of euros worldwide. The counterfeit market represents 5 to 10% of global trade. This results in a significant loss in taxes and customs duties.

iii. Similarly, there is a risk to the health and safety of consumers. Products are manufactured without being controlled by the relevant authorities and do not always meet quality standards.

iv. Counterfeiting and piracy have an especially negative impact on innovation and investment. Companies are less inclined to invest in research and development if the results are not efficiently protected.

v. An effective way to fight piracy is therefore extremely important. In the wake of international and European

---

[19]
http://economie.fgov.be/en/entreprises/Intellectual_property/Innovation_et_propriete_i ntellectuelle/Protection/#.VsyGfH196t

treaties, Belgian legislators have thus come up with a variety of different ways to prevent copyright violations.

vi.   The licenses given to IP owners use to get violated and abused time to time which is in itself a major threat to every economy whether Indian or American etc

13 National IPR Policy of India and Technology Issues:

Indian government is in the process of formulating the National Intellectual Property Rights (IPRs) Policy of India and preliminary formalities have already been completed in this regard. A group of experts have been brought together in the form of a think tank that would assist the government in this regard. This move of Indian government is appreciable and it a general hope that the proposed national IPR policy of India would be released very soon. With the experts on the board, the proposed IPR policy would be drafted with best intentions and in the most appropriate manner, it is presumed that the think tank would also consider the technological aspects of intellectual property rights while drafting the policy document. "For instance, issues pertaining to domain name dispute resolution, cyber squatting, online copyright violations and their redressals, pirated TV broadcasting, industrial espionage, e-books, anti piracy redressal mechanism, online brands infringements and their management, international exhaustion of trademarks, challenges of new GTLDs, etc must also be considered while formulating the proposed national IPR policy of India. Public awareness about IPRs protection and management in India is very low. At time companies and individuals take actions that are clearly illegal. Similarly, many times stakeholders are not aware that they are actually violating the IPRs of others. In many cases IPR protection under patent law of India is lost for improper handling of the product to be patented. Conflict of laws in cyberspace also requires compliance with laws of other jurisdictions to get appropriate relief. The proposed national IPR policy of India also needs to cater technological issue of IPR in India"[20]

---

[20] *http://iprsi.blogspot.in*

14 Suggestions for protection of intellectual property:

i.   Compulsory licensing of copyright, patents and other intellectual properties is important for the protection and it will prevent the abuse and violation.

ii. Securing and registration of patents, trademarks, and copyrights in key foreign markets to prevent the regular abuse of IP Products[21]

iii. The public should be knowledgeable and educated in real sense on the basics of trademarks, copyrights, patents, and trade secrets breeders rights[22]

iv. Conduct an audit to identify all your registered and unregistered trademarks and copyrights

15. Conclusion:

It seems apparent that the competition authorities need to ensure the co-existence of competition policy and intellectual property laws, they need not overlook the fact that the objectives of the two policies, though complementary, can also be conflicting, in which case there could be harm to society in terms of reduced welfare, and on the other side it also stated that the MNCs and the business globetrotters and trade giants abuse their power by their worldwide connectivity and by that the revenues and control is reduced hence development process is not completed as the revenue resources are curbed by the MNCs. Although putting exemption clauses in competition laws to cater for IPRs is a noble idea, the exemption should ensure that it leaves room for competition authorities to carefully implement a rule of reason approach, on a case by case basis, to ensure that the innovation objective, which is the basis for IPRs, does not result in practices that are in violation to the competition laws. It will also be equally important that in the drafting of the IPRs in the countries with competition laws, some references also be made to corresponding competition provisions to ensure co-existence. Ownership of both tangible

---

[21] *http://www.uspto.gov/patents-getting-started/international-protection/protecting-intellectual- property-rights-ipr*

[22] *http://www.inc.com/kelly-fitzsimmons/ten-ways-to-protect-your-intellectual-property.html*

and intangible property equally provides the right to exclude others from the use or exploitation of the property, subject to limitations imposed by the general and basic law.

Some of the important cases like Bajaj auto limited, Bayer corporation case, Novartis, Merck vs Glenmark, Ericsson vs Xiaomi etc have shown great impetus on infringement issues and increasing patent and copyright litigation in the present scenario.

On the whole it is specifically seen that the GDP of the countries are increasing but the violations are rampant and they need to be controlled as everybody is of the knowledge that intellectual property are proving profitable in the developmental and economic growth of every country worldwide but their abuse is also increasing and the breach of law ultimately turns in the infringement of laws and in case of infringements it is getting necessary to provide relevant and adequate remedies to the specific IP owners for achieving the ends of Justice. The latest IP Crime Report was published on 29 July 2013. The report specifically have highlighted the current and emerging threats surrounding theft and piracy, including those conducted by the internet. The report also contains statistical data and enforcement activities from UK law enforcement agencies such as trading standards, police and HM Revenue and Customs along with industry bodies

Patents act, Information Technology Act, Design Act, Geographical Indications of Goods Act, Trade Marks Act in India and Berne convention for the Protection of Literacy and Artistic Works ,Hague Agreement concerning the International Deposit of Industrial Designs. The WIPO treaty, The Anti-Counterfeiting Trade Agreement (ACTA) at the international level have provided effective enforcement to intellectual property rights for economic growth across all industries throughout the world.

16 POVERTY ALLEVIATION IN INDIA AFTER INDEPENDENCE IN VIEW OF GROWTH WITH JUSTICE

(By: Mr. Swadesh Deepak* and Prof. A. B. Siddiqui**)

Abstract

*T*he planners and policymakers in India have been underscoring higher economic growth as an outcome as well as a prime-mover of development policies. However, while discussing about the economic growth both as an instrument and outcome, the question that inherently arises is whether economic growth has actually been poor and inclusive in nature. In order to understand the nature of poverty alleviation process in Indian context, an assessment of poorness of economic growth is all the more essential.

In India, a stated objective of economic policy planning is achievement of high rates of growth of the economy and sustained improvement in the standards of living of people. A rapid growth in employment opportunities for all sections of the society, associated with rising GDP growth is essential to realize this objective as also to achieve the goal of Inclusive Growth. However, despite impressive economic growth over the years, the situation on employment front leaves much to be desired.

Keywords: Poverty Alleviation, Economic Growth

* Assistant Professor, Department of Management, Unity Degree College, Lucknow, India
** Principal, Unity Degree College, Lucknow, India

1. Introduction:

In India, a stated objective of economic policy planning is achievement of high rates of growth of the economy and sustained improvement in the standards of living of people. A rapid growth in employment opportunities for all sections of the society, associated with rising GDP growth is essential to realize this objective as also to achieve the goal of Inclusive Growth. However, despite impressive economic growth over the years, the situation of employment front leaves much to be desired.

The twin objectives of ensuring economic growth with equity and social justice have guided India's strategies for planned economic development since independence. The initial Five Year Plans, however, focused essentially on realizing a high rate of growth while poverty alleviation through generation of employment opportunities was viewed as a natural outcome of this development process. The so-called trickledown theory, an acronym for the

Mechanism of economic processes through which the benefits of growth percolate down to the lowest ranges of the social classes and groups, was thought by planners to adequately address the problem of high unemployment and poverty in the country. Overtime, however, it was realized that these economic processes were too slow and uneven and hence incapable of solving the problem of unemployment and poverty itself despite the economy registering economic growth. Economic growth itself was moderate and shied away from the steady state growth path due to many reasons and tended to hover around a low equilibrium growth rate of 3.5 percent dubbed by some economists as the "Hindu Rate of Growth". This was thought to be far short of the rate which could make a tangible dent on the massive problem of unemployment and hence poverty in the country.

2. Intersectoral Structural Change and Growth:

In parallel with broad sectoral changes at the economy-wide levels the micro economic foundations of structural change also merit attention. Restructuring within the industrial sector itself can impact on macroeconomic growth. The intra-industry product cycle is driven by the emergence of new product groups within each industrial sector, i.e., from simple items to complex goods, while the inter-industry product cycle entails a shift in the relative mass of production from consumer to capital goods. Each product cycle, whether intra- or inter-industry, passes through a three-stage import-production-export sequence.4 The country begins to import foreign goods, then begins itself to produce the imported manufactured goods (import-substituting production), and finally begins to export the excess production of these goods. During the cycle the efficiency, competitiveness and as a result value added is enhanced. If efficiency and competitiveness can no longer be enhanced, the industry ceases to exist. The interaction between the inter-industry and intra-industry stimulates the industrial development of the national economy.

Another approach identifying 'leading industries' within the industrial sector and their growth effects highlights the importance of linkages among sectors, and has popularized the terms such as 'forward and backward linkages. The basic idea is that there are technical complementarities among the various industries and that the growth of one industry is linked to other industries through these complementarities. Leading sectors can however vary across countries depending on the level of industrial development.

Education and Economic Growth in India:

The link between public spending on education and economic growth is by now well-established in the literature. Starting with the work of Schultz (1961) education has been viewed as investment in human capital rather than considered to be consumption good under Keynes' influence. Subsequently, Blaug et al (1969), Tilak (1987) and Psacharopoulos (1993) show that investment in education yields a higher rate of return than investment in physical capital. Romer (1986) and Lucas (1988) have propounded the new growth theories in which sustained long-run growth of per capita income is explained by the likelihood of investment in human capital generating constant or increasing returns. Empirical studies in the literature on education and economic growth also find compelling evidence for the hypothesis that a substantial proportion of the growth of the economies is attributable to the rise in the educational levels of the workforce. Lau et al (1993) attribute almost 25 percent of the economic growth in Brazil to the increase in the average education of the workforce. The success stories of the East Asian miracle economies are also replete with references to mass primary education programmes pursued by their governments (World Bank, 1993). In India, Mathur (1993) has shown that a positive association exists between stocks of human capital and economic development and that the association becomes stronger at higher levels of education. Mathur and Mamgain (2002) find the influence of both technical and general education on per capita income to be positive with that of the former being more powerful. In agriculture, Chaudhri (1979) finds that primary schooling affects productivity positively, particularly in times of rapid technological change.

3. Issues in Macroeconomic Policy and Poverty

The gradual but steady reform process since 1991 in a large democracy with high incidence of poverty naturally led to a wide debate on the effects of liberalisation. There is consensus that trend growth in GDP has improved to about 6 per cent per annum. But, attempts to quantify change of poverty in the post reform period have not led to general agreement on magnitude of poverty reduction. Some major macroeconomic policy issues emerging in the context of poverty reduction relate to:

- Effects of changing structure of production and income generation process on poverty and inequality.

- Adequacy of social sector expenditure by the state governments who have primary responsibility for education and health sectors.

- Changing labour market conditions and casualisation of labour.

- Role of public investment in infrastructure and irrigation.

- Effectiveness of credit delivery system to underdeveloped regions after liberalization of the financial sector.

- Whether macro policies affect poverty primarily

through growth or they play additional role in addition to the growth effects.

- Some states have made substantial progress in poverty reduction while others continue to stay on almost where they were a decade ago. Which forces have contributed to this situation: structural factors, inadequacy of resources or governance issues?

4. Minimum Wages Policy in India:

India was one of the first developing countries to introduce a minimum wage policy. According to J. John (1997), the enactment of the Minimum Wages Act in 1948 was the result of both internal and external factors. Internal factors included the increase in the number of factories and wage-earners during the first half of the 20th century, as well as the

Growing number of industrial unrests and strikes of workers who rebelled against their starvation wage. The most significant external factor was the adoption by the International Labour Organization (ILO) in 1928 of Article 1 of Convention No. 26 on minimum wage fixing in trades in which no effective collective bargaining takes place and where wages are exceptionally low. Until this day, the Minimum Wage Act of 1948 is still considered to be one of the most important pieces of labour legislation.

But India's system of minimum wages is also one of the most complicated in the world. The 1948 legislation determines that the —appropriate government‖ should fix minimum wage rates payable to employees in a number of listed (or —scheduled‖) employments. This has at least three important implications:

- firstly, minimum wages are set by different authorities in different types of companies;

- secondly, the minimum wage is set only —in certain employments or occupations‖ and so not all wage-earners are covered:

- thirdly, there exist now a large number of rates which sometimes differ widely across states, even for the same occupation.

Thus, India has a complex system of minimum wages, which are not applicable to all workers and set up often arbitrarily by different authorities, making it difficult to monitor and enforce the innumerable minimum wages.

5. Minimum Wages and its Effects on Poverty Reduction:

Has the minimum wage the ability to help workers who live in poor households? In the literature, it is often argued that minimum wages benefit workers in the formal economy who usually live in non-poor families. However in India, as in other developing countries, a relatively high proportion of poor, low-skilled people in both rural and urban areas are wage-earners. Our analysis of Indian data for 2004-05 shows that about 30 per cent of salaried workers and 40 per cent of casual workers who earn below minimum wages belong to poor families (and that among the workers belonging to poor families, about 50 per cent earn below the minimum wage). If these poor workers were to receive at least the minimum wage, it would presumably help them and their families move out of poverty.

Assuming complete compliance with a national minimum wage for all wage workers at 2004-05 level, we can estimate the potential impact on workers' probability of being poor (i.e. living in poor household). Our findings show that for salaried workers, the fact of being paid below the minimum wage currently increases the probability of being poor by 9 to 10 per cent. For casual workers, not receiving the national minimum wage raises the probability of living in poverty by 7 to 8 per cent. These results indicate that the enforcement of national minimum wages would reduce the probability for wage-earners of being poor by anywhere between 7 to 10 per cent. 17 Similarly, complete compliance or enforcement of state-level minimum wages would reduce the probability for wage-earners being poor by 3 to 6 per cent. The marginal effects of the probate estimates also bring out that minimum wage is the third most important factor in reducing the poverty risk for the wage-earner household after education and location, if extended to all workers. Clearly this is a significant effect and strongly suggests that minimum wages, whether national or state level, may help in lifting a significant number of low-income families out of poverty.

6. Summary and Concluding Remarks:

India is the second most populous country in the world. After its independence in 1947 from about two centuries of colonial rule, it adopted a mixed economy model with a key role to the state in industrial production and heavy reliance on an import substitution policy. This policy helped to lay the foundation for industrialisation, but overall economic growth was low with a trend growth rate of 3.5 per cent per annum which translated to only about 1.5 per cent in per capita terms. As a result, majority of the people remained below the poverty line till mid-seventies. Starting with similar level of living in the 1950s, the outward oriented East Asian economies grew fast taking advantage of world trade expansion and investment flows.

India was a latecomer in initiating market friendly economic reforms in 1991. The reform process has continued slowly but steadily over the years in several spheres of the economic activities. The various components include liberalisation of international trade by gradual removal of all import quotas and reduction of tariff rates to moderate levels, abolition of the industrial licensing system, market determined foreign exchange rate subject to Central Bank's checks on volatility, promotion of foreign investment to modernize technology and take advantage of global division of labor, disinvestments of government equity in public sector enterprises, and financial sector liberalisation. These wide ranging measures have changed the basic economic policy making framework of the country.

In India, the Minimum Wage Act of 1948 is perceived as being of great importance, particularly to the unorganized casual workers which – as our paper calculates account for two-thirds of all wage-earners and a total number of about 116 million workers. Understandably, therefore, there have been many discussions and arguments about the minimum wage over the years. One important discussion has revolved around the question of what is the appropriate level of the minimum wage to prevent labour —exploitation‖ and provide a decent standard of living. Another debate concerns the way to increase compliance by elevating the minimum wage to a fundamental right, even equating noncompliance with a form of forced labour. Finally, in India, policy-makers have also discussed for years the possibility of simplifying and extending the coverage of minimum wages to the whole labour force.

Our paper provides a contribution to this last issue, mostly leaving aside the other important policy debates. We attempt to provide some benchmark figures on the possible effects of either making the national minimum wage floor compulsory or extending the coverage of state-level minimum wages. We find that such a policy decision, if fully implemented, would have a significant impact on inequality and poverty in India. The large impact can be easily explained by our finding that an extension of either system of minimum wages could potentially improve the wages and the lives of about 73 to 76 million low-paid workers.

References

- Ahluwalia, Montek S. (1978): "Rural Poverty and Agricultural Performance in India", Journal of Development Studies, Vol. 14, April.

- Bandyopadhyay K R - Poverty Alleviation and Pro-poor Growth in India(2007), Asian Institute of Transport Development

- Blaug, M, P R G Layard and M Woodhall (1969), "The Causes of Graduate Unemployment in India", Allen Lane the Penguin, London

- Deaton, Angus and Valerie Kozel (ed), "The Great Indian Poverty Debate", Macmillan India, Delhi.

- Dev, Mahendra S. and Jos Mooij (2005): Patterns in Social Sector Expenditure: Pre- and Pot-reform Periods", in Kirit S. Parikh and R. Radhakrishna ed., India Development Report 2004-05, Oxford University Press.

- Dollar, David and Aart Kraay (2002): "Growth is Good for the Poor", Journal of Economic Growth, Vol.7.

- EPW Research Foundation (2003): "Domestic Product of States of India 1960-61 to 2000-01", EPW Research Foundation, Mumbai.

- Government of India (2010) Report on Employment & Unemployment Survey Ministry of Labour & Employment Labour Bureau Chandigarh October.

- Lau, L J, D T Jamison, S C Liu and S Rikvin (1993), "Education and Economic Growth : Some Cross-Sectional Evidence from Brazil" Journal of Development Economics, vol. 41, 45-70.

- Mathur, A (1993), "The Human capital Stock and Regional Economic Development in India" in Nuna, S C (ed.) Regional Disparities in Educational Development, South Asia Publishers, New Delhi.

- Mathur, A and R P Mamgain (2002), "Technical Skills, Education and Economic Development in India", The Indian Journal of Labour Economics, vol. 45, no. 4.

- Mid-Year Economic Analysis (2014-15) Ministry Of Finance Department Of Economic Affairs Economic Division

- Ojha V. P., Pradhan B.K.- National Council Of Applied Economic Research (NCAER), New Delhi Paper Human Capital Formation and Economic Growth in India: a CGE Analysis.

- Planning Commision Govt. Of India Report on Human Development in India Analysis to Action October 2010.

- Psacharopoulos, G (1993), "Returns to Investment in Education: A Global Update", PPR Working Paper No. WPS 1067, World Bank, Washington, D.C.

- Romer. P M (1986), "Increasing Returns to Long-Run Growth", Journal of Political Economy, vol. 94, 1002-10037.

17 THE NEW FACE OF BANKS' LENDING TO THE PRIORITY SECTOR

(By: Dr. Tahira Akhtar*)

Abstract

*F*inance is the life blood of economic activity. This is because it provides access to all other resources required in economic activities. No business enterprises can start and continue its operation without sufficient funds at its disposal. Financial system contributes to growth and development of the economy by mobilizing saving and then efficiently allocating these savings across investment projects. The Bank is an intermediary between those having resources and those requiring resources.

Sector wise distribution of bank credit provides an outstanding contribution towards economic growth and financial inclusion as well as its role in ensuring financial stability. Various efforts have been done to increase formal credit to key priority sectors. An internal working group (IWG) was set up in July 2014 by RBI to revisit the existing priority sector lending guidelines. The diversification and development of our Economy and the acceleration of the Growth process are in no small measure due to the active role the banks have played in financing economic activities in different sectors specially priority sector.

---

* Assistant Professor, Department of Commerce, Unity Degree College, Lucknow, India

A compendium of papers presented for the national seminar of April 10, 2016 organised by the LEAD Trust and Unity Degree College, Lucknow, India

Banking system is no longer confine to metropolitan cities and large town, Infact Indian banks are now spread out into the remote corners of the country, even more significant achievement is the close association of India's banking system with India's developmental efforts. The target set for advances to the agriculture sector raises concern from the point of view of equitable distribution of credit to productive sector of the economy. Therefore non-adherence to the agricultural lending target raises concern as till a large proportion of India's population depends on the agricultural sector for livelihood.

This paper provides an overview of the targets to priority sector lending by commercial banks in India set by RBI. The present study ensures growth with justice by taking into account all sectors of the economy.

Keywords: Banking sector, priority sector and credit.

1. Introduction:

In today's world, the Banking System plays an important role in the economic development of a country. Banking in India is fairly mature in terms of supply product range and reach even in rural India. The reserve Bank of India is an autonomous body which in collaboration with Government of India, work for achieving the growth of the India economy.

At the meeting of the National credit council held in July 1968, the Government of India emphasised that Commercial banks should increase their involvement in the financing of priority sectors. The description of the priority sector was later formalised in 1972 on the basis of the report submitted by the informal study group on statistics relating to advances to the priority sectors constitutes by the Reserve Bank of India in May 1971. Based on this report, the Reserve bank prescribed a modified return for reporting on the priority sector advances and certain guidelines issued in this connection indicating the scope of the items to be included under the various categories of priority sectors. Although initially there was no specific target fixed in respect of priority sector lending, the Reserve bank advised the banks in November 1974 to raise the share of these sector in their aggregate advances to the level of 33 and one-third percent by March 1979.

At a meeting of the Union Finance Minister with the CEOs of Public sector banks held in March 1980, it was agreed that banks should aim at raising the proportion of their advances to priority sectors to 40 percent by March 1985. Based on the recommendations of the working group on the modalities of implementation of priority sector lending and the twenty points economic programme by banks, all commercial banks were advised to achieve the target of priority sector lending at 40 percent of the aggregate bank advances by 1985. Sub target were also specified for lending to agriculture and the weaker sections within the priority sector. Since then, there have been several changes in the scope of priority sector lending and the target and sub target applicable to various bank groups.

The Reserve Bank of India set up an Internal Working Group (IWG) in July 2014 to revisit the existing priority sector lending guidelines.

2. Objectives:

For the easy approach of the subject to its culmination and to find out the ultimate results of the research the following objectives are preferred

a. To learn the concept of priority sector.

b. To know the priority sector lending by the banking sector.

c. The Reserve bank of India guidelines on priority sector lending and the latest developments in this field.

d. To discuss that the banking sector ensures growth with justice by taking into account all sectors of the economy.

3. Research Methodology:

Research methodology is a way to systematically solve the research problem. These are various methods used in conducting research in order to precede the research. In this particular work, the research preferred to use secondary data, collected from various publications, Reserve Bank of India annual report, books, magazines, journals etc. Here descriptive method is followed to justify the topic.

4. Significance of the methodology:

Though recently a large number of studies, evaluating the performance of commercial banks have come up yet, certain important aspect like the priority sector lending by commercial banks ensuring growth with Justice have remain untouched. Thus for measuring the lending performance to priority sector by commercial banks, a present study is conducted and using the research methodology is justified. Research methodology inculcates scientific and inductive thinking and it promote the development of logical habits of thinking and organisation.

The role of research methodology on several fields of applied economics, whether related to business of the economy as a whole, has greatly increased in modern times. The increasing complex nature of business and government has focused attention on the use of research in solving operational problems. It is an aid to the researcher thus gained importance.

The researcher decided to use the aforesaid method to make analysis of the data so as to which design would be prove to be more appropriate for the research project.

5. Salient features of the guidelines are as under:

(i) Medium Enterprises, social Infrastructure and renewable energy is now included in the priority sector a part of the existing one.

(ii) A difference between direct and indirect agriculture is dispensed with

(iii) Agriculture will also include bank loan to food and agro based units.

(iv) A target of 8 percent of ANBC or credit equivalent to balance sheet exposure, whichever is higher for small and marginal farmers to be achieved.

(v) No change for weaker section, it will remain 10 percent of ANBC or credit equivalent to balance sheet exposure, whichever is higher.

(vi) A target of 7.5 percent of ANBC or credit equivalent to balance sheet exposure, whichever is higher has been prescribed for micro enterprises.

(vii) Foreign banks with 20 branches and above have already target and sub target for priority sectors (agriculture and weaker section) to be achieved by 31 March 2018 and 40 percent of ANBC or credit equivalent to balance sheet exposure, whichever is higher by 2019-20.

(viii) The loan limit for housing under priority sector has revised.

(ix) Export credit upto 32 percent of ANBC or credit equivalent to balance sheet exposure, whichever is higher, under priority sector for foreign banks with less than 20 branches.

(x) Non achievement of the priority sector will be assessed on quarterly basis from 2016-17 onward, instead of annual basis.

6. Categories under priority Sector:

(i) Agriculture

(ii) Micro, small and Medium enterprises

(iii) Export credit

(iv) Education

(v) Housing

(vi) Social infrastructure

(vii) Renewable energy

(viii) Others

7. **Target/Sub-targets for priority sector:**

(i) The target and sub target set under priority sector lending for all scheduled commercial banks are as follows:

categories	Domestic scheduled commercial Banks and foreign banks with 20 branches and more	Foreign banks with less than 20 branches
Total Priority Sector	40 percent of ANBC or credit equivalent to balance sheet exposure, whichever is higher. Foreign banks with 20 branches and more have to achieve the target within maximum period of five years starting from 1 April 2013 to 31 March 2018.	40 percent of ANBC or credit equivalent to balance sheet exposure, whichever is higher to be achieved by 2020.
Agriculture	18 percent of ANBC or credit equivalent to balance sheet exposure, whichever is higher Foreign banks to achieve the target within maximum five years starting form 1 April 2013 to 31 march 2018.	Not Applicable

Micro enterprises	7.5 percent of ANBC or credit equivalent to balance sheet exposure, whichever is higher to be achieved by March 2016 and 7.5 percent by March 2017. Foreign banks would be made applicable after a review in 2017.	Not applicable
Advances to weaker Sections	10 percent of ANBC or credit equivalent to balance sheet exposure, whichever is higher Foreign Banks to achieve the target within a maximum period of five years starting from 1 April 2013 to 31 march 2018 as per the approval of RBI.	Not applicable

Source:RBI report on Priority Sector lending-target and classification.

(ii) The total priority sector target of 40 percent for foreign banks with less than 2o branches has to be achieved in the following manner as under:

Financial Year	The total Priority Sector as percentage of ANBC or credit equivalent to balance sheet exposure, whichever is higher
2015-16	32
2016-17	34
2017-18	36
2018-19	38

2019-20	40

Source: RBI report on Priority Sector lending-target and classification.

8. **Description of the eligible categories under priority sector**

(i) **Agriculture:** It includes farm credit, agriculture infrastructure, Ancillary industry

(ii) **Micro, small and medium enterprises (MSMEs):** It includes manufacturing enterprises, service enterprises, Khadi and Village industries sector, other finance to MSMEs.

(iii) **Export Credit:** It include pre shipment and post shipment export credit and customer services to exporters.

(iv) **Education:** Loans to individual for education purpose including vocational courses upto rs. 10 lakhs.

(v) **Housing:** Loans to individuals, loans for repairs to damaged dwellings, housing projects, housing finance companies

(vi) **Social infrastructure:** schools, hospitals, drinking water facilities, sanitation facilities.

(vii) **Renewable energy:** Solar based power generation, wind mill, street lighting system, remote village electrification, electricity for individual household.

9. **Weaker sections:**

(i) Small and Marginal Farmers

(ii) Artisans, village and cottage industries

(iii) Scheduled caste and schedules tribes

(iv) Self help groups

(v) Persons with disabilities

(vi) Minority communities

(vii) Individual women beneficiaries

(viii) Distressed farmers

(ix) Distressed person other than the farmers

10. Conclusion:

With the significant changes in the economic environment and the thrust given by the Government of India for doubling of agriculture in the tenth five year plan, it is important to increase the farmers' participation in the existing extension system. The Reserve bank of India has advised banks to form farmers' advisory committee in all rural branches. This committee will play a vital role in the rural development and it will not only strengthen the extension system, but will also make it more reliable and transparent by proper planning and resource allocation. A branch advisory committee comprising of selected elected representatives, including women leaders of local panchayat raj institutions, within the service area of the branch, is established at every rural branch. It should meet at least once in a quarter. These meetings are made mandatory and are to be attended by the controlling official of the bank.

The priority sector has been extended by the Reserve Bank of India. The commercial banks enlarge the credit to the priority sector and ensures that priority sector advances constitutes 40 percent of the net bank credit and that substantial portion is directed to the weaker sections, this ensures that growth is accelerating with justice.

11. Findings:

(i) Various purposes for which banks are granting to agriculture and other allied activities.

(ii) How is the bank credit essential for development of our economy keeping in view our large population, rural base of the economy?

(iii) The recent development in priority sector lending by commercial banks with a view to bringing farmers in general and the rural poor in particular within the reach of the extension system and the enhanced flow of bank credit.

(iv) Various features like target and sub target assigned to both domestic and foreign banks under each sector and sub sector are also discussed

(v) Priority sector and their relevance to the overall economic development.

References:

(i) Indian Institute of Banking and Finance (2008), 'Principals of Banking', Macmillian Publishers India Limited.

(ii) Kothari, C.R.(2007), 'Research methodology methods and Techniques', New age International Publishers.

(iii) Shahjahan, K.M. (1998), 'Priority Sector Bank lending, some important issues', Economic and Poilitical weekly, Oct,17th -24th ,Vol-XXIII, No. 42-43, Page No. 2749-56

(iv) https://www.irbi.org.in/scripts/annualpublications.aspx ?head=A+profile+of+banks

(v) https://www.irbi.org.in/scripts/BS_viewmMasCircular details.aspx?id=9046

18 GROWTH WITH JUSTICE: CONSTITUTIONAL SAFEGUARD TO CHILDREN AND THEIR GROWTH

(By: Ms. Kamini Vishwkarma [*])

" *If the law fails to respond to the needs of changing society, then either it will stifle the growth of the society and choke its progress or if the society is vigorous enough, it will cast away the law which stands in the way of its growth. Law must therefore constantly be on the move adapting itself to the fast changing society and not lag behind."*

............................*Justice Bhagwati*

Jeremy Bentham who has propounded a utilitarian theory said that law should be such which gives more pleasures to more members of society[1].According to him function of law is to emancipate individual from the bondage and restraint upon his freedom. The proper end of every law is the promotion of the greatest happiness of the greatest number. Bentham defined utility as the property or tendency of happiness of the greatest number[2].Bentham agreed with irrational Hans Kelson who said absolute justice is an irrational ideal an illusion one of the eternal illusion of mankind. He held justice as primarily a quality of social order regulating mutual relations of men. Justice is nothing but social happiness guaranteed by protecting

[*] Assistant Professor, Unity Law College, Lucknow, India
[1] Malik &Raval , 'Law and social transformation in India' P 2
[2] Dr. N.V. Pranjape, 'Sudies in Jurisprudence &Legal Theory'PP 17

of interests of society.[3]Other Jurists and legal reformers notably Llewellyn, Roscoe Poun, Max Weber also supported the contention that the law can be extensively used as tool of social change as it is an effective way of social control[4].

In United States and other advanced countries law is being pragmatism and rationalized thinking .The process has begun in India ever since its independence but the progress is rather slow perhaps because of the vast gap between the law as it exist and as it ought to be implemented[5]. As law is an effective instrument of growth of society as well individual, Indian constitution also underlines the growth by incorporating 'We the people of India' which aims to achieve justice: social ,economic and political. Justice is the spirit and vision of our constitution and it obligates social growth and social order by protecting rights of individual and providing them equal opportunities to them. Beg, J referring to the preamble as well as provision of part III and IV of Constitution opined that it seeks to express the principle *Salus Populi Suprema Lex* the good of the mass of citizens of our country is supreme law embodied in constitution.[6] The universal prayer to mother goddess *'Sarve Bhavantu Sukhina Sarve Santu Niramayah, Sarve Bhadrani Pashyantu Ma Kanchit Dukh Bhag Bhavet'* (it is not enough if alone we are happy those around us should also be happy then whole world will be happy) contains very essence of growth[7]. Indian constitution also embodied the concept of growth which means optimum participation and involvement of the people in the process of the country contributing to prosperity of nation and prosperity of any nation depends upon the growth of its children. Children are important asset of nation and the potential future careers of the social structure. They shape the future of nation. Their solitude and nurture are our responsibility. Children's program should find a

---

[3]*op.cit.Malik&Ravak p 18*
[4] *Llewellyn:some Realism About Realism,44Har .LR (1931)1222*
[5]*op.cit Malik & Raval. P 409*
[6] *AIR(2014) vol. 101-part 1201 jour 6*
[7] *Dr. Shyamlha Pappu Padmashri,All India Seminar on Directive Principle of State Policy & Inclusive Growth held on 28 Sep 13,Vigyan Bhawan,New Delhi*

prominent part in our national plans for the development of human resources, so that our children grow up to become robust citizens, physically fit and healthy, mentally alert and also endowed with the skills and talent required for the development of society.[8] They are beautiful gift of nature .Growth of nation depends upon the healthy growth of children. To have it in mind constitution makers made provision for children. The constitutional provisions are as follows[9]:

Art 15(3): The article provides right of equality without any discrimination but empowers the state to make special provision for children.

Art. 21: No person shall be deprived of his life or personal liberty except procedure established by law.

Art. 21-A: The state shall provide free and compulsory education to all children below the age of six to fourteen in such manner as the state may determine.

Art 23: Traffic in human beings and beggar and other similar form of forced labour prohibited and any contravention of this prohibition shall be an offence punishable in accordance with law.

Art.24: No child below the age of 14 years shall be employed to work in any factory or mine or engaged in other hazardous employment.[10]

Art.39(e): Article Says that the children of tender age are not abused and that citizens are not forced by economic necessity to enter avocations unsuited to their age or strength.

Art. 39(f): The state shall, in particular, direct its policy towards securing that children are given opportunities and facilities to develop in a healthy manner and in conditions of freedom and dignity; and that childhood and youth are protected against exploitation and against moral and material abandonment.

Art. 45: The state shall endeavor to provide early childhood

---

[8] O p.citMalik & Ravalpp 213-214
[9] Bakshi,M.P. 'TheConstitution of India Law',Universal Law publishing Co.
[10] Hazardous employment includes construction work,match box and fireworks

care and education for all children until they complete the age of six years.

Art. 51A(k): It shall ne the duty of every citizen of India, who is parent or guardian to provide opportunities for education to his child or ward as the case may be between the age of six to fourteen years.

The Supreme Court of India also held first time in case of Mohini Jain[11] that Right to life U/A 21 and individual dignity cannot be attained without providing right to education .The Court also recognizing importance of education in securing goal of Indian constitution that is growth with justice.

Apart from Indian constitution there is The **Child Labour (Prohibition and Regulations)Act,1986** which prohibits employment of children in certain specific hazardous occupations and processes. Section 3 of newly created Right of Children to free and compulsory Education Act 2009 provides right to free and compulsory education to all the children of 6 to 14 years in a neighboured school till the completion of elementary education.

Though there are so many laws for educating children but in practical underprivileged kids lag at all stages of education. When earning a livelihood and taking care of the members of family become a primary concern in one's life, education become a primary stand a little or very often no chance of pursuance. For the million of underprivileged people in India, education is a high priced luxury and this negative outlook continues on with every new generation. Poverty damaged childhood with significant effect on a child's physical and mental health as well as educational achievement. It limits the expectations of the child' ability to perform well in school constantly reminding him/her of the minuscule chance he/she has to overcome adversity and poverty.[12]

A 2011 census of India found that the total number of child labour aged 5-14 to be at 4.35 million and the total child population to be 259.64 million in that age group.[13]India is the hotbed of child labour worldwide, with over 45m children

---

[11] *Mohini Jain v. State of Karnataka ,AIR 1992 SC 802*
[12] *www.smilefoundationindia.org/child_rights.htm*
[13] *www.wikipedia.org/wiki/child_labour_in_india*

involved in forced labour. We say children are forced to work because none of them is a free individual at this age; they depend on their parent and their environment who makes decision for them. These are kids forced into labour by circumstances imposed on them at birth. Laws and government bans against child labour only have a very limited impact and in some case they aggravate the situation causing poor families to end up poorer. In India, it also reveals the lack of worker's rights but also problems of law enforcement.[14] The surveys of the mega cities make shocking revelations. Mumbai has the largest number of child labourers. In Saharanpur, 10,000 child workers are engaged in the wood carving industry, working for 14 hours a day and getting just seven to eight rupees in a day. In Delhi 60,000 work in *dhabas*, tea stalls and restaurants on a daily wages of ₹8 or 10. In the mining sector 56 percent of workers are children below 15. Child labour is inextricably linked to bonded labour. In Andhra Pradesh, 21percent of bonded laboures are under 16. In Karnataka, 10.3 percent and in Tamil Nadu, 8.7 percent belong to this group.

The only way to deal with the non access of children to education and child labour is to do some agrarian reforms such as employment creation scheme, dissemination of improved technology among the poor, promotion of informal sector and creation of cooperatives and social security programmes and most importantly to make awareness programmes about laws. To end up saying of Gabriel Mistral: Nobel Prize winner is worth mentioned here:

"We are guilty of many errors and faults but our worst crime is abondoning the children, neglecting the foundation of life. Many of the things we need can wait. The child cannot; right now is the time his bones are being formed, his blood made and his senses are being developed. To him, we cannot answer tomorrow. His name is today."

---

[14] *www.poverties.org/child-labor-in-india.html*

19 SOCIETAL DEVELOPMENT OF HUMAN LIFE WITH THE DEVELOPMENT OF MATERIAL AND MACHINERY

(By: Dr. A. K. Srivastava [*])

Abstract

*T*he Human development (HD) and Economic Growth (EG) both are interrelated activities and several studies of the society tells us that humans get several things directly and indirectly with the development of the economic status.

The chronological order of the development of materials and machinery can be evaluated in so many ways in the support.

The foreign traveller 'Fa-hein' elaborated the developed stage of the India in his literature. He stated that the life of humans were so prosperous and healthy that could be seen by seeing the economic development of the society of that time.

Our study is focused on the development of life of a particular segment of the society and their social and economical growth. This segment of the society was the most backward and most sufferer in the society since the beginning of the caste system. Although they were living in the cities but were having several problems.

Every coin is having two sides. It depend upon us which

[*] Assistant Professor, Department of Management, Unity Degree College, Lucknow, India

sides we want to see or like. This is general behavior of humans that on some occasion under some circumstances we may like the things and on the other hand we may dislike the same things.

Nobel Prize is very prestigious and honorable award in the global platform. But the history attached to it having some other sides.

Similarly, this has been debatable topic since long whether the development without the development of human life is the development of the society or not.

The deadly diseases like Malaria, Tuberculosis and chickenpox now have been controlled by the development of medicine and science.

There are number of cases filled in the society where human life has been getting so many things and their life becoming easy.

The chronological order of the development of materials and machinery can be evaluated in so many ways in the support.

The foreign traveler 'Fa-hein' elaborated the developed stage of the India in his literature. He stated that the life of humans was so prosperous and healthy that could be seen by seeing the economic development of the society of that time. It means he wanted to state that the development of humans was to the parallel to the economic development. The advance stage of the society was depicted by various ways.

The disintegration of the Political system in India year by year upto the advent of the industrialization era, it was the society which suffered a lot in all sphere of life including the social life, spiritual life and health of the humans.

However, the Human development (HD) and Economic Growth (EG) both are interrelated activities and several studies of the society tells us that humans get several things directly and indirectly with the development of the economic status.

A study conducted by GUSTAV RANIS (Yale University, New Haven, Connecticut, USA), FRANCES STEWART (University of Oxford, UK) and ALEJANDRO RAMIREZ (United Nations Development Program, New York, USA) in the "Economic Growth and Human Development" state the co-relation of these two. The two chains theory is explained in this support.

A. Chain From EG to HD

B. Chain from HD to EG[1]

Here, our study is focused on the development of the life of a particular segment of the society and their social and economical growth. This segment of the society was the most backward and most sufferer in the society since the beginning of the caste system. Although they were living in the city with having several problems.

The sweeper community has been the most beneficiary with the economic growth. The latest machinery and equipment have made their life more easy and respectable in the society in the comparison of their earlier life of past generations.

The *Balmiki* are one of the largest socially stigmatized Dalit groups numbering nearly 1.5 million in Uttar Pradesh alone and constitute about 16 % of India's population. They occupy the lowliest position of the caste system. During the colonial period they were brought from villages to remove human excrement and clean the cities. They became an urban community. In time, with the introduction of septic latrines, the practice of carrying buckets of excrement on their heads is gone but they still work to clear blockages in sewers where they are half submerged in filth. The stigma remains as they are still identified with the work they perform and considered untouchable and treated as such. They have always been marginalized and treated as outcasts socially, economically and culturally. Sweepers are now referred to as '*safai karamcharis*' or 'sanitary workers'.

The *Balmiki* make up a cluster of communities – a few of whom are the *Bhangi, Mehtar, Chuhra, Lal Beghi* and *Halalkhor*. They have united to form one community and claim a common origin from the saint Balmiki. Balmiki is thought to be the first Sanskrit poet and author of the holy Hindu epic Ramayana and was brought up by a sweeper woman although he was a Brahmin (highest Hindu caste) mendicant's son.

They were given names contrary to their position to give them dignity despite their lowly status – like *Chuhra* meaning beautiful and *Mehtar*, a Persian word meaning prince or leader. However *Bhangi*, the most widely used name is a Hindi word meaning one addicted to drinking bhang (a drink made from marijuana leaves).

These communities can be found throughout the states of Uttar Pradesh, Haryana, Punjab, Delhi, Gujarat, and the union territory of Chandigarh where they are locally known by various names mentioned above.

Balmiki's are employed as sweepers in municipalities, hospitals and government offices. Some Balmiki are engaged in agricultural or contract labour. Pig rearing, bamboo basketry, and poultry farming are some ancillary occupations. Some *Balmiki*, such as the *Mehtar* men of Bihar, play drums at weddings and festivals, while women are midwives.

Post-independence, the Indian government's affirmative action policies have seen an increase of *Balmiki* emerge as political leaders in regional and national levels. A prominent example is Buta Singh, from the *Bhangi* community in Punjab, who was an MP in parliament from the early sixties and became a Union Minister of Home Affairs. The *Balmiki* who work at municipalities have formed unions to help them be treated fairly. The *Balmiki* have also formed an association for their caste at a national level called the All-India *Safai Mazdoor* Congress with a head office in Bombay and branches in other states. The objectives of the association are to strengthen the economic, social, educational and political status of all sweeper castes in India and to remove all social discrimination.

Literacy rates among the *Balmiki* are low because they cannot afford it, though they view education favorably. In recent years, especially in urban areas like Delhi, girls are educated. They visit doctors and use traditional medicines as well. They have begun to value and practice family planning. They have started to utilize the government's developmental programs provided for Scheduled Castes.

A major problem among the *Balmiki* is debt. A common saying of the *Bhangi* is that they are born in debt, live in debt and will die in debt. Social customs that require money for dowries, marriages, death rites, help for extended family and poor health all contribute to debt. Money is borrowed from a money lender at very high interest rates. Gambling is seen as a way out of poverty that leads them further in debt.

The *Balmiki* have a diet that includes wheat, millet and rice. Pork is eaten by all and beef is eaten by Gujarati *Balmikis*. Men drink homemade alcohol and women are allowed to drink at ritual celebrations only. The *Balmiki* accept water and food from almost all other communities but other communities make it a point not to reciprocate. Wherever they are, the *Balmiki* live in squalid, overcrowded segregated areas.[2]

The endeavors done by Mr Robert Owen and Mr J R D Tata are the example to tell that the Growth of Enterprises has been initiating several things for the growth and development of humans since long time.

The Robert Owen had raised the demand for ten-hour day in year 1810, and instituted it in his New Lanark cotton mills. By 1817 he had formulated the goal of the 8-hour day and coined slogan 8 hours labour, 8 hours recreation, 8 hours full rest.

Women and children in the England were granted the ten-hour day in 1847. The 8-hour day movement forms part of the early history for the celebration of the Labour Day, and the May Day in many nations and cultures.

Robert Owen (1771-1858), social and educational reformer, remains a controversial and enigmatic figure. Having profited enormously from enterprise in the early Industrial Revolution he set about trying to remedy its excesses through environmental, educational, factory and poor law reform. Synthesizing reformist ideas from the Age of Enlightenment and drawing on his own experience as an industrialist he constructed A New View of Society (1816), a rallying call for widespread social change, with education at its core. New Lanark, the test-bed for his ideas, became internationally famous.

Robert Owen moved on to the world stage, using New Lanark, however inappropriate, as a model for his Village Scheme, where rather than profit mutual co-operation would be the prevailing ethos. Owen later translated his ideas to the United States, attempting to establish a Community of Equality at New Harmony (1824-28) in Indiana. This was followed by a fantastic and abortive scheme to colonise part of the new Mexican republic on communitarian principles.

Robert Owen returned to Britain, continuing his propaganda campaign, by promoting labour exchanges, consumer co-operatives, trade unions and other Owenite organisations. By the 1830s the man had become a movement headed by Owen as Social Father. Always education, for what Robert Owen was by then calling the New Moral World, was central to his thinking.

Robert Owen was a man ahead of his time. During his lifetime, he endeavoured to improve the health, education, well-being and rights of the working class. This driving ambition to create a better society for all took him around the world, from a small mill village in Lanarkshire in Scotland to New Harmony, Indiana in America with varied success. Although, he encountered much criticism and opposition in his lifetime, he influenced reformers who came after him and many of his views are as relevant and resonate today in their modernity and progressive.

Robert Owen often talked of the new Millennium time when society would be greatly improved.

When he opened the Institute for the Formation of Character on the New Year's Day 1816, he gave an Address to the Inhabitants of New Lanark, in which he outlined his hopes for the Millennium, his plans, and his notion that education was the means of achieving a better and fairer society.

The Address included these memorable words: "What ideas individuals may attach to the term "Millennium" I know not; but I know that society may be formed so as to exist without crime, without poverty, with health greatly improved, with little, if any, misery, and with intelligence and happiness increased a hundredfold: and no obstacle whatsoever intervenes at this moment except ignorance to prevent such a state of society from becoming universal".

Owen's extremely advanced system of factory management, which he pioneered at the New Lanark Mills gained him credibility, not only as a successful businessman, but also as a benevolent employer. He proved that commercial success could be achieved without exploitation of those employed; his approach to social and economic organisation was extended beyond the mill floor into every aspect of village life.

"The working classes may be injuriously degraded and oppressed in three ways:

1. When they are neglected in infancy

2. When they are overworked by their employer, and are thus rendered incompetent from ignorance to make a good use of high wages when they can procure them.

3. When they are paid low wages for their labour". (On the employment of children in manufactories, 1818)

"The lowest stage of humanity is experienced when the individual must labour for a small pittance of wages from others".[3]

"Eight hours' daily labour is enough for any human being, and under proper arrangements sufficient to afford an ample supply of food, raiment and shelter, or the necessaries and comforts of life, and for the remainder of his time, every person is entitled to education, recreation and sleep".[4]

Robert Owen's views had particular appeal for women. At a time when men were hostile to women's rights, he courted controversy by denouncing marriage, as it then existed, as a form of slavery for women.[5]

"Women will be no longer made the slaves of, or dependent upon men.... They will be equal in education, rights, privileges and personal liberty".[6]

The health of the employee by the employer was the most social aspects of a businessman in the era of industrialization. He first time realized the importance of the healthy life of their employee which indirectly helped a lot to make him No. 1 businessman in the India. J R D Tata opened a hospital in 1935 in his factory to provide all necessary hospital facilities free of cost to his employee when the whole word was trying to earn profit more and more by exploiting humans.

When JRD took over Tata Group as its chairman in 1938, he started on with 14 enterprises under his leadership. After 50 years of his leadership in 1988, Tata & Sons was a corporation of 95 enterprises including the ones they either started or in which they had controlling interest.

For nearly 50 years, JRD Tata was the trustee of Sir Dorabji Tata Trust which was set up in 1932. The trust established Asia's first cancer hospital, the Tata Memorial Center for Cancer, Research and Treatment, Bombay, 1941 under the guidance of JRD Tata.

While in 1945, JRD founded Tata Motors; in 1948, he launched Air India International as India's first international airline. JRD Tata was appointed as Chairman of Air India and a director on the Board of Indian Airlines in 1953 by the Government of India. He served this position for 25 years. He was also conferred with the title of Honorary Air Commodore of India for his greatest achievements in the field of aviation.

JRD Tata was always concerned for his employees and therefore he instigated a program of closer 'employee association with management' in 1956, in order to give workers a stronger voice in the affairs of the company. JRD Tata believed in employee welfare and advocated the principles of an eight-hour working day, free medical aid, workers' provident scheme, and workmen's accident compensation schemes for employees, which were later adopted as statutory requirements in India.[7]

Work enables people to earn a livelihood and be economically secure. It is critical for equitable economic growth, poverty reduction and gender equality. It also allows people to fully participate in society while affording them a sense of dignity and worth. Work can contribute to the public good, and work that involves caring for others builds cohesion and bonds within families and communities. Work also strengthens societies. Human beings working together not only increase material well-being, they also accumulate a wide body of knowledge that is the basis for cultures and civilizations. And when all this work is environmentally friendly, the benefits extend across generations. Ultimately, work unleashes human potential, human creativity and the human spirit. This year's Human Development Report explores how work can enhance human development, given that the world of work is changing fast and that substantial human development challenges remain. The Report takes a broad view of work, including voluntary work and creative work, thus going beyond jobs. And it examines the link between work and human development, focusing on care work as well as paid work and discussing sustainable work. The Report also makes the points that the link between work and human development is not automatic and that some work, such as forced labour, can damage human development by violating human rights, shattering human dignity and sacrificing freedom and autonomy. And without proper policies, work's unequal opportunities and rewards can be divisive, perpetuating inequities in society. The Report concludes that work can enhance human development when policies expand productive, remunerative and satisfying work opportunities, enhance workers' skills and potential and ensure their rights, safety and well-being. The Report also pursues an action agenda based on a New Social Contract, a Global Deal and the Decent Work Agenda. People are the real wealth of nations, and human development focuses on enlarging people's choices Twenty-five years ago the first Human Development Report presented the concept of human development, a simple notion with far-reaching implications. For too long, the world had been preoccupied with material opulence, pushing people to the periphery. The human development framework, taking a people-centred approach, changed the lens for viewing development needs, bringing the lives of people to the forefront. It emphasized that the true aim of development is not only to boost incomes, but also to maximize human choices— by enhancing human rights, freedoms, capabilities and opportunities and by enabling people to lead long, healthy and creative lives. The human development concept is complemented with a measure—the Human Development Index (HDI)—that assesses human well-being from a broad perspective, going beyond income. With this simple but powerful notion of people-centred development, nearly two dozen global Human Development Reports and more than 700 national Human Development Reports have been produced over the past 25 years. They have contributed to the development discourse, assessed development results, spurred research and innovative thinking and recommended policy options. Work, not just jobs, contributes to human progress and enhances human development From a human development perspective, the notion of work is broader and deeper than that of jobs or employment alone. Jobs provide income and support human dignity, participation and economic security. But the jobs framework fails to capture many kinds of work that have important human development implications —as with care work, voluntary work and such creative work as writing or painting. The link between work and human development is synergistic. Work enhances human development by providing incomes and livelihoods, by reducing poverty and by ensuring equitable growth. Human development—by enhancing health, knowledge, skills and awareness—increases human capital and broadens opportunities and choices.[8]

Conclusion:

There is no doubt that Trade and business have been providing several things to the society apart from the commercial benefits to the humans. The spiritual benefits, cultural benefits, benefits from the development of material and machinery humans have been getting several benefits. Their living standard and status with minimum hurdles have been improving day by day.

References:

1-http://www.elsevier.com/locate/worlddev

2-http://www.peoplegroupsindia.com/profiles/balmiki

3-From a Paper Dedicated to the Governments of Great Britain, Austria, Russia, France, Prussia and the United States of America, London 1841)

4-From the Foundation Axioms of Owen's "Society for Promoting National Regeneration", 1833

5-https://sites.google.com/site/whatishumanresource/robert-owen

6-From a Book of the New Moral World: Sixth Part, 1841

7-http://www.indiatvnews.com/business/india/lesser-known-facts-about-business-tycoon-jrd-tata-18515.html

8http://hdr.undp.org/sites/default/files/2015_human_developm ent_report_1.pdf

20 THE GLOBAL IMPACT OF THE MINIMUM WAGE POLICY

(By: Dr. Shashank Shekhar* and Mr.Swadesh Deepak**)

Abstract

*W*ith the expansion of global labour markets, more countries are looking for policy tools to address growing low-wage work and working poverty. Does the "living wage" movement offer a path to reducing poverty and inequality? The term "living wage" was first used in the 1800s, as scholars and activists argued that the spread of wage labour should come with a mandate for employers to pay employees wages high enough to support themselves. There was never a consensus on how to define a living wage, although several governments and administrative bodies took up the task of developing complex formulas.

The minimum wage also enters strongly into debates about the impacts of mandated nonwage benefit payments and other regulations on labor demand. If, for instance, the worker fully values the health insurance provided by the employer, then, in a market with no rigidities, his or her wage will fall by an equivalent amount. However, in the presence of a wage floor, the mandated benefit raises total costs to the worker and hence reduces total demand. In reality, most regulation can be

* *Head-Law, Unity Degree College, Lucknow.*
** *Asstt. Professor- Dept. of Management, Unity Degree College, Lucknow.*

imagined as a tax on firms whose incidence depends partly on how much workers value it and partly on rigidities in the nominal wage.

Keywords – Minimum wage, Labor demand.

1.   Introduction:

In recent years, there has been growing interest in the role of minimum wages in promoting social justice by improving the lives of low-paid workers, and also in rebalancing national economies. In Brazil, a stronger national minimum wage – a conditional cash transfer programme – are two of the most widely credited measures to explain the reduction of poverty, which has fuelled the country's economic engine.

1 - In China, coordinated minimum wage increases across Provinces have been a key part of a strategy to reduce inequality and rebalance the economy, encouraging stronger domestic consumption in the face of falling export demand and reduced scope for investment-led growth. In the United Kingdom, where minimum wages were introduced at the beginning of the twentieth century, abolished in the 1980s and reinstated in the 1990s, a survey of political experts has identified the national minimum wage as a successful Government policy.

2 - In the United States too, a higher minimum wage has come to be seen by many as a way to reduce poverty and inequality and provide a stimulus to the economy with potentially favorable including through reduced costs of anti-poverty programs and increased tax revenue

In developing countries, minimum wages have the potential to reduce inequality and distribute income to low paid workers, so as to ensure that it meets their basic minimum needs. From a policy perspective, minimum wage is an important labor market instrument and is often introduced with a clear welfare objective of raising the wages of low-paid workers and improving the wage distribution. However, there has been an over emphasis on the employment effects of minimum wages in the literature, which has to a large extent overshadowed the redistributive impacts and its effects on the wage distribution. The literature focusing on employment effects often also ignores the impact of minimum wages on the wage distribution, wherein some of the low wage workers potentially earn better wages due to the existence of minimum wages or increase in minimum wages. In this regard, Dickens et al. (2012) recently have pointed out that "if the impact on wage inequality and not employment is the first-order effect of the minimum wage then the existing literature on the minimum wage has been poorly focused". There is a renewed interest since the 2008 economic crisis on minimum wages as a useful and relevant policy tool as more and more countries experience increase in both income and wage inequality. A number of emerging and developing economies have been more active in revising the minimum wages on a regular basis and even in advanced countries, like Germany the UK and the USA minimum wages have gained importance to address income inequality. There has been some effort in studying the impacts of minimum wage increases or the introduction of minimum wage in advanced countries, but there is no systematic analysis on the impact of minimum wages on the wage distribution across developing countries.

Analyzing for a later period, 1996 to 2001, showed that minimum wages pushed up wages at the bottom of the wage distribution, as it was binding for many low-wage workers but there was no impact on wages of workers at higher quartiles. The exclusion of time effects increased the impact on wages for formal sector workers and the impacts declined further up the wage distribution. When formal and informal sector workers were combined with time effects, then the effects were positive and significant till the 20th percentile and afterwards there was a decline, while for the formal sector it was positive only at the 10th percentile.

2. Minimum Wage Enforcement Issues:

One of those variables is enforcement. In most developing countries, non-compliance with labor regulations is common. Whether minimum wages affect the job market depends a lot on the extent to which legislation is enforced. This, in turn, is a function of the local political economy. Chronic shortages of labor inspectors and corruption can further subvert the best intentioned law.

The issues are particularly relevant as emerging and

developing countries strive to achieve rapid economic growth that is socially inclusive. This has renewed interest in minimum wages policies. On one hand, there are strident calls to make labor markets more flexible. On the other, there is increased recognition of minimum wages as a tool for reducing "unfair" pay practices and raising the incomes of the poor. According to Ravi Kanbur, professor of economics at Cornell University "In the policy arena, the debate on minimum wages is emblematic of the broader debate on labor regulations, and regulations in general. Intellectually, the issue of minimum wages and labour regulations generally raises a whole host of very interesting and intricate theoretical and empirical analytical problems".

3.   Effect of Minimum Wages on the Wage Quintiles:

To analyse the marginal effect of the minimum wages at different quintiles, we run the quintile regression of log hourly real wages on the effective minimum wage and the vector of personal characteristics. As the analysis is undertaken for all wage workers in Brazil and Mexico, and for those who are covered by the minimum wage legislation in India, Indonesia and South Africa. As a result, while in Brazil and Mexico all wage workers are distributed across the different quintiles, in India, Indonesia and South Africa only the sample of wage workers covered by minimum wage legislation are distributed across the different quartiles. This could result in marginal effects being higher at the higher quartiles, which needs to be carefully interpreted. The marginal effects of the minimum wage are significantly positive around the 20th quintile of the conditional wage distribution for all the counties in both years. The marginal effects of the quintile regression in Brazil show that a 1% increase in the effective minimum wage will lead to a 0.20% increase in wages around the 20th quintile, ceteris paribus in 2005. This effect reduces at the 40th quintile reaching to 0.07% and is significantly negative in absolute value at the 60th and 80th quartiles. In 2009, the marginal effect is positive and significant across all quartiles in the wage distribution and the magnitude is higher compared to 2005. However the effect is much stronger around the 20th quintile (0.42%) and it declines gradually to 0.07% around the 80th quintile. The results for Brazil indicate that a 1% increase in the effective minimum wage leads to an increase in wages around the 20th quintile, ceteris paribus than at the 80th quintile, which could imply that there is a 'squeeze' in the wage distribution. These results are quite consistent with Limos (2007) who also observed that minimum wages compresses the wage distribution in the eighties and nineties. In India, the marginal effects for both years are significantly positive for all the quartiles. Across the two years the marginal effects has increased by 0.14% at the 20th and 40th quintile for a 1% increase in the effective minimum wage. The comparatively lower effect in 2004-5 could be due to the lower rate of compliance, which was only about 31.9%. However, with the implementation of the National Rural Employment Guarantee Act (NREGA) in 2005 now known as Mahatma Gandhi National Rural Employment Guarantee Act (MNREGA), there has been an effort to ensure enforcement of at least state level minimum wages in rural areas. It is also possible that the average wages in general were also growing due to better economic growth. This seems to have given an impetus for improved enforcement as the compliance rate increased to 61% in 2009-10. The marginal effects of the quintile regression are much stronger at the bottom quartiles and it declines marginally at upper quartiles in 2009-10. A 1% increase in the effective minimum wage leads to a 0.47% increase in wages around the 20th quintile ceteris paribus, while the effect around the 80th quintile is about 0.41% in 2009-10.

4.   Marginal Effects of Minimum Wage for all Wage Workers in India:

We further try to analyze the impact of the minimum wages on all workers irrespective of whether they are covered by minimum wage legislation or not. To illustrate what the impacts could be we undertake the analysis only for India where the coverage is incomplete. For workers who are not covered by the minimum wage legislation, we allocate the state level minimum wages based on the state in which the worker resides, which are available from the labour bureau on an annual basis. We then run the quintile wage regression for all wage workers. For 2004-05, the marginal effects of the effective minimum wage increases gradually as we move towards the 80th quintile. A 1% increase in effective minimum wage leads to an increase in wages by 0.23% around the 20th quintile, ceteris paribus and by 0.34% around the 80th quintile. The direction of the results is quite similar and the magnitude of the effects is higher in 2009-10 till the 60th quintile but thereafter the marginal effect declines. A 1% increase in effective minimum wage leads to an increase in wages by a 0.32% at the 20th quintile, ceteris paribus and by 0.34% around the 80th quintile for 2009-10. However, the differences in the marginal effects across the wage distribution are not very big in 2009-10 compared to 2004-05. These results suggests that when all workers are not covered by minimum wages, and there is only partial coverage then wage inequality could increase, as a large proportion of low-paid workers are not able to avail minimum wages. The results are also quite useful for the on-going debate in India about covering all wage workers and making the national or state minimum wage floor binding, so that low-paid workers could benefit.

5. Effects of Minimum Wage on Formal and Informal Sector:

The literature on legal minimum wages in developing economies generally assumes that minimum wages are likely to be enforced only in larger firms and among unionized workers in the urban formal sector and enforced weakly or not at all in the rural or urban informal sectors. It also showed that across selected developing countries the compliance rates were higher among workers engaged in the formal sector than in the informal sector. However, despite the weak enforcement of minimum wages in the informal sector, it still has an impact across the quartiles in the wage distribution The marginal effects of the quintile regressions for the formal and informal sector shows a positive effect of the minimum wages on wages around the quartiles and the effects are quite stronger for the workers in the informal sector compared to the formal sector in Brazil, India and Mexico. These results are quite intuitive in the sense that informal sector wages are in general quite low, so an increase in effective minimum wage would have a positive effect on the wages of informal sector workers than for those in the formal sector workers. In India, comparing the results for the formal and informal sector reveals that the positive effects for the overall sample is mainly due to the informal sector rather than the formal sector. This is not far from expectation as the minimum wage schedule of India is set mainly to protect the informal workers (casual workers) in different sectors. However, in Indonesia and South Africa the marginal effects in the formal sector are stronger or are quite similar across both the sectors. There is no negative marginal effect observed in the regressions for the informal sector. The marginal effects of the effective minimum wage tends to decline across the quartiles as we move towards the higher quartiles in all countries except Indonesia in the informal sector. This could be due to the high level of minimum wage. However, in the formal sector in Indonesia, the marginal effects decline as we move towards 80th quintile. Overall, the wages of the workers in the formal sector are comparatively less affected by minimum wages in all countries except Indonesia and South Africa.

6.   Concluding Remark:

The analysis of the marginal effect of the minimum wages at different quintiles shows that despite less than perfect compliance, minimum wages are quite effective in improving the wages of the workers at the lower quintiles in all the countries under study. The marginal effects of a 1% increase in the effective minimum wage for the overall sample around the 20th quintiles varied between 0.15% (Mexico) to 0.99% (Indonesia) in the late-2000s and the marginal effects increased over the two points of time. The reason for this huge variation could be due to the levels at which the minimum wage are set. In Brazil and Mexico, the marginal effects declined gradually moving up the wage distribution, while in India, Indonesia and South Africa the marginal effects remained at almost similar levels albeit declining slowly. This could be because in the latter three countries, as the analysis is only undertaken for the sub-sample of covered workers, they are redistributed across the different quintiles. In Brazil, we find positive effects at the lower quintiles and negative effects at the upper quintiles in the mid-2000s indicating a squeeze in the distribution, and the effects in the late-2000s are positive throughout the wage distribution but they decline gradually. For sectors (formal and informal) the analysis shows that the marginal effects are relatively stronger for the workers in the informal sector compared to the formal sector in Brazil, India and Mexico. However, in Indonesia and South Africa the marginal effects are stronger or quite similar across both the sectors. Finally, for India the analysis shows that when only a sub-sample of wage workers who are covered by minimum wage legislation are considered then the marginal effects are similar and quite moderate across the different quintiles compared to other countries. This could suggest that there is a potential for wage inequality to decrease as a result of a 1% increase in the effective minimum wage. However, when we take into consideration all the wage workers into the analysis, we find that the marginal effects are comparatively low. The marginal effects also increase across the quintiles as we move up the wage distribution. The reason for this trend is largely because a substantial proportion of low-paid workers are not covered by minimum wages or schedule of employment. As a result, due to partial coverage we observe that wage inequality could increase. These results also suggest that for minimum wage to be a useful tool for income distribution, but it is essential that all workers are covered by minimum wages.

References

-Alaniz, Enrique, T.H. Gindling, and Katherine Terrell (2011) 'The impact of minimum wages on wages, work and poverty in Nicaragua.' Labour Economics 18(S1), S45–S59

-Gazette Govt. of India

-The effects of minimum wages throughout the wage distribution.' Working Paper 7519, National Bureau of Economic Research, February

-Rani, Uma, and Patrick Belser (2012) 'The effectiveness of minimum wages in developing countries: The case of india.' International Labour Review 4(1), 45–66

-Koenker, Roger W, and Gilbert Bassett (1978) 'Regression quintiles.' Econometrical 46(1)

- International Journal of Labour Research 2012 Vol. 4 Issue 1.

-Saget, C. 2006. Wage fixing in the informal economy: Evidence from Brazil, India,

Indonesia and South Africa, ILO Conditions of Work and Employment Series No. 16.

21 THE PRESENT SCENARIO AND FUTURE PROSPECTS OF HIGHER EDUCATION IN INDIA

(By: Dr. Dinar Fatima and Ms. Binish Fatima[*])

Abstract

*E*ducation is one of the significant factors instrumental to the development of a country. It should be transformed to the needs of the time and changing scenario of the world. In particular, the higher education and the mode of its delivery should be tuned time and again for greater development and changes to cope with such challenges. In this backdrop, given the present scenario of Indian higher education, there needs a paradigm shift in the higher education system.

The higher education system in India has grown in a remarkable way, particularly in the post-independence period, to become one of the largest systems of its kind in the world. However, the system has many issues of concern at present like financing and management including access, equity and relevance, reorientation of programmes by laying emphasis on health consciousness, values and ethics and quality of higher education together with the assessment of institutions and their accreditation. These issues are important for the country, as it is now engaged in the use of higher education as a powerful tool to build a knowledge-based information society of the 21st

---

[*] Both Assistant Professors, Unity Degree College, Lucknow.

century. It is also seen that the bad precedent set by the existing institutions dissuade serious investments. These factors have led to specific problems for serious investors in this sector in India. The paper identifies these problems and suggests that a possible change in perception towards higher education would be most desired in the current milieu. Certain contours of change in perception are identified. To meet the futuristic prospects of Indian higher education, teachers should not be spared in such meaningful reforms since teachers provide with the best trained manpower for a nation such as technologists, scientists, doctors, engineers, policy makers, businessmen etc. It is therefore teachers too should be empowered as a part of reforms for Indian higher education meeting the growing demands of liberalization and globalization going on in the world. Hence, the emerging Indian society needs to make the system of their higher education must innovative and futuristic to face the changing demands of the modern Indian society.

1 Introduction:

Higher education in India has experienced phenomenal expansion since independence. India has produced scientists, engineers, technologists, doctors, teachers and managers who are in great demand all over the world. Now it is one of the top ten countries in our industrial and technological capacity because of the significant contribution of manpower and tools provided by higher education, especially technical education. Methods of higher education also have to be appropriate to the needs of four pillars of education, learning to learn, learning to do, learning to be and learning to become (Ganihar & Bhat 2006). Student centered education and the employment of dynamic method of education will require from teachers new attitudes and skills (Saravana Kumar & Mohan 2008). Methods of teaching through lectures will have to be supplemented with the methods that will lay stress on self study, personal consultation between teachers and students and informative sessions of seminars and workshops. India will have to decide on what knowledge and or skills would be most helpful to prepare students for adjustments to continuing change. The impact of continued change will be visible in the content of the curriculum, its form and the process of decision making that shapes it.

2   The status quo of higher education in India:

The system of Indian higher education has experienced an enormous success after independence and emerged the largest in the world. More than 20 million of students are pursuing their higher studies in around 700 degree awarding institutions and 35500 affiliated colleges. This is a huge potentiality for the rapid development and research for the country. For the entry into Indian higher education institutions, a student needs to get through senior secondary examination conducted by the states or the central board of school education. The duration of the first degree is of three years in general education in Arts, Science, and Commerce followed by two years of masters degree level courses and three to five years of degree in the interested field.

Table 1: Higher Education Institutions (Universities & Colleges) in India

Type of Institutions	Number
Central Universities (Public)	44
State Universities (Public)	306
State Universities (Private)	154
Deemed Universities (Private or Public)	129
Institutions of National Importance (Public)	67
Total Degree-granting Institutions	700

Affiliated Colleges (Public or Private)	35,539

Source: Statistics on Higher Education, 2012-13 from http:\\\www.dreducation.com/2013/08/data-statistics-india-student-college.html.

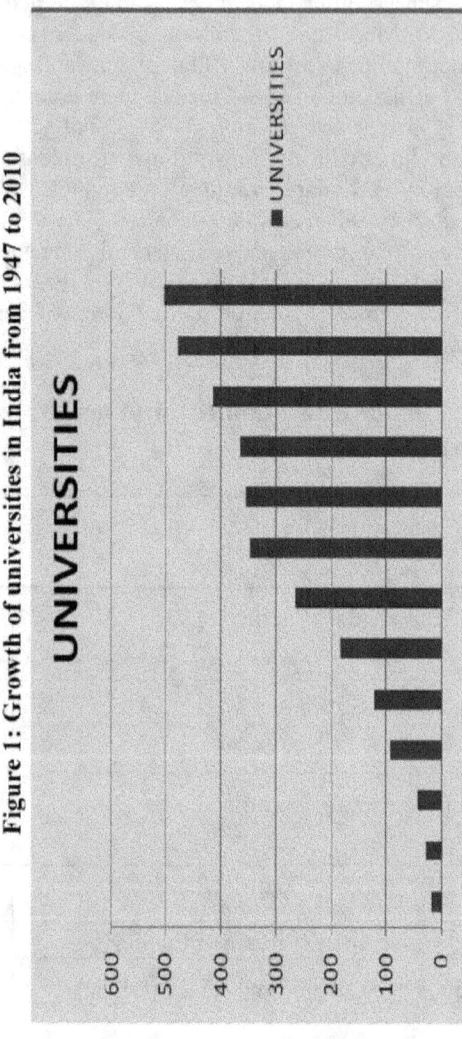

Figure 1: Growth of universities in India from 1947 to 2010

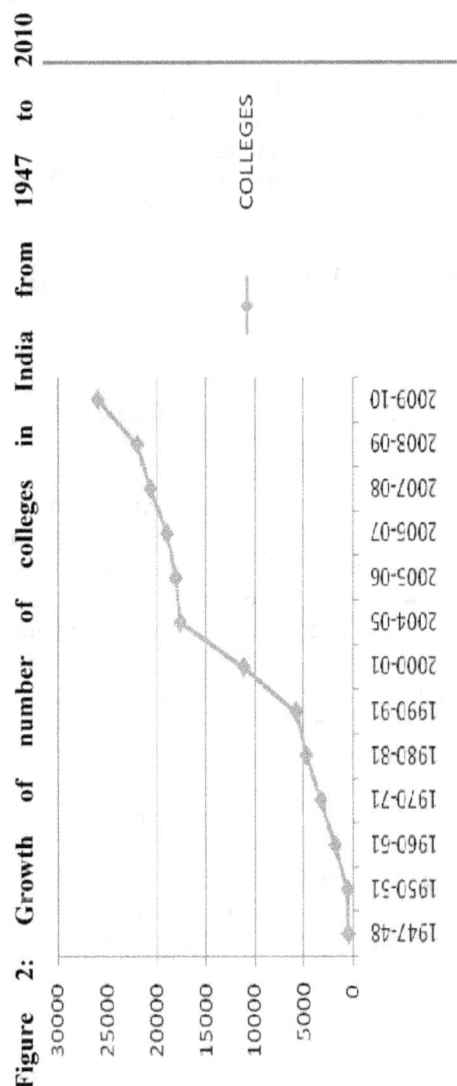

Figure 2: Growth of number of colleges in India from 1947 to 2010

Before Independence, access to higher education was very limited; there were only 496 colleges and 20 odd universities. Since independence, the growth has been very impressive. The number of universities in year 1971 has increased rapidly to 93 colleges and 3227 universities which is great achievement for our nation. In the year 2000-01 the growth of universities and colleges are appreciated, it has increased by a large number. Year by year educational institutes are growing gradually. In its size and diversity, India has the third largest higher education system in the world, next only to China and the United States.

3   Higher Investment in Higher Education:

The growth of higher education has led to the higher investment in higher education. A large number of private colleges and universities cropped up and are in the recent years providing quality education from degree to doctoral degree in the variety of fields. The opportunities for higher education have been recently due to the private participation. In terms of expenditure incurred on education, particularly on higher education during the year 2010–11, the government spent around Rs.15, 440 crores which is about 85 per cent of the revised budget estimates for the year. The recent 66th round of NSSO survey reveals that between 1999 and 2009, spending on education in general jumped by 378 per cent in rural areas and 345 per cent in urban areas of the country. The survey further reveals that spending on children's education underlines sharp increase – 63 per cent for rural and 73 per cent for urban families. However, if we measure the expenses on education as a percentage to GDP, India lags behind some developed/developing nations (Table 2). We recognize that the gap in investments in education in India can perhaps be filled by private sector playing a crucial role.

Table 2: Expenditure on Education

Country	Spending on education as a percentage of GDP
Switzerland	5.2
South Africa	5.9
U.S.A	5.6
U.K.	6.2
Thailand	3.8
France	5.9
Chile	4.1
Brazil	5.8
Malaysia	5.1
Mexico	5.3
India	3.3

Source: UN data from http://data.un.org/Data.aspx?d=UNESCO&f=series%3AXGDP_FSGOV (last accessed on 17/5/2014)

4   Gross enrolment patterns in higher education in India:-

At present, in India, there are about 1.46 crores of students enrolled in various streams of higher education including business management. Despite the large number of students studying in various streams, we have not seen any major shift in the productivity as skills and talents are deficient to support economic activities and, hence, there is a serious concern on employability of these educated persons. The gross enrolment ratio (GER) for higher education in India was 19.4 in 2010-11. However; the enrolment level varies across states. We also need to recognize that our enrolment level is far below several other countries. For example, according to a report, GER is 23 per cent for China, 34 per cent for Brazil, 57 per cent for U.K., 77 per cent for both Australia and Russia and 83 per cent for the U.S (Fig. 2). In this context, the attempt of Government authorities to increase the number of students by 2020 so as to reach GER of 30 per cent becomes a big challenge. As a positive step, for the remaining duration of Eleventh Five Year Plan, the Government has taken initiatives to incentivize states for setting up/expansion of existing educational institutions, establishment of 8 universities, expansion of colleges to achieve a target of 1 lakh students enrolment and schemes for setting up model colleges in regions which are below national average of GER.5 UGC Annual Report, 2009-106 All India Survey on Higher Education by MHRD, 2010-

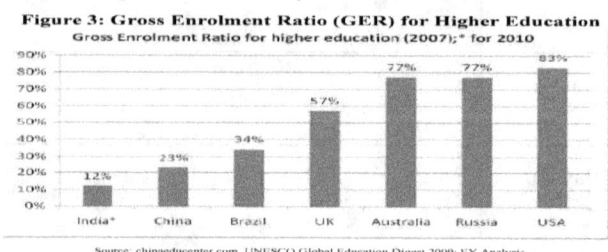

Figure 3: Gross Enrolment Ratio (GER) for Higher Education
Gross Enrolment Ratio for higher education (2007);* for 2010

Source: chinaeducenter.com, UNESCO Global Education Digest 2009; EY Analysis

5   Capacity Utilization:

Another challenge to be addressed in strengthening the Indian education system is to improve the capacity utilization. For example, a recent study on capacity utilization in India for higher education indicates that the capacity utilization in case of MBA is about 57 per cent in Maharashtra and 72 per cent in Haryana (Fig. 3). In case of certain states, there are a lot of unfilled seats in institutions. On the one hand, we need to improve our GER, and on the other, we need to ensure that institutions/ colleges/schools created for providing higher education fully utilize the capacity created.

6   Higher Education Hub:

India is attracting a large number of foreign students to their central, state and private universities and colleges from several parts of the world. Asian and western students find India a place of higher education hub due to the fact that the education provided here is inexpensive, higher quality and in the learner friendly environment.

This trend evinces that Indian higher education has more potentialities to cater to the need of growing global demand. It is high time the UGC on the one hand has to encourage private participation in awarding quality and inexpensive higher degrees in the multi-disciplinary domains to attract even more foreign students and on the other hand, the establishing world class schools of higher education will prevent the students, the younger generation in particular, from being attracted by foreign institutions.

7   Problems of higher education in India:

(I) Co-modification of education: Higher education is becoming a marketing commodity. It is a multi-billion dollar business. Foreign universities are trying to have a share of Indian educational markets and have prepared for this during the last decade or more. This shift from education as a social good to marketable commodity is against the Indian culture and sufferers in these changes will be poor and disadvantaged people of India.

(II) Global competitiveness: The competition will essentially be for offering quality education recognized at the International level and relevant to the local needs the major issue is how to raise the quality and standards of Indian education and make it globally competitive, locally relevant and enable it to offer marketing paradigm appropriate for developing societies.

(III) Concerns of weaker institutions: High disparities in educational standards and quality of education offered by Indian universities and colleges is of great concern to all. National and global competition may create problems of survival of weaker universities and colleges.

(IV) Developmental disparities and unsolved Indian problems: Many colleges and universities were started in India for removing regional imbalances and for supporting education of weaker and disadvantaged classes, particularly of women. These institutions and other developmental programs for weaker classes are still facing resource constraints, which are further aggravated by ignorance, poverty and disadvantages of the people they serve. This is resulting in widening divides and in keeping many educated from weaker and disadvantages sections outside the job and employment markets. The challenge of these marginalized and deprived to the system of education is enormous.

(V) Weak linkage of education with developmental processes: It is creating frustration amongst graduates when they find that education is not so useful in employment and in work situations. A challenge is to transform the system from its present model of education to developmental education linking education to developments in society, industry and services sectors.

(VI) Shortage of teachers: Economic growth led by industrial and service sector during the last decade has created more opportunities and faster career growth for the young talent. Further, the lucrative salaries and glamour has acted as catalyst in attracting talent to such fast growing sectors. Higher education in India which has been passing through transition on account of privatization and withdrawal of financial support from the government has been finding it difficult to attract adequate number of young talent to teaching job. It is a big challenge for higher education sector to sustain in future due to lack of availability of faculty.

(VII) High cost of higher education: The unit cost of traditional education, particularly of professional education, is quite high and has gone out of reach of the Indian middle and lower classes. Many private entrepreneurs have started educational institutions for offering creamy courses with marketing approach; and have raised fees not affordable to majority. Subsidy to the education by the state is not the right solution in the present situation, when numbers aspiring for higher education is large and ever increasing. The deprived are already creating pressure on the state to make education accessible and have raised an issue of socio-economic equity and justice.

8   SWOT Analysis:

Despite the huge potential in the higher education sector, not everyone has been able to achieve success. The challenges/threats which the private sector players face in India are significant and therefore, approaching the market with a well thought-out strategy is advisable.

8.1 Strengths:

• Few globally renowned educational institutions.

• Huge demand – estimated 150 mn populations in 18-23 age groups.

• Growing middle class with increasing incomes.

• Growing economy with numerous employment opportunities.

• Huge demand for Indian students in overseas markets.

8.2 Weaknesses:

• Lack of infrastructure.

• Shortage of trained faculty to meet the increased demand.

• Highly complex and unclear regulatory framework at Central & State level.

• Regional imbalances.

• "Not for profit" tag in formal education.

8.3 Opportunities:

• Unsaturated demand for quality global education.

• Low GER of 15% in Higher education as compared to 84% in USA.

• Sharp decline in dependency ratio predicted in the next 30 years.

• India is expected to emerge as a Global hub in education in Asia Pacific region.

• Low focus on R&D.

8.4 Threats:

• High time lags in introduction of reforms due to various reasons.

• Deterioration in quality of education especially in private sector due to lack of availability of trained faculty.

• Over regulation – Control over course curriculum, entrance tests, fees etc

9 Suggestions for Higher Education in India:

1. Promoting and coordinating university education.

2. Determining and maintaining standards of teaching, examination and research in universities.

3. Framing regulations on minimum standards of education.

4. Monitoring developments in the field of collegiate and university education; disbursing grants to universities and colleges.

5. Accreditations are also made mandatory for any higher educational institutions to receive the title of a university.

6. Launching of a new scheme of interest subsidy on educational loans taken by professional courses by the economically weaker students.

7. The higher education of India needs mechanisms to improve the quality of education provided through universities and other degree awarding institutions. The mechanism should pay attention on refining, diversifying, and upgrading higher education and research programmes.

8. The higher education of India needs mechanisms to improve the quality of education provided through universities and other degree awarding institutions.

The mechanism should pay attention on refining, diversifying, and upgrading higher education and research programmes.

9. For making education affordable all such schemes are introduced keeping in mind about the growing need of education and in parlance to the concept of "education for all".

10. Teachers are the most important factors for any innovative society because teachers' knowledge and skills not only enhance quality and efficacy of education, but also improve the potential for research and innovation.

10 Conclusion:-

To sum up, we need to recognize that the knowledge, skills and productivity of our growing young and dynamic work force form the backbone of our economy. To reap the benefits of such a young work force, we need to implement the reforms in the education system and also bring forth new factors of production, namely knowledge, skills and technology which have the ability to unleash the productive frontiers of the economy in the most efficient and dynamic way. Besides, taking a leaf from the western hemisphere, India should try to become "knowledge economy" to promote inclusive growth.The three major areas to be focused to ensure that our education system is sustainable and meets global standards:

*   Quality of Education – in terms of infrastructure, teachers, accreditation, etc.

*   Affordability of Education – ensuring poor and deserving students are not denied of education.

*   Ethics in Education – avoiding over-commercialization of education system.

Our education system is different from the developed countries, so, it is time to bring in the changes that will give us the momentum to find a place in the global scenario. Govt. and public both should work hand-in-hand to support each other and look for the required upliftment of education. Change in the GER will not come in a year, but it can be achieved by consistent persuasion, Using of state-of-the-art infrastructure allied with ICT and a developed curricula for industry-ready candidates seems to be the dream of the country and its people, but, the possibilities of such extent need to be channelized and it is make sure that everyone do get the opportunity to be a part of such system. Bringing in quality teachers from outside may cost us heavily but providing with the required amenities, we can have quality teachers to educate the society.

References :-

1.Deloitte (November 2013), Annual Status of Higher Educations of States and UTs in India (ASHE 2013), retrieved from http://www.deloitte.com/assets/Dcom-India/Local%20Assets/Documents/Thoughtware/AnnualSstatu sof Higher Education of StatesandUTsinIndia,%202013.pdf

2. Dept. of Higher Education, MHRD, Govt. of India (2010-11), Final report on All India Survey on Higher Education (AISHE 2010-11), retrieved fromhttp://mhrd.gov.in/sites/upload_files/mhrd/files/AISHE20 1011.pdf

3.Takwale, R., (2006) Challenges and Opportunities of Globalisation for higher Education in India- Alternative through e- Education, retrieved from www.ugc.ac.in ugc-pro.pdf. pp 10-11.

4.Bharath Joshi, "State spending Rs 60k on each student in Govt Engg colleges", The New Indian Express, April 9, 2014. http://www.newindianexpress.com/cities/bangalore/State-Spending-Rs-60k-on-Each-Student-in-Govt-Engg-Colleges/2014/04/09/article2157934.ece

5. Proceeding of the Social Sciences Research ICSSR 2014 (e-ISBN 978-967-11768-7-0). 9-10 June 2014, Kota Kinabalu, Sabah, MALAYSIA. Organized by http://WorldConferences.net

22 FEMINIST PEDAGOGY: A NEW WAY TO EDUCATIONAL GROWTH

(By: Dr. A. H. Rizvi*)

Abstract

*F*eminist practice and theory have always conferred value on narrative knowledge produced through storytelling, mainly because of its ability to stimulate reflexive thought. In our contribution we intend to present and discuss a training methodology founded on memory work and designed to stimulate an individual and group reworking of the leadership dimension, and of the gender and leadership relationship. We will describe a narrative workshop conducted with groups of women working in managerial positions and based on the perspective of workplace learning through experiential reflexivity. The narrative methodology proved to be a particularly effective tool: it gave the participants a chance to conduct retrospective analysis of their past work experiences (individual and organizational), and it generated —due to the interaction with other stories (those furnished in the training activity and those provided by other trainees) — different interpretative perspectives and new meaning configurations in order to face working life and organizational dynamics.

Keywords: narrative knowledge, gender, memory work, storytelling.

---

* Maulana Azad National Urdu University, Hyderabad mail:drahrizvi110@gmail.com

1. Introduction

Feminist practice and theory have always conferred value on narrative knowledge produced through storytelling, mainly because of its ability to stimulate reflexive thought. In our contribution we intend to present and discuss a training methodology founded on memory work and designed to stimulate an individual and group reworking of the leadership dimension, and of the gender and leadership relationship. We will describe a narrative workshop conducted with groups of women working in managerial positions and based on the perspective of workplace learning through experiential reflexivity. The training objective was to address the issue of leadership as situated practice. To this end, narrative stimuli were given to the participants in order to prompt more general reflection about male and female modes of power management (and about the connected practices of domination/exclusion). The purpose was to highlight the social and cultural factors that influence these differences, and to offer perspectives alternative to dominant patterns. The narrative methodology proved to be a particularly effective tool: it gave the participants a chance to conduct retrospective analysis of their past work experiences (individual and organizational), and it generated — due to the interaction with other stories (those furnished in the training activity and those provided by other trainees) — different interpretative perspectives and new meaning configurations in order to face working life and organizational dynamics.

2. Reflection, reflexivity and narrative in feminist pedagogy:

What is meant by retrospective thought can be illustrated by referring to the story of the stork told by Karen Blixen in Out of Africa (1938).

The story runs as follows. A man lived in a small house near a pond. One night he was woken up by a loud noise. He ran out of his house and in the darkness headed towards the pond, repeatedly tripping, falling and getting up again. Following the noise he found a leak in the pond wall, which he repaired and then went back to bed. When he looked out of the window the next morning, he saw that his footsteps had traced the outline of a stork on the ground. In this short story, retrospective glance is metaphorically represented by the man looking out of the window. His work of the night is finished, and it is only a posteriori, in the marks left on the ground, that he gives meaning to his movements, sees a pattern, shapes his experience. It is through recounting that the signs and traces of experience are pieced together and acquire complete meaning. The pattern of a life or an event emerges retrospectively when thought becomes reflexive, when it turns onto itself to compose a narrative, to give shape to what was indistinct. Besides the backward introspection that induces reflexive thought to appropriate or re-appropriate personal history, also of especial importance in feminist methodology is «memory work».

3. Leadership as a situated and gendered practice:

Leadership has long been a topic of central concern for organizational studies. However, with the course of time attention has shifted from the role and function of the leader to the practice of leadership, from a personalized and functionalist view to one that emphasises the relational and constructive dimension of leadership action and the process of the collective creation of meaning and consensus (Alvesson, 1992; Piccardo, 1998). Among the emergent features of this new view of leadership there are some that we believe to be particular significant.

The first is the growing awareness that leadership is not so much a personality trait or a natural gift as a relational practice, something that «one does» by relating to others (Manz and Sims, 1991). Thus, a prescriptive approach intended principally to identify categories and models (the charismatic leader, the participative leader, the transactional leader, and so on) is replaced by an experiential one in which the focus is on experiences of leadership, the relational dynamics involved in leadership, its motivational and emotional features, and especially its relationship with power. The interweaving between leadership and power has been stressed by several authors (Kets de Vries, 1993; Sievers, 1996), but in this case the object of analysis is the subjective relationship with power and its implications for interpersonal relations.

The second emergent feature is connected to the «situatedness» of leadership (Bruni, Gherardi and Poggio, 2005). Like every practice also leadership has a situated nature, in the sense that it cannot be conceived in absolute and general terms but must be contextualized in specific relational situations and systems. Situated leadership means that it is situated in a physical context, in the dynamics of interactions, in the language and in the body.

Therefore, leadership is also gendered. It has been historically constructed as a male sub-text by producing images of leadership which are difficult to relate to femaleness (Alvesson and Billing, 1997) or by describing styles and models of female leadership which stand as alternatives to traditional leadership (Hegelsen, 1990; Loden, 1985). A frequent finding of these studies is that, whereas men are mainly characterized by a «transactional» style of leadership (involving the exchange of results for rewards and command through control), women display distinct abilities in «transformational» leadership: a management style which emphasizes relationality and seeks to foster positive interactions and trust relations with/among subordinates, to share power and information and to encourage employees to subordinate their personal aims and interests to collective ends. In short, these studies relate female leadership styles to a specific (natural or socialized) orientation of women towards communication, cooperation, affiliation and attachment, and to a conception of power as control not over the group but by the group.

4. A workshop on leadership:

In recent years feminist critiques within organization studies (Gherardi, 2003) have led to a redefinition of the concept of leadership and a redefinition of training practices. Approaches more oriented to relationality, empowerment and reflexivity have appeared and therefore courses and methods designed to re-elaborate personal and professional experience, to create sense and consensus collectively, to develop creativity, and to foster autonomy and self-awareness. The aim is no longer to teach efficacious leadership styles or models, nor to define skills to be developed; rather, it is to stimulate individual and collection reflection, for example, through the sharing of leadership stories recounted by the trainees. A reflexive approach to leadership enables individuals, and women in particular, to start from personal experience and from self-awareness to question the traditional paradigms of «objectivity» and «detachment» that support the dominant models of knowing in organizations and producing knowledge on organizations.

Reflection and individual or group analysis of situations in which the participants have wielded authority in organizations furnish occasions for self-knowledge or even its redesign which involve not only the cognitive, cultural and affective dimensions of the individuals concerned but also the strategic and structural ones of the organization. The assumption is that the group is a crucial learning resource because it enables different experiences to be shared and compared.

We now describe a specific instance of a narrative workshop based on some of the assumptions just outlined, and the focus of which was the relationship between leadership and gender. Four editions of the workshop were organized, each of them attended by twelve women with managerial positions in the local administration in Hyderabad.

The course was designed around a number of themes representing the core of leadership in traditional textbooks: rationality, control, decision making, strategic thinking. Each of them was framed in relations to its opposite (the suppressed term). On this basis, the workshop was divided into five day-long sessions entitled:

1.   The retrospective gaze,

2.   Leadership in the feminine,

3.   The Myth of control

4.   Rationality and emotionality.

5.   Designing the future.

Each session required the participants to read and to write stories, according to the following schema:

— The facilitator read aloud «the story of the day», a literary passage intended to introduce the proposed theme in a imaginative way and in the context of wordly life.

— Following the narrative stimulus, each participant was invited to write a short story relating to her professional experience in the organization and which centred on the topic of the day.

— The stories were told, exchanged and analysed in smaller groups. The group as a whole worked together in order to bring out shared and divergent views on the experience narrated, the plots used the processes by which meaning had been reconstructed and attributed, and the underlying cultural models.

— Cutting across the various themes addressed provided the stimulus to reflect on a number of issues intrinsic to the topic of leadership: its relationship with power, recognition of its conflictual dimensions, and the importance of learning to recognize and understand the emotions connected with the exercise of authority in the participants' organizational contexts.

The key component of the workshop was reflexive learning, defined as «a process which involves dialogue with others for improvement or transformation whilst recognizing the emotional, social and political context of the learner». Narrating leadership and analysing it collectively and in relation to organizational change is a way of constructing a more or less shared understanding of what leadership is and how it may be «done» in a shared workplace. Storytelling provides not only the opportunity to discuss «things that happened or could happen», but also the opportunity of performing one's identity as power holding in situated circumstances.

5. The use of narrative pedagogy

This section presents one day, and one theme, in our narrative workshop, in order to illustrate the process and reflect on managerial education. The subject of the day (the second in the course) was the relationship between gender and leadership.

The stimulus for reflection, narrative writing and storytelling in groups was a story entitled «Fanta-Ghiro» taken from Italo Calvino's Italian Folktales, of which a summary follows.

A king had three daughters but no sons. The king was of a

sickly disposition. One day a Turkish king declared war against his land, but the king was too ill to take command of his army. So his three daughters offered to take his place. The father at first refused, because commanding an army was not women's work. But then, given the seriousness of the situation, he agreed to send his eldest daughter, but on the condition that she dressed and behaved like a man. He warned her that if she started talking about women's things, his trusted squire would bring her straight home. The daughter left for the war, but during the sea voyage she saw a gaily coloured fish and remarked that she wanted a ball gown in the same colours. So the squire took her straight back home. The same thing happened to the second daughter. During the voyage, when Papers 93 001-181: Papers 2/10/09 10:21 Página 60 Tales of Ordinary Leadership. A Feminist Approach to Experimental Learning Papers 93, 2009 61 she saw the colourful sails of the fishing boats, she began talking about the fabrics she wanted to decorate her bed chamber. So the third daughter, Fanta-Ghiro, then set off to fight the war, even though she was still so small that her armour had to be padded before she could put it on. The sea voyage passed without incident, and the young princess went to parlay with the enemy king. The king was intrigued by the «iron general» and set traps to see whether he was not really a woman. He took Fanta-Ghiro into the armoury and then into the garden, asking question to catch her out. Fanta-Ghiro passed all the tests until the king invited her to go for a swim. This forced her to find an immediate excuse to return home But she left behind a letter explaining who she really was. The king, by now in love, followed Fanta-Ghiro and asked her to marry him. Peace was made, of course, and when Fanta-Ghiro's father died he left his kingdom to his son-in-law.

This story was particular stimulating for the participants, owing to various features which emerged very clearly from both the narratives produced during the workshop and the group and plenary discussions. The first of these features concerned the symbolic order of gender apparent in the story, which the participants recognized as an organizational archetype (gender segregation) and a dilemma (adopt male or female behaviour?) that all of them had encountered to some extent in their professional lives.

6. Conclusion

In this paper we have sought to demonstrate the importance of a narrative methodology in generating reflection and reflexivity with respect to working and organizational experience, and to leadership processes in particular. Our treatment has been based on feminist practice and theory, and the emphasis that these have placed on the centrality of reflexive thought and memory, as well as on the need to redefine the mainstream models of leadership aimed at maintaining and reinforcing hegemonic masculinity. From this perspective, experiential learning is based on the interaction between two processes distinctive of narrative workshops: narrating and listening. It is, in fact, above all in this interaction that individual identities, as relational and per formative processes, are produced and negotiated and that the meaning of experience is constructed. The collective processing of common experiences elicited in the workshops through the reciprocity of narrating and listening, stimulates the participants to reconsider their positioning in individual, professional and organizational relations and to redefine the meaning of their experiences, generating transformative practices and processes. By describing our reflexive workshops on leadership, therefore, we have sought to show how storytelling stimulates reflection and reflexivity, or retrospection and reflective learning from experience on the one hand, and storytelling as a means to reflect on current practices and to create further contexts on the other.

References

- Alvesson (1992). Leadership as social integrative action: A study of a computer consultancy company». Organization Studies, 13, 2, p. 185-209.

- Gherardi, Silvia and POGGIO, Barbara (2006). Feminist challenges to mainstream leadership trough collective reflection and narrative. In: BOUD, D.; CRESSEY, P. and DOCHERTY, P. (eds.). Productive reflection and learning at work. London: Routledge, p. 181-192.

- Hegelsen, Susan (1990). The female advantage. New

York: Currency Doubleday.

- Kets De Vries, Manfred F. R. (1993). Leaders, fools and imposters. San Francisco: Jossey-Bass.

- Loden, Marilyn (1985). Feminine leadership or how to succeed in business without being one of the boys. New York: Times Books.

- Manz, Charles C. and Sims, Henry P. Jr. (1991). «Superleadership: Beyond the myth of heroic leadership». Organizational Dynamics, 19, p. 18-35.

- Piccardo, Claudia (1998). Insegnare e apprendere la leadership. Milano: Guerini.

- Poggio, Barbara (2004). Mi racconti una storia? Il metodo narrativo nelle scienze sociali. Roma: Carocci.

23 GROWTH OF HIGHER EDUCATIONAL INSTITUTIONS TO BRING OUT THE EQUAL OPPORTUNITIES AMONG THE EDUCATION SEEKERS

(By: Ms. Zia Afroz * *and Ms. Rupali Sharma* * * *)*

Abstract

*E*ducation is the basis of all the development and growth. And for the growth of the education, educational institutions become vital. Especially when we talk about the Higher education the need of higher educational institutions including college, universities and technical education institutions with the full equipped and facilitating infrastructure and quality education comes in our mind. This paper is an attempt to analyse the relevance of the establishment of these institutions and to examine the relationship between the enrolments of students with these institutions. As India is the second highest populated country in the world and India has a bulk of the population which belongs to education seekers group.

1. Introduction:

It is well known education and development are intertwined. Through education, a country develops its

---

* Research Scholar (MANF & ICSSR), Department of Applied Economics, University of Lucknow, Lucknow.
** JRF, Faculty of Special Education, Dr. Shakuntala Misra National Rehabilitation University, Lucknow

productive human resources that serve as the engine of social and economic transformation and carry forward national development. Only when human resources-their skills, talents, energies, and knowledge are effectively developed and harnessed, a nation can attain the capability and credibility to bring about positive social changes and much needed economic growth. To achieve the development of the country we need skilled, knowledgeable manpower. Only quality education can ensure expected level of human resource (Md. Abu Naser, 2013).

Despite the rapid increase in the enrolment in higher education during the last decade the quality of education remains a serious cause of concern. Education especially higher education has an important role for the development of a country. The basic objectives of the universities are providing education, conducting research and creating new knowledge. Andaleeb (2003) says that, higher education is of strategic importance not only as an engine for human resource development and as a facilitator of growth through forward and backward linkages, it also serves as an incubator and repository of knowledge with untold potential.

2.   Research methodology:

The study is of analytical and theoretical in nature. This paper is basically based on the secondary data and the limitation of this study up to the exactness of the data.

3.   Objectives

1- To find out the relevance of the establishment of Private and Deemed University.

2- To find out the existing situation of the balance between Enrollment of students and University.

4.   List of state wise universities:

State	Central universities	State universities	Deemed universities	Private universities	Total
Andhra Pradesh	0	20	5	0	25
Arunachal Pradesh	1	0	1	7	9
Assam	2	12	0	4	18
Bihar	3	15	1	0	19
Chandigarh	0	1	1	0	2
Chhattisgarh	1	12	0	8	21
Delhi	5	7	10	0	22
Goa	0	1	0	0	1
Gujarat	1	26	2	23	52
Haryana	1	14	6	18	39
Himachal Pradesh	1	4	0	17	22
Jammu and Kashmir	2	7	0	0	9
Jharkhand	1	7	2	3	13
Karnataka	1	24	14	12	51
Kerala	1	13	2	0	16
Madhya Pradesh	2	20	3	15	40
Maharashtra	1	19	22	0	42
Manipur	2	0	0	1	3

State	Central universities	State universities	Deemed universities	Private universities	Total
Meghalaya	1	0	0	8	9
Mizoram	1	0	0	1	2
Nagaland	1	0	0	2	3
Odisha	1	12	2	3	18
Puducherry	1	0	1	0	2
Punjab	1	9	2	12	24
Rajasthan	1	21	8	42	71
Sikkim	1	0	0	5	6
Tamil Nadu	2	22	28	0	52
Telangana	3	16	2	0	21
Tripura	1	0	0	1	2
Uttar Pradesh	5	24	10	24	63
Uttarakhand	1	10	3	11	25
West Bengal	1	25	1	7	34
Total	46	342	125	227	740

- This list is current as of 31 December 2015.

- It does not include the National School of Drama, which changed status on 7 October 2011; its current status is unclear.

- Source: UGC and Higher Education in India, Annual Reports (2014-2015) (Universities include central, state, Private, Deemed and also institution of national importance established both by the central and state legislatures).

5.   Types and numbers of higher education institutions in India:

Type of Institution	Number	E.g.
Central Universities (Public)	44	University of Delhi
State Universities (Public)	306	University of Mumbai
State Universities (Private)	154	Amity University
Deemed Universities (Private or Public)	129	Tata Institute of Social Sciences
Institution of National Importance (Public)	67	Indian Institute of Technology
Total Degree-granting Institutions	700	
Affiliated Colleges (Public or Private)	35,539	

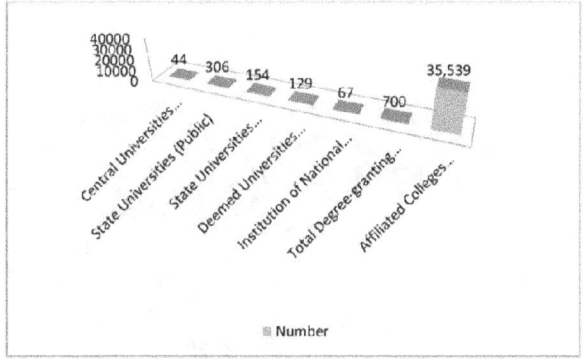

In India the total numbers of Central universities are 44 and the example of central university is University of Delhi, the total numbers of State universities which are public are 306 like University of Mumbai and private state universities are 154 like Amity University. And number of Deemed Universities private or public are 129 for example Tata Institute of Social Sciences (TISS). The numbers of Institution of National Importance (Public) like Indian Institute of

Technology (IIT) are 67. The total Degree granting Institutions are 700 and the total numbers of Affiliated Colleges (Public or Private) are 35539.

6.   **Enrollment of Indian students by level of education:**

Level	Number ('000)	% of Total
Graduate (Bachelor's)	17,456	86%
Post-Graduate (Master's)	2,492	12%
Research (Doctoral)	161	1%
Diploma/Certificate	218	1%
Total	20,327	

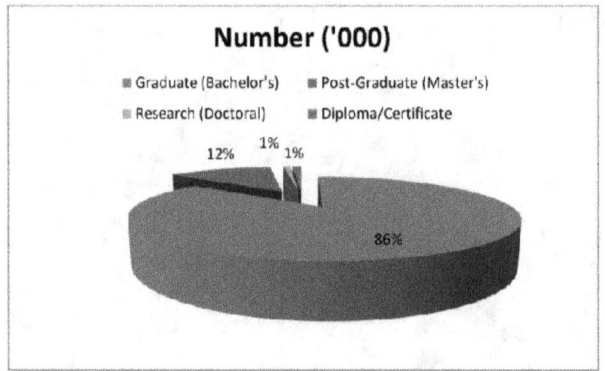

If we see the enrollment of Indian Students in higher education we find that 17456000 which is approx. 86% of total enrollment is in Bachelor's, 2492000 enrollments in Post-Graduate which is approx. 12% of total and 161000 enrollments in Research which is approx. 1% of the total. And we see approx.1% which 218000 enrollment in Diploma or Certificate.

7. Enrollment of Indian students by fields of study:

Field	Number ('000)	% of Total
Arts	7,539	37%
Science	3,790	19%
Commerce & Management	3,571	18%
Engineering & Technology	3,262	16%
Education	733	4%
Medicine	716	3%
Law	373	2%
Others	218	1%
Agriculture	97	0%
Veterinary Science	28	0%
Total	20,327	100%

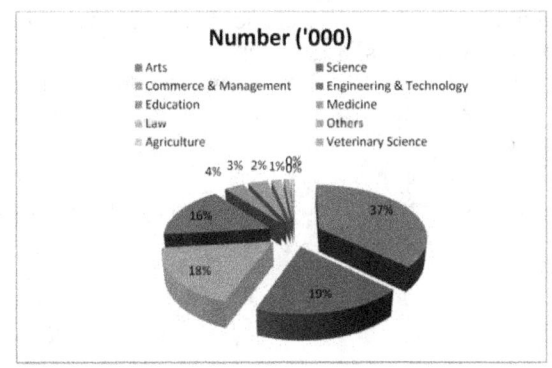

After analyzing the above chart we found that maximum number of students are enrolled in arts which is approx. 37% of total enrollment and then 19% in science and then 18% in Commerce & Management and 16% in Engineering & Technology and then 4% in Education, 3% in education, 2% in law, 1% in others and less than 1% in agriculture and Veterinary Science.

We can clearly see that there are total 504 Central and State universities altogether, which is definitely a very less in number and not capable of providing the quality education to all the education seekers, whereas the total population of the India is so high, so to fulfill this requirement the establishment of private and deemed university was a very good and necessary step, and even to provide the part-time education to the education seeker who are not able to earn it as on regular basis.

8.   Conclusion

The goal of higher education is not only to create new knowledge and disseminate it, but also create skilled forces for the country to face development challenges. Quality and balanced education system can help to achieve this goal. In job market, job providers do not think graduates/post- graduates have same skill from every university. Only few universities graduates/post -graduates have high demand in job market and they are capable enough to fight in global market. Researcher and academician said that though few universities of India have gained both national and international reputation, but not all of them are functioning with the same level of efficiency, but here according to the analysis of the total number of university and the number of students, first of all we should bother about providing the education to all along with quality education. After going through the above analysis we can conclude that no doubt that there has been tremendous increase in the number of educational institutions still there is a gap between the availability of the institutions and the education seekers.

References

1. Amlanjyoti Goswami (2012), "Higher Education Law and Privately-Funded University Education in India; Towards a Vision?", India Infrastructure Report 2012.

2. Andaleeb, S. S. (2003), "Rejuvenating the Nation"s Higher Education System", Proceeding of the workshop organized by International University of Business Agriculture and Technology, Dhaka, Bangladesh.

3. Coombs, P. H. (1985), "The world crises in education: The view from the eighties", Oxford University Press, New York.

4. Hafiz. G.A. (2006), "A morning with Dr. Hafiz G.A. Siddiqi", Vice Chancellor of North South University. Retrieved March 5, 2009, from http://www.thedailystar.net/campus/2006/09/02/academicicanspeaks.htm

5. info@iiep.unesco.org, www.unesco.org/iiep

6. Downloaded at: www.unesco.org/iiep/en/publications/pubs.htm © IIEP 2007

7. Jamal, Shawkat A. N. M., (2002), "Role of Private Universities in Human Resource Development", Retrieved February 24, 2009, from

8. http://www.international.ac.uk/resources/ROLE%20O F%20PRIVATE%20UNIVERSITIES%20I N%20HUMAN%20RESOURCE%20Development %20in%20Bangladesh.pdf

9. Md. Abu Naser (2013), "Education Quality of Private Universities in Bangladesh: faculty resources and infrastructure perspective", Department of General and Continuing Education (GCE), North South University Dhaka, Downloaded from Google 12 aug.2013.

10. National Council of Educational Research and Training (NCERT) (1986), "National Policy on Education", http://www.ncert.nic.in/oth_anoun/npe86.pdf (accessed

8 November 2012).

11. Oxford (2003), "The Oxford Compact English Dictionary", Oxford University Press, New York "Private sector participation in Indian higher education", FICCI Higher education summit 2011.

12. Pounder, J. (1999), "Institutional Performance in Higher Education: is Quality a Relevant Concept? Quality Assurance in Education".

13. World Bank (2000), "The Task Force on Higher Education and Society, Higher Education in Developing Countries: Peril and Promise", Washington, DC, USA.

14. https://www.arcjournals.org/pdfs/ijhsse/v1-i9/19.pdf

15. www.ugc.ac.in

16. http://www.dreducation.com/2013/08/data-statistics-india-student-college.html

17. https://www.arcjournals.org/pdfs/ijhsse/v1-i9/19.pdf

18. http://mhrd.gov.in/sites/upload_files/mhrd/files/statistics/AISHE2011-12P_1.pdf

24 GUARANTEED SUCCESS WITH RSETI

(By: Mr. S. K. Singh *)

Abstract

*W*hile training the unemployed youth in various skills for catering to the growing needs of industrial and service sector for skilled manpower, is one of the options , promoting Self Employment is yet another viable option to address the unemployment problem.

Government of India, after recognizing the successful model of giving training by RUDSETI for Entrepreneurship Development, has decided to open one such institute i.e. RSETI in each District of the Country. At RSETI - TRAINING, FOODING, LODGING IS FREE OF COST to all trainees irrespective of caste / category.

RSETIs are managed by Bank Officials posted on deputation as Directors. These Directors are assisted by Faculty Members who are postgraduates with an inclination to involve in Rural Developmental activities. The Directors and Faculty Members have to play the role of Motivators, Trainers & Facilitators in promoting Entrepreneurship Development besides taking care of all other activities of institute. Since RUDSETI/ RSETI Model is unique, NACER Bengaluru gives 2 week training to all Trainers of RSETIs to achieve the desired objectives.

At RSETIs we give emphasis on Hard skill development

---

* Director, PNB RSETI, Ramgarh, Jharkhand, India

(70%) and on Soft skill development (30%).Hard skill is given by specialist of that field, whereas soft skill is given by Director and Faculty members. It has been observed that without soft skill it is very difficult to excel in business. On first day MICROLAB / ICE BREAKING EXERCISE is administered. It unfreezes the participants for upcoming training through varieties of activities / games. In this process participants interact with each other and open up. Now they are ready to grasp what we want to give them. We give soft skill training through different business games such as Risk Taking /Goal Setting Exercise, Boat making Exercise, Tower Building Exercise and other techniques such as how to solve problem , how to manage time, be creative, be innovative. Personality of the trainees is build and improved through communication classes in between the training.

Typical day at RSETI during training period begins with *Shramdan, Yoga*, Breakfast then classes. Class begins with Meditation, prayer, MILLY (Most Important Lesson Learnt Yesterday). In the evening, where residential facility is available, some cultural programmes are organized every day to improve personality of participants. During training period all trainees are given equal opportunity to learn.

During the training period trainees are exposed to their related field through MARKET SURVEY and UNIT VISIT to get the reality check of the situation which they have to face after they are trained.

RSETI not only train the candidates but make them future ready to become a successful entrepreneur. After completion of training, trainees are followed for a period of 2 years in which they are motivated to start their own business by taking loans from concerned banks. In this process trainees are guided time to time in case they face any difficulty.

All the data/details related to RSETI training programmes are uploaded in best ever software developed by CREDO INFOTECH. More than 70% of RSETI trained candidates are reported to be settled i.e. they have started income generating activity of their own. Some of them have excelled in their field making us proud.

25 INDUCED EMPLOYMENTS FOR GROWTH AND JUSTICE

(By: Mr. Shailendra Srivastava *)

Abstract

*P*ure justice only can be expected from ISHWAR-ALLAH-GOD OR NATURE. But for waves of growth reaching all corners of society there must be an honest intent to reach till the last man in the circle.

In my opinion this is possible only through "Induced Employment".

Since Origin human family has travelled a long way in developing the Civil Society". They have developed many human physical & Life sciences. The growth is improvement over to past level of living.

During these developments man has evolved Money as a means of medium measure exchange & store. The human activities are governed by the force of money. Circular force of money has created wealth & capital.

Initially human beings were provoked by hunger to do the activities but at present human wants are complex.

Growth is a continuous process of variant rate. But distortions of distributions have created classes in human society here we cry for growth with justice.

---

* Former Manager, Punjab National Bank

"Laissez faire" growth to me deems a very long term invisible hand justice course. However an human being has a limited life span how he can wait for thousand years to reap the benefits of growth. Here instead of invisible hand the role of government comes into being. The government only can demolish the distortions with force of law so that instead of weak. Waves of growth reaching all corners of society their must be an honest intent to reach till the last man in circle.

In my opinion this is possible only through "Induced Employment".

"Induced Employment" means employment of working force over and above to cost analysis employment. Initially induced employment will be a burden upon the governments but in 15-20 year it will be adjusted in increased demand. The growth with justice will be visible in 15 to 20 years in within the life span of every human being born in society.

26 GLOBAL MEASURES OF GENDER INEQUALITY WITH SPECIAL REFERENCE TO INDIA - AN ANALYSIS
(By: Mr. Syed Ali Akhtar*)

Abstract

*G*ender based inequalities are undeniable fact which existed in every society and continues to exist even today in most parts of the world. History is full of instances where females were subjected to atrocities through many ways at different times. The history is nothing but the traces of past and the dark history of women is found in the writings of many notable ancient scholars. Female Infanticide, Early Marriages, Glorification of Sati and Dowry Death are few examples of degradation to women which existed with full recognition in previous times. Around the globe, problems like inferior status of women, less legal rights, no independent identity and unequal treatment has deteriorated the status of women in all spheres of life. Convention on the elimination of all forms of discrimination (CEDAW), Vienna Convention and other international measures paved a way to get rid of this problem. In the context of Indian situation, factors that are driven by gender inequality include less access to education, unemployment, economic restraints, unawareness, constraint in sustainable development and growth of this country. Legal position of women in India changed after various amendments to laws, judicial activism and constitutional provisions in

* Student of B.A,LL.B (HONS),Faculty of Law, Unity Degree College, Lucknow

favour of females. Considering all these facts, empowerment of women both on National and International plane is the task of policy makers for better and productive future because the growth is impossible without justice.

Keywords – Gender inequality, Women in India, Growth

1 Introduction

Gender inequality has been a long debated topic all over the world. A brief history of gender inequality in various parts of the world, international measures in this regard taken by United Nation and legal position of women enshrined in Indian constitution are discussed in this paper. Lastly it discusses how gender inequality affects the growth of a country and what measures could be taken to eliminate gender inequality.

This starts with the legal position of women in previous times. This paper also presents some historical known facts and figures in order to better understand the true situation of gender inequalities existed in ancient times.

While describing the role of United Nation, conventions like Convention on the elimination of All forms of Discrimination against women, 1979 (CEDAW) are discussed. Various articles of CEDAW convention which are connected to our study are briefly explained to some extent. The effect of these initiatives by United Nation at world level, especially in case of reservation is analyzed.

To study this topic in depth, we have also looked into the legal provision of Indian constitution and judicial activism in order to better understand the true legal position of women in India. In this context, various articles of fundamental rights and directive principles are explained. A brief account of judicial activism through some notable case laws of this country is also added.

Lastly it has been described why gender equality is necessary for sustainable development and growth of a country. And what will be the consequences if equal rights and opportunities are not given to both sexes. Some suggestions on this issue have also been made while concluding this paper.

2 Historical account of gender injustice

It is undisputed fact that the ancient authors considered women inferior to men. This fact is evident from the writings of various authors. Aristotle believed that all things derive their character from their function. Thus, his approach to women is functional.(Rao,2008) He believed that the head of the household is unmistakably man who rules it, women may be said to be an inferior man. (Bodenheimer Edgar, 1974). In fact Rousseau's view represents the whole western world. And he too branded qualities like feminity, modesty and meekness as womanly and natural for the female sex. The ideas of Hobbes, Locke, Bentham and John Stuart Mill are however advanced. As Locke felt that the familial authority belonged to the mother as much as to the father. Hobbes implied that paternal power was not derived from fatherhood as such. It could therefore be inferred that women were considered subordinate to men in previous times.

As English jurist William Blackstone famously put it in his commentaries on English law (1765-1769) "by marriage, the husband and wife are one person in the law. That is, the very being on legal existence of the women is suspended during the marriage, or at least is incorporated and consolidated into that of husband: under whose wing, protection, and cover, she performs everything." This assertion leaves no doubt in mind that in British Colonial Era, women have no independent identity. In Colonial laws of England, married women could not own property independently unless she entered into special contract termed as 'Marriage Settlement' which was rare at that time and also illegal in some states. All properties women brought to her marriage or earned during the marriage including wages were the property of her husband. He could use it or give it away as he chose without consulting her. However a husband was duty bound to maintain his wife according to his social status otherwise a wife could sue and win the support of the courts. Despite this fact that the courts created obligation on the part of husband but could not stop them from gambling and bad investments and wife had to survive with bare necessities of life. This was generally defined as two dresses (as she would have one to wear while other is being washed) , cooking, utensils and bed. (*Salmon,1998*). It shows that the most of the rights were denied to women and were exclusively given to men. Despite all this discrimination based on gender, few rights like child custody was given preferably to women in most parts of USA. (Salmon, 1998)

The atrocious practice of female infanticide has become the ultimate symbol of women's oppression in pre-Islamic Arabia. Female infanticide was promoted because of two reasons namely poverty and disgrace in earlier tribes. The Quran admonishes the Arabs against killing their children for fear of poverty and promises sustenance for them: "Hence, do not kill your children for fear of poverty: it is we who shall provide sustenance for them as well as for you. Verily, killing them is a great sin." Quran (17:31). With the advent of Islam the situation of women improved dramatically but later deteriorated due to the restrictive interpretation of Quran by many Muslim scholars. According to William Montgomery Watt, Islam improved the status of women by 'instituting rights of property ownership, inheritance, education and divorce.' Despite having improved in many spheres, women had to suffer discrimination on many account. It was not until 2011 that a woman could drive car in Saudi Arabia. Thus, it could be summarized that the position of women was not satisfactory in ancient Arab societies.

As historian Romilla Thapar remarks: "within the Indian subcontinent there have been infinite variations on the status of women diverging according to cultural milieu, family structure, class, caste, property rights and moral." The Vedic period could be truly called as the era of women. In the Rigveda, the wife has been blessed to live as queen in the house of her husband. However in post-Vedic period, women's rights and privileges were restricted by Manu. Women and shudras were not allowed to study Vedas therefore the door of formal education was closed to women at that time. (Rao,2008) In the medieval period, the legal status of women was further degraded. Various social evil like Sati, child marriages etc. were prevalent. Later, Social Reform Movement of nineteenth century & Nationalist Movement of twentieth century affected the status of women. Both these movements helped equalizing the status of women in almost every sphere.

3 International measures on gender equality

The establishment of UNO in 1945 and its main focus on women especially in late 19th century changed the legal, economic and political status of women in most part of the world. *Later more and more governments responded to the call of United Nation to secure women's right.*

As the international feminist movement began to gain momentum during the 1970s, the General Assembly declared 1975 as the International Women's Year and organized the first World Conference on Women, held in Mexico City. At the urging of the Conference, it subsequently declared the years 1976-1985 as the UN Decade for Women, and established a Voluntary Fund for Decade. (un.org)

In 1979, the General Assembly adopted the Convention on the Elimination of All Forms of Discrimination against Women (CEDAW), which is often described as an International Bill of Rights for Women. In its 30 articles, the Convention explicitly defines discrimination against women and sets up an agenda for national action to end such discrimination. The Convention targets culture and tradition as influential forces shaping gender roles and family relations, and it is the first human rights treaty to affirm the reproductive rights of women. (un.org)

UN convention on elimination of all forms of discrimination, 1979 and various other conventions helped to ensure basic rights to women. According to the UN Division for Women in its review of the four World Conferences:

"The fundamental transformation that took place in Beijing was the recognition of the need to shift the focus from women to the concept of gender, recognizing that the entire structure of society, and all relations between men and women within it, had to be re-evaluated. Only by such a fundamental restructuring of society and its institutions could women be fully empowered to take their rightful place as equal partners with men in all aspects of life. This change represented a strong reaffirmation that women's rights were human rights and that gender equality was an issue of universal concern, benefiting all."

CEDAW, 1979 creates an obligation on state parties to implement the provision of the convention. Till now 187 countries of the world have ratified the convention. Only 134 countries have ratified the convention without reservation and 52 countries have ratified with some sort of reservation to this convention. (United Nation,2016)

4   Effect of reservation:

Many states have become party to CEDAW convention in name only. They have no goal what so ever to promote equality to women. Reservations tends to allow states to become parties to convention, while not making changes into the laws of their country and the practices of society which is necessary to promote equality of women. A reservation is any statement made when ratifying a treaty that "purports to exclude or to modify the legal effect of certain provisions of the treaty in their application to that State."(Vienna Convention, 1980).

Article 2 of CEDAW convention provides:

States Parties condemn discrimination against women in all its forms, agree to pursue by all appropriate means and without delay a policy of eliminating discrimination against women and, to this end, undertake:

 (a) To embody the principle of the equality of men and women in their national constitutions or other appropriate legislation if not yet incorporated therein and to ensure, through law and other appropriate means, the practical realization of this principle;

(b) To adopt appropriate legislative and other measures, including sanctions where appropriate, prohibiting all discrimination against women;

(c) To establish legal protection of the rights of women on an equal basis with men and to ensure through competent national tribunals and other public institutions the effective protection of women against any act of discrimination;

(d) To refrain from engaging in any act or practice of discrimination against women and to ensure that public authorities and institutions shall act in conformity with this obligation;

(e) To take all appropriate measures to eliminate discrimination against women by any person, organization or enterprise;

(f) To take all appropriate measures, including legislation, to modify or abolish existing laws, regulations, customs and practices which constitute discrimination against women;

(g) To repeal all national penal provisions which constitute discrimination against women.

Articles 2 and 16 are considered by the Committee to be core provisions of the Convention. (un.org) The Committee holds the view that article 2 is central to the objects and purpose of the Convention. (un.org CEDAW committee) According to committee, States parties which ratify the Convention do so because they agree that discrimination against women in all its forms should be condemned and that the strategies set out in article 2, subparagraphs (a) to (g), should be implemented by States parties to eliminate it. (un.org). Under CEDAW, as well as under the Vienna Convention on the Law of Treaties, a reservation is impermissible if it "is incompatible with the object and purpose of the treaty."(Vienna Convention) Thus, the Committee has concluded that reservations to CEDAW Articles 2 and 16 are impermissible. Though there are instances of reservation by states parties on these core articles too. This kind of reservation at the time ratification shows the unwillingness of states to accept and promote women right.

In addition to reservation to article 2 and 16, some states have gone beyond this. For example, take Saudi Arabia, It ratified with the reservation, '[i]n case of contradiction between any term of the Convention and the norms of Islamic law, the Kingdom is not under the obligation to observe the contradictory terms of the Convention.' (U.N Women, 2016) Similarly, Mauritania agreed to be bound to the treaty "in each and every one of its parts which are not contrary to Islamic Sharia and are in accordance with our Constitution."(U.N Women, 2016) there is no binding force of CEDAW. As a result, the Committee is left to repeatedly request states parties to remove such reservations, either in its general comments or in responses to individual state reports. (Keller, 2014)

5 Legal position of women in Indian constitution:

The fact remains that the law cannot change the society overnight, but it can definitely formulate certain principles and make laws to ensure justice specially gender justice. As the gender injustice has been the most challenging issue in India, the law makers have put certain special provisions for women while drafting the constitution, so that equality at every level may be achieved. A few provision of Indian constitution are mentioned in brief:

5.1 Fundamental rights (part iii):

5.1.1   Article 14 of the constitution provides for the equality of law and equal protection of law.

5.1.2   Article 15(1) prohibits discrimination on the ground of sex and Article 15(3) empowers the state to make special provision for women.

5.1.3   Article 16 guarantees equality of opportunity for all citizens in matters of 'employment' and 'appointment'. However this is article is confined to employment and appointment only.

5.2 Directive principles (part iv):

5.2.1   Article 38 of constitution speaks for the social justice. As observed in Air India Statutory Corporation v. United Labour Union by Apex Court, "the concept of social justice consists of diverse principles essential for the orderly growth and development of personality of every citizen. Social justice is then an integral part of justice in the generic sense. Justice is the genus, of which social justice is one of the species."

5.2.2   Article 39 put down the principles of policies to be followed by state to secure economic justice. Equal pay for equal work, equal right of men and women to adequate means of livelihood, and healthy condition of workers are some principles of policy which should be implemented by state.

5.2.3   Article 42 directs the state to make provision for securing just humane condition and for maternity benefit.

5.3 Constitution 73rd and 74th amendments acts:

These two amendments have served as a major breakthrough to enhance political participation of women in India. These two amendments have provided for reservation of 33.33% of elected seats for women at different levels of local bodies in both rural and urban areas. This has dramatically increased the participation of women in governing bodies. It has also changed the position of women in rural areas.

5.4 Judicial activism:

5.4.1   The Supreme Court in VISHAKHA v. STATE OF RAJASTHAN AIR 1997 SC 3011 observed that when women are subjected to gender specific violence, the equality in employment is impaired. Therefore the Apex court of the country issued guidelines of mandatory nature against this exploitation at work place. These guidelines are considered as law and still continue to be considered as law until parliament makes any law on this issue.

5.4.2   In AMMINI E. J v. UNION OF INDIA AIR 1995, the Kerela High Court while referring the life of Christian wife being compelled to live as wife against her will observed that it will be humiliating and oppressed life without freedom to remarry and enjoy life in the normal course. It will be a life without freedom to uphold the dignity of the individual in all respects.... The court then quashed the impugned provision as violative of article 14, 15 and 21 of constitution.

6   Relation of growth with gender equality:

The role of women in economic development continues to occupy centre stage in policy debates. As has been shown in World Bank's recent World Development Report 2012, gender inequality in terms of access to education, health, formal sector employment, and income remains a significant constraint to growth in many countries.

The *Gender Inequality Index (GII)* is an index for measurement of gender disparity that was introduced in 2010. (Wikipedia) According to GII reports in 2012 Norway,

Australia and Switzerland are top three countries in terms of gender equality. (UNDP) India ranks 130 in gender inequality index in 2015. (UNDP) According to census of India 2011, literacy rate of female is 65.46% compared to males which are 82.14%. Several other factors like dowry deaths, gender based violence, patriarchal society system etc. contribute to the gender inequality.

The growth of a country highly depends on its workforce. Due to the prevalent gender injustice in India, half of its work force seems to be inactive. This is the most relevant factor which hinders the economic growth of this country. Women are still considered as the home keeper or responsible only for house hold chores. Granting rights only on paper can't help country to grow, as much of the rights have been granted to women by the constitution and various other laws. But this is high time to implement these laws. The growth of this country in reality can only be achieved when the equality is practiced at every level. In short, gender inequality served as a constraint to the sustainable development and growth of this country.

7   Suggestions:

No problem exists without a solution whether we know it or not. The solution lies to this problem of gender injustice too. In my opinion, it is we who can bridge this gender gap than policy makers. Society at large should take initiatives in this regard and support the cause of gender equality leaving behind their cultural patterns of living, superstitious religious beliefs and traditional approach as all these hinder growth of the country and promote gender inequality. The policies of law makers can only be implemented when society at large wills to accept it. No society can grow in real sense unless its mothers are educated. Therefore education, awareness, and participation in social gathering should be promoted among girls so that they may give their hand to the growth of this country. Non Governmental Organization should also take steps to eradicate this problem from its root. Law makers should take this problem seriously and make strategies as well as policies to stop this atrocious evil practice. These policies should not be made only on paper but with the intent to promote and support this cause then only positive results could be seen. Man and Woman are like two wheels of a carriage. The life of one without the other is incomplete.

Bibliography:

1. Bodenheimer edgar, Jurisprudence, Harvard University Press, Cambridge, 1974.

2. Census of India 2011, http://censusindia.gov.in (retrieved on 16 January 2016).

3. Dr. J. N. Pandey, 'The Constitutional Law Of India, Central Law Agency, 48th Edition 2011.

4. Full Text Of Convention in English, UN Women, http://www.un.org/womenwatch/daw/cedaw/text/econ vention.htm#article2 (retrieved on 18 January).

5. Linda M. Keller, 'THE IMPACT OF STATES PARTIES'RESERVATIONS TO THE CONVENTION ONTHE ELIMINATION OF ALL FORMS OF DISCRIMINATION AGAINST WOMEN', 2014 MICH. ST. L. REV. 309

6. Mamta Rao, 'law relating to women & children' Eastern Book Company, 2nd Edition 2008.

7. Marylynn Salmon, 'the legal status of women, 1776-1830', https://www.gilderlehrman.org/history-by-era/womens-history/essays/legal-status-women (retrieved on 18 January, 2016).

8. Reservation to CEDAW, UN Women, http://www.un.org/womenwatch/daw/cedaw/reservatio ns.htm (retrieved on 17 January 2016.

9. State Parties, UN Women, http://www.un.org/womenwatch/daw/cedaw/reservatio ns.htm (retrieved on 17 January 2016).

10. The Holy Quran.

11. "Table 5 Gender Inequality Index 2015". United Nation Development Programme (retrieved on 20 January 2016).

12. Vienna Convention on the Law of Treaties art. 2, May 23, 1969, 1155 U.N.T.S. 331 (entered into force Jan. 27, 1980).

13. William Blackstone, 'Commentaries on English Law (1765–1769).

14. Women, http://www.un.org/en/globalissues/women/ (retrieved on 15 January 2016).

15. Wikipedia.

27 INDIAN LEGAL SYSTEM AS A SAVIOUR OF "GROWTH WITH JUSTICE"

(By: Ms. Maria Fatima*)

Abstract

*G*rowth with justice has been proclaimed as the basic objective of India since the inception of planning. Like most other colonies, India greatly lagged behind economically as well as socially compared to the developed world. Periodic estimates of national income available since mid-nineteenth century indicate that the per capita income virtually stagnated in India till independence when world income grew several fold due to industrial and technological revolution. A large part of the population was living in appalling conditions. The leaders of the Indian national movement had pledged on the eve of Independence of wiping tear from each eye and the Nation would dedicate itself to the service of millions of poor who suffer. Rapid growth combined with active and purposive state intervention would, it was believed, make it possible to achieve over a period of time a more equitable distribution of wealth, income and economic opportunities without attempting any drastic changes in the social and economic structures. Social inclusion, social justice, secularism and tolerance are some pivots around which this idea needs to be formed. The year 2016 marked the sixty sixth year of the working of the Indian Constitution. The Constituent Assembly, elected to frame a suitable constitution for free*

---

* Student of B.A,LL.B (HONS), Faculty of Law, Unity Degree College, Lucknow

India, made sure that the new constitution did cater to the needs of Indians from all walks of life. To make sure that this end was achieved specific provisions were incorporated for the upliftment of the weaker sections and bridging the gap between the rich and the poor. Most of these provisions have been protected by the judiciary which bracketed them as the basic structure of the law of the country. Hence, the Indian Constitution envisages India which propels growth as well as idealises justice. At a time when there are so many ideological clashes, rising intolerance among people of various communities, growing inequality, suppression of women's rights, it is only the Constitution of our country that can bind everyone together and help find solutions to various problems. In these difficult times, it is important to have knowledge and a better understanding of the Constitution because a country can only be called a "developed nation" only if it has informed citizenry.

"If the society cannot help the many who are poor, it cannot save the few who are rich."

-Robert F. Kennedy

When it comes to setting up an appropriate economic policy for a developing country, like ours, the terms "growth" and "justice" are often conceived as conflicting ideas. Amartya Sen, a Nobel Prize Winner in economics and a professor of economics and philosophy at Harvard University, believes that India should invest more its social infrastructure to boost the productivity of its people and thereby raise 'growth'. On the other hand, Jagdish Bhagwati, a professor of economics at the University of Columbia, argues that only a focus on growth can yield enough resources for investing in social structure schemes[1]. Investing in health and education to improve human capabilities is central to Sen's scheme of things. Without such investments, inequality will widen and the growth process itself will falter, Sen believes. Bhagwati argues that growth may raise inequality initially but sustained growth will eventually raise enough resources for the state to redistribute and mitigate the effects of the initial inequality (Bhattacharya, 2013).

---

[1] *"Everything you wanted to know about Sen-Bhagwati Debate", Pramit Bhattacharya.*

The International Monetary Fund, which is often identified as the 'hard-nosed promoter of efficiency' (See Sen (1999), has also recognised that "as a matter of social justice, all members of society should share in the benefits of economic growth...poverty in the midst of plenty is not socially acceptable..."(Fisher, 1999).[2]

1   Indian perspective

"The future beckons to us. Whither do we go and what shall be our endeavour? To bring   freedom and opportunity to the common man, to the peasants and workers of India; to fight and end poverty and ignorance and disease; to build up a prosperous, democratic and progressive nation, and to create social, economic and political institutions which will ensure justice and fullness of life to every man and woman."

-Pt. Jawaharlal Nehru

India is a democratic state with 29 states and 6 union territories. Like most other colonies, India greatly lagged behind economically as well as socially compared to the developed world. Periodic estimates of national income available since mid-nineteenth century indicate that the per capita income virtually stagnated in India till independence when world income grew several fold due to industrial and technological revolution. A large part of the population was living in appalling conditions. The leaders of the Indian national movement had pledged on the eve of Independence of wiping tear from each eye and the Nation would dedicate itself to the service of millions of poor who suffer. Gandhi had envisioned India of his dreams in which the poorest shall feel that it is their country. The national government formed after independence placed priority on 'economic growth with social justice'. A mixed economy model with a major role for the state in industrial production was adopted. This was based on what was popularly known as "Nehruvian Socialism".

Nehruvian Socialism, it was not socialism upon the economy, but an aspiration of Indian National Congress to bring Socialistic pattern of society.

---

[2] *"Economic Policy and Social Justice in India: An Agenda for the millennium", Dr. Narendra Jadhav*

What is socialistic pattern of society? Economy as such is not made socialistic but the goal is bringing equity through Socialistic means. Eg: Mixed economy with reservations. Mixed economy: State (Brings equity) + Domestic Private players (enhance production). Reservations: Socialistic methodology of State to bring equity.

How Nehruvian socialism differs from Traditional socialism?

Socialism in the economy: Traditional Socialism. Socialism in the society + Mixed economy: Nehruvian Socialism.

Nehruvian socialism didn't aim to bring down the rich classes but to bring up the poor classes.

While this policy helped to lay the foundation for industrialization and technological change, national income growth remained low at about 3-4 per cent per annum for several decades. Finally, in the wake of a balance of payments crisis in 1991, Indian policy makers initiated a process of wide ranging economic reforms to shift to a more market friendly trade and industrial policy regime. The economic reform process has been steady but gradual because of a need for wide consultation and broad consensus so necessary in a democratic society. The process of consultation and debate has contributed to non-reversal of policies even under different political parties that have formed the government after the reforms. Whether and to what extent India has achieved the stated objective of higher growth and faster poverty removal during the post-reform period has been a matter of intense debate. These developments make India an interesting case study for examining issues in macroeconomics of poverty reduction. The aggregate estimates routinely brought out by the Central Statistical Organisation (CSO) show a "feel good factor" — that real per capita income has been growing rapidly. But there is little evidence on (a) how this growth has been shared among households in rural India versus urban India and (b) whether households belonging to different socio-religious groups have grown together. (Dubey & Vanneman, 2014)

2 Legal basis of "growth with justice"

Growth with justice has been proclaimed as the basic objective of India's development policy since the inception of planning. Rapid growth combined with active and purposive state intervention would, it was believed, make it possible to achieve over a period of time a more equitable distribution of wealth, income and economic opportunities without attempting any drastic changes in the social and economic structures. Hence, the concept would help in bridging the gap between the rich and the poor which would otherwise hamper development. Social inclusion, social justice, secularism and tolerance are some pivots around which this idea needs to be formed. In a socially just society, there exists, in addition to basic human rights, a realization of human potential, social benefits, an equitable distribution of resources, equal opportunities and obligations, and security[3]. In fact, the Indian Constituent Assembly had this in mind while they were drafting a Constitution which could successfully work in the Indian setup. Part III of the Indian Constitution embodies the Fundamental Rights of the citizens which have been can be enforced by the Indian courts. Some of the provisions worth mentioning here are as follows-

(i)Article 19 enshrines the fundamental rights of the citizens of this country. The seven sub-clauses of Article 19(1) guarantee the citizens seven different kinds of freedom and recognise them as their fundamental rights. Article 19 considered as a whole furnishes a very satisfactory and rational basis for adjusting the claims of individual rights and the claims of public good.

(ii) Article 23 and 24 provide fundamental rights against exploitation. Article 24, in particular, prohibits and employer from employing a child below the age of 14 years in any factory or mine or in any hazardous employment.

(iii) Article 31 makes a specific provision relating to right to property and deals with the vexed problem of compulsory acquisition of property.

---

[3] *"Social Justice and Economic Growth: Strange Bedfellows or Partners in Prosperity", Epaminondas Farmakis.*

(iv) The social problems presented by the existence of a large number of citizens who are treated as untouchables has received special attention of the Constitution. Article 15(1) prohibits discrimination on the grounds of religion, race, caste, sex and place of birth only. The state would be entitled to make special provisions for women and children, and also for the advancement of educationally and socially weaker sections.

A similar exception as been provided to equality of opportunity provided by Article 16(1) in as much as Article 16(4) provides for reservation of appointments and posts in favour of the backward classes which in the opinion of the state has not been adequately represented in the services.

(v) Article 17 proclaims that untouchability has been abolished and its practise in any form is prohibited. It provides that enforcement of untouchability shall be an offence punishable by law.

(vi)Article 38 requires that the state should make an effort to promote the welfare of the people by securing and protecting ,as effectively as it may, a social order in which justice social, economic as well as political shall inform all the institutions of national life.

(vii)Article 39 clause (a) says that the state shall secure the operation of a legal system which promotes justice on the basis of equal opportunity and shall, in particular, provide free legal aid, by suitable legislations and schemes, or in any other way, to ensure that opportunities for securing justice are not denied to any citizen by reason of economic or any other disability.

(viii)Article 41 recognises the right of every citizen to work, to education and to public assistance in cases of unemployment, old age, sickness and disablement and in other cases of undeserved want.

(ix)Article 42 stresses the importance of securing just and humane conditions of work and for maternity relief.

(x)Article 43 holds before the working population the ideal of the living wage.

(xi)Article 46 emphasises the importance of the promotion of educational and economic interests of the scheduled castes and scheduled tribes and other weaker sections.

Hence, this is the code of provisions dealing with the problem of achieving the ideal of socio-economic justice in this country which has been prescribed by the Constitution.

The main instrument for a sustainable and inclusive growth is assumed to be productive employment[4]. Employment growth generates new jobs and income for the individual - from wages in all types of firms, or from self employment, usually in micro firms - while productivity growth has the potential to lift the wages of those employed and the returns to the self-employed. After all, in many low-income countries the problem is not unemployment, but rather underemployment. Hence, inclusive growth is not only about employment growth, but also about productivity growth. Moreover, it is not only about wage-employment but also about self-employment which means that returns to capital, land and other assets matter to the income potential of the focus group as shown in the identity above. The ability of individuals to be productively employed depends on the opportunities.

3   Social justice and empowerment:

"In a real sense, all life is interrelated. The agony of the poor impoverishes the rich; the betterment of the poor enriches the rich. We are inevitably our brother's keepers because we are our brother's brother. Whatever affects one directly affects all indirectly."

-Martin Luther King

The concept of inclusiveness must go beyond the traditional objective of poverty alleviation to include equality of opportunity, as well as economic and social mobility for all sections of society, with affirmative action for SCs, STs, OBCs, minorities and women. There must be equality of opportunity to all with freedom and dignity, and without social or political obstacles. This must be accompanied by an improvement in the opportunities for economic and social

---

[4] *According to the Growth and Development Commission Report (2008), sustained high growth requires rapid incremental productive employment.*

advancement. In particular, individuals belonging to disadvantaged groups should be provided special opportunities to develop their skills and participate in the growth process. This outcome can only be ensured if there is a degree of empowerment that creates a true feeling of participation so necessary in a democratic polity. Empowerment of disadvantaged and hitherto marginalized groups is therefore an essential part of any vision of inclusive growth. India's democratic polity, with the establishment of the third layer of democracy at the Panchayati Raj Institution (PRI) level(73rd Amendment) , provides opportunities for empowerment and participation of all groups with reservations for SCs, STs, and women. These institutions should be made more effective through greater delegation of power and responsibility to the local level.

4 National Human Rights Commission

The Human Rights Act, 1993 seeks to provide regulatory framework for protection of rights related to life, liberty, and quality, dignity of individuals guaranteed by the constitution or embodied in the International Covenants and enforceable by courts in India. Section 3 of the Act provides for constitution of National Human Rights Commission and section 21 provides for constitution of State Human Rights Commission. In pursuance of section 3, a National Human Rights Commission is already in existence since 12th October, 1993. It takes up the cases regarding human rights violations addressed to it and through its own initiative. As atrocities on SCs are violation of Human Rights, it intervenes in complaints relating to them also. The Commission is also required to submit a report annually which is laid on the table of both Houses of Parliament.

5 National Commission for Women

Section 3 of National Commission for Women Act, 1990 provides for the constitution of National Commission for Women to investigate and examine all matters relating to safeguards provided for the women under the Constitution and various other laws. The First National Commission was constituted on 31st January, 1992. It takes up Social Justice. The Legal Instruments complaints of women referred to it for redressal irrespective of caste. Accordingly, problems of SC women including those of physical violence against them are also dealt with by it. As other statutory Commissions, the commission has to submit a report annually which is laid on the table of both the Houses.

6   National Commission for Backward Classes

This is basically an Indian Statutory body established in 1993 which considers inclusions in and exclusions from the lists of communities notified as backward for the purpose of job reservations and tenders the needful advice to the Central Government as per Section 9(1) of the NCBC Act, 1993.. Similarly, the states have also constituted commissions for BC's. As of 24 July 2014 over two thousand groups have been listed as OBCs. Both the National Commission for Backward Classes and National Commission for Scheduled Castes have the same powers as a Civil Court.

Besides these measures the Parliament had enacted several legislations to secure equilibrium in the society. The new labour laws are meant for revamping the conditions of workers in trade and industries. The freedom of contract has been regulated between the employee and employer in the interest of workers and an attempt has been made to assure to every worker condition of work ensuring a decent standard of life. A number of important enactments such as the Industrial Dispute Act 1947, Minimum Wages Act 1948 ,the Plantation Labour Act 1951, the Maternity Benefit Act 1961 have been designed to curb if not eradicate the urge to exploit the workers. The **Bonded Labour System (Abolition) Act, 1976** abolished all agreements and obligations, including customary sanctions which permit bonded labour system in various forms. The Act also released all such labourers from these obligations, cancelled their outstanding debts and prohibited creation of any new bondage agreement. The Act also mandatorily provided for economic rehabilitation of freed bonded labour by the State. Keeping a bonded labour is a violation of law and is punishable with sentence of 3 years imprisonment and a fine of Rs. 2,000/- Ministry of Labour operates a centrally sponsored scheme for rehabilitation of released bonded labours. **Debt Relief Legislations**- Indebtedness is a chronic problem of all poor persons but it affects SCs/STs more severely.

293

Indebtedness arises because of their poverty and therefore need to borrow for subsistence and to meet other emergent social expenditure like illness, marriage, etc. Report on Prevention of Atrocities against SCs & STs since no such credit is available from institutional sources; money is borrowed from private money lenders who charge exorbitant rates of interest. Due to their inability to pay back, the borrowers are enmeshed in a vicious cycle of debt-bondage.

7 The incumbent five year plan

The *visible hands* of the state as expressed in innumerable affirmative actions and pro-active policies with reinforcement from the NGOs cannot certainly go totally waste. Indeed, they have been successful, at least, in triggering the process of emancipation of the disadvantaged, albeit the process remains highly limited in terms of coverage and achievements so far. What follows is a snapshot of the outcome of such efforts in terms of an update of the status of the disadvantaged. The presentation, however, deals with only SCs and STs in the absence of reliable information for OBCs (Jadhav). India is currently operating under its 12th Five Year Plan. In December 2012, the Planning Commission published the near final draft 12th Five Year Plan- *Faster, More Inclusive and Sustainable Growth.* The 12th Plan says that '*[it] must be guided by a vision of India moving forward in a way that would ensure a broad-based improvement in living standards of all sections of the people through a growth process which is faster than in the past, more inclusive and also more environmentally sustainable'.*

The main objectives of this five year plan have been described as:-

- Better performance in agriculture
- Faster creation of jobs in manufacturing
- Wider industrial growth
- The creation of appropriate infrastructural facilities to enhance agricultural and manufacturing growth
- Stronger efforts at health education and skill development

- Reforming the implementation of flagship programs

- Special challenges focused on vulnerable groups and back ward sections.

The unfathomable and unprecedented victory of the Bharatiya Janta Party in the elections of May 2014 clearly indicated that the young aspiring Indians were eagerly waiting for some good reforms in the pattern of governance. However, since Mr. Narendra Modi became Prime Minister, there has been almost no talk of 'parivartan' or 'vikas' from him. Instead he has taken to talking about 'the poor' in much the same way as Congress leaders always have. Other than the abolition of the Planning Commission, there have been no economic reforms. He promises that India will become the easiest country in the world for business but nothing has really changed in his government's behaviour except in small ways. Reform in education and healthcare policies is desperately needed and there are no signs of new policies. And in vital economic ministries, dealing with such important things as energy, there are no signs of change. Moreover, India has been ranked very low[5], mostly in the bottom half, globally on most of the parameters for inclusive growth and development even as it fares much better internationally when it come to business and political ethics. India's overall place in the Global Competitiveness Index 2014–2015 rankings is 71 out of 144 countries (India ranks low on inclusive growth, development on WEF, 2015). And still many sections of the society have not seen their incomes rise for years. The gap between rich and poor has widened, with those at the top capturing the 'lion's share' of growth. Rising inequality in earnings and in wealth is a major concern, but money is just one aspect of people's well-being. In just about every area, whether it be education, life expectancy, or employment prospects, success is determined by socio-economic status, wealth and assets, sex, age or the places where people live. In many countries, people have not seen their incomes rise for years. The gap between rich and poor has widened, with those at the top capturing the 'lion's share' of growth. Rising inequality in earnings and in wealth is a major concern, but money is just one aspect of people's well-being. In just about every area, whether it be education, life

---

[5] *World Economic Forum Report 2015*

expectancy, or employment prospects, success is determined by socio-economic status, wealth and assets, sex, age or the places where people live. It is in fact baffling and at the same time depressing that even with such a spectacular legal system we have not been able to pass through the dark passages of injustice and inequality. Indians need to introspect because the problem lies within. As Dr. Bhimrao Ambedkar remarked, *"By independence, we have lost the excuse of blaming the British for anything going wrong. If hereafter things go wrong, we will have nobody to blame except ourselves."*

Bibliography

1. Bhattacharya, P. (2013). Everything you wanted to know about Sen-Bhagwati debate. Retrieved from www.livemint.com.

2. Dubey, A., & Vanneman, R. (2014). An Inclusive Growth Policy.

3. Fisher, Stanley (1999), 'A View from the IMF', in Economic Policy & Equity, edited by Tanzi, V., Chu, K., and Gupta, S. (1999), IMF, Washington D.C.

4. India ranks low on inclusive growth, development on WEF. (2015). *The Hindu* .

5. Jadhav, D. N. (n.d.). Economic Policy and Social Justice in India.

6. Sen, A. K. (1999), 'Economic Policy and Equity: An Overview', in Economic Policy & Equity, edited by Tanzi, V., Chu, K., and Gupta, S. (1999), IMF, Washington D.C.

28 TECHNOLOGICAL ASPECTS OF GROWTH WITH JUSTICE

(By: Ms. Nabiha Khwaja)*

Abstract

The purpose of this paper is to throw light on the various means of technology that have led us to a new era, i.e., the Digital Era and done justice alongside. We can see that how much impact the technology has made in our life. Nowadays, we can see many technological inventions, without which, we cannot imagine our life. Everybody has his hands on technology from peasants to presidents. It has become a necessary evil. The more the availability of new technological inventions, the more our lust for facilitators escalates. Technology has been continuously in the phase of development since its inception in Stone Age. The invention of various tools and techniques and the background knowledge helps the people to develop new things. Technology had converted fairy tale fancies to reality. The development of technology has been found spreading justice in many sections of society like printing gave power to the Bible and led directly to the Protestant Reformation in Northern Europe and DNA which made possible the tracing of Heredity and helps identifying criminals.

So growth with justice can be ensured if we work towards developing technology and appropriately allocating it to

---

* Student of B.A,LL.B (HONS), Faculty of Law, Unity Degree College, Lucknow

various sections in society.

1. Introduction:

If we talk about the historic era i.e. the olden times, we come across many examples to state how technology has contributed to justice. In the fourteenth century, the new technology of printing changed the face of Europe, bringing books and education out of monasteries and spreading them as far wide among the people. Printing gave power to the Bible and led directly to the Protestant Reformation in Northern Europe[1]. Recent technologies that contributed in a practical way to justice were those of Public health-clean water supplies, sewage treatment, vaccination, antibiotics .These technologies were effective in protecting people from contagious diseases and sickness. Even if the rich receive preferential treatment, the benefits of public health technology are not beyond the reach and threshold of everybody. And in countries where public health technologies are enforced by law, there is no large gap in life expectancy between rich and poor. Household appliances are another technology with a tendency towards justice. Around three decades ago our daily household chores like washing clothes, utensils and so on were done manually and many a times servant were employed to do these works but with the march of time and advent of technology led to the invention of washing machine, dish washer and many other electric appliances which eventually replaced the manual labour and the household chores could be done more effectively. This also led to justice in a way as the servants in the olden times were treated cruelly and were not valued and were also required to do the pettiest and nauseous jobs which was unfair, human scavenging is the heinous of jobs both socially and ethically but now with hygiene awareness and latest sanitation technology and stringent laws the practice has become extinct .New schemes of literacy and employment provided by the government to the citizens it is evident that most of the people have risen financially and also in terms of literacy which has led to the reduction of poverty in the long run and also elevated the academic standards.

Radio and television brought a renaissance in

---

[1] *www.carnegiecouncil.org*

society the greatest technological advent that reach out to the masses, not only spread awareness about health and education but also educates the population about their rights and duties. This has reduced exploitation to a great extent and people could move to any court of justice to avail their rights and to seek justice in case of harassment or assault.

2. In the field of agriculture:

If we deal with the sphere of agriculture in terms of Technological aspects of growth with justice we come across many potential developments like that of the modern tubewells, Drip irrigation/micro spray heads and the Sprinkler system. These modern equipments of agriculture has undoubtedly led to the welfare of farmers and made agriculture convenient for a country like India where nearly 70% of the population is engaged in agriculture. Though, for many farmers these modern equipments are far out of reach but due to the conscious and effective measures of government the farmers are being provided with these convenient equipments. The Government has laid emphasis to provide financial assistance to the farmers and other target groups for purchase of different kinds of farm equipment, demonstration of new equipment among farmers for spread of new technology, human resource development in operation, maintenance/ repairs and management of agricultural machinery and the quality improvement through testing and evaluation besides institutional credit & fiscal measures. The Farm Machinery Training & Testing Institutes at Budni (M.P.), Hissar (Haryana), Garladinne (A.P.) and Bishwanath Chariali (Assam) established by the Government have playing a vital role in promoting agricultural mechanization. Efficient farm management and resource efficiency – As mentioned earlier, a declining percentage of farmers in the world have to produce more for a growing population. Fortunately, advances in technology can have significant impact, as did irrigation systems, tractors, and other mechanical innovations in the 19th and 20th Centuries. Further, a "whole farm approach" optimizes the farmer's efficiency, including use of water, waste, soil, energy, and most importantly, time. Precision agriculture technologies, for example, can optimize fertilizer applications, saving time and money by creating a more productive field. Throughout history, scientific and technological advances have greatly impacted the agriculture industry. Early farmers improved their crop production by inventing the first hoes. Today, farmers improve crop production through the use of global positioning systems. How did these changes happen? How did people learn about new ideas? How have these ideas changed farming methods?

Early advances were shared by word of mouth. As new ideas were tried out and applied to growing crops and livestock, they were shared and passed to the next generation as parents taught their children. Neighboring tribes exchanged ideas with one another and with new settlers. In more recent times, scientists studying at universities devote their lives to research and development of farming products and practices. Iowa farmers and agricultural scientists have benefited and contributed to the ever-evolving science of agriculture.

3. New Ideas and Inventions:

One milestone in the evolution of technology in Iowa occurred with the completion of rail lines across the state. By 1870 transportation had been greatly expanded—which made it easier for farmers to market their products outside the Midwest. Transportation advances greatly impacted the life of an Iowa farmer. Another event that affected farm life was the commercial production of barbed wire. As the land became more settled and there were fewer and fewer acres of open prairie, farmers needed a way to keep their own cattle at home. Barbed wire was the answer. Instead of grazing on open prairie, cattle were fenced in the farmer's own field and fed with corn. This allowed Iowa farmers to transition from cattle grazing to cattle raising.

4. Saving paper (thus preventing deforestation):

With the advent of the Digital revolution and evolution of EBooks, books are being preferably read more on tablets, kindles, etc. It is gradually replacing the big hefty bundle of papers combined together. It is beneficial in a way as it discourages the cutting down of innumerable number of trees to produce paper out of it and the biggest irony I have ever come across is the cutting of trees to make paper out of it and writing save trees on the same. Articles and stories are easily available online and are very convenient to store and keep a record and keep them in order rather than managing big bundles of books arranging which requires a lot of effort. This is one of the main factor when we deal with Technological aspects of growth with justice as it prevents the ecological imbalance too by discouraging deforestation.

5. Biological aspects:

The most potential example is of DNA **(Deoxyribonucleic acid)** is a molecule that carries most of the genetic instructions used in the development, functioning and reproduction of all known living organisms and many viruses. Forensic scientists can use DNA in blood, skin, saliva or hair found at a crime scene to identify a matching DNA of an individual, such as a perpetrator. This process is formally termed DNA profiling, but may also be called "genetic fingerprinting". In DNA profiling, the lengths of variable sections of repetitive DNA, such as short tandem repeats and mini satellites, are compared between people. This method is usually an extremely reliable technique for identifying a matching DNA. The development of forensic science, and the ability to now obtain genetic matching on minute samples of blood, skin, saliva or hair has led to a re-examination of a number of cases. Forensic scientists can analyze types of DNA: nuclear DNA or mitochondrial DNA; nuclear DNA can individualize evidence, while mitochondrial DNA, or mtDNA, can only classify the maternal inheritance of the sample taken in for analysis. Evidence can now be uncovered that was not scientifically possible at the time of the original examination. Combined with the removal of the double jeopardy law in some places, this can allow cases to be reopened where previous trials have failed to produce sufficient evidence to convince a jury. People charged with serious crimes may be required to provide a sample of DNA for matching purposes. The most obvious defence to DNA matches obtained forensically is to claim that cross-contamination of evidence has taken place. This has resulted in meticulous strict handling procedures with new cases of serious crime. DNA profiling is also used to identify victims of mass casualty incidents. As well as positively identifying bodies or body parts in serious accidents, DNA profiling is being successfully used to identify individual victims in mass war graves – matching to family members. DNA profiling is also used in DNA paternity testing in order to determine if someone is the biological parent or grandparent of a child with the probability of parentage is typically 99.99% when the alleged parent is biologically related to the child. Normal DNA sequencing methods happen after birth but there are new methods to test paternity while the mother is still pregnant. Thus, in other words DNA has indefinitely led to justice by making it possible to identify criminals and punishing them thus ensuring justice to the victims. The invention of new gadgets has travelled a long way to help the authority (police). For instance, police frequently had been looking for technology for enhancing their effectiveness. The advent of fingerprinting in the 1900s and of crime laboratories in the 1920s greatly augmented the police capacity to solve crimes. The introduction of the two-way radio and the widespread use of the automobile in the 1930s multiplied police productivity in responding to incidents. The use of high-technology equipment and applications is essential to the efficient practice of community policing. Without high technology, officers would find it difficult to provide the level and quality of services the community deserves. Computer-aided dispatching, computers in patrol cars, automated fingerprinting systems, and online offense-reporting systems are but a few examples of the pervasiveness of technology in agencies that practice community policing. The advent of technology has helped in almost all spheres of justice. It did not only came handy to the authority but also to the general public facing the threat of being attacked. Assailants are not invited, motives to steal and extort for valuables can drive them anytime and so it led to the invention of 'Pepper Spray'. Pepper spray, also known as OC spray (from "oleoresin capsicum"), OC gas, and capsicum spray, is a lachrymatory agent (a chemical compound that irritates the eyes to cause tears, pain, and temporary blindness) used in policing, riot control, crowd control, and personal self-defense, including defense against dogs and bears. Its inflammatory effects cause the eyes to close, taking away vision. This temporary blindness allows officers to more easily restrain subjects and permits people using pepper spray for self-defense. The latest in the list of crimes is cyber crime which is actually a gift of technology, the internet which has shrunken the world has also shrunken the geographical limits of crime, but again for the lock the key are cyber experts who through their excellent skills in the field of computers manage to track down the cyber criminals and get them behind the bars. The boon of technology should be utilized under a protocol because as the technology increase the side effects and potential hazards also increase. Technology is a queer thing. It brings you great gifts with one hand but if used unwisely, it stabs you at the back. After all, technology gives us power but it does not and cannot tell us how to use that power. Thanks to technology through which we can instantly communicate across the world but it still does not help us to know what to say. It is in our hands to use it as such that its side effects and potential hazards do not escalate. Stringent laws should be framed for the proper usage of every new technology.

6. Conclusion:

We should work to create a world in which technology can capably wipe social evils of our society and end poverty along with providing a sustainable future for everyone. In today's world, 1.3 billion people do not have access to safe water, 2.5 billion people live without sanitation and 1.1 billion still lack access to electricity. Technology can be considered as the heart of human development. It enables people to produce food, access water and energy and maintain good health. But access to technology and its benefits are not fairly shared and if it is not changed then will lead to drive injustice and inequality and so it is time to halt pondering and work to overhaul how technology and innovation are governed in order to ensure the well-being of the people. Practical action will indefinitely overcome injustices by leading a change in the way the world approaches and governs technologies.

Technological aspect of growth with Justice allows people to use technology to improve their lives and it is focusing research and innovation to meet humanity's basic needs and protect the planet. It should make sure that technologies do not harm others, now or in the future. An objective of Technology to ensure Justice can be to ensure that everyone globally can achieve a minimum standard of living. Technological aspects of growth with justice are ensured when everyone has access to existing technologies that are essential to life; and the focus of efforts to innovate and develop new technologies is firmly centred on solving the great challenges the world faces today: ending poverty and providing a sustainable future for everyone on our planet.

Bibliography:

1. http://infohub.practicalaction.org/oknowledge/handle/1 1283/5/93516

2. http://investeddevelopment.com/blog/2013/06/the-impact-of-technology-in-agriculture/#sthash.q6F0G0c6.dpuf

3. Nuwer, Rachel (18 July 2015). "Counting All the DNA on Earth". The New York Times (New York: The New York Times Company). ISSN 0362-4331. Retrieved 2015-07-18.

4. "Pepper Spray". Llrmi.com. Retrieved 2011-12-02.

5. practicalaction.org

6. Walker, Samuel (1992). "Origins of the Contemporary Criminal Justice Paradigm: The American Bar Foundation Survey, 1953-1969". Justice Quarterly 9 (1): 47–76. doi:10.1080/07418829200091251

29 EDUCATIONAL ASPECTS OF GROWTH WITH GENDER JUSTICE WITHIN UTTAR PRADESH

(By: Ms. Novaira Masih *)

Abstract

*A*fter independence, the state of UP has continued to take investment over the years in all the sectors of education and has achieved significant success in overcoming general educational backwardness and illiteracy.

But, the differential between female and male literacy remained high. Similarly, the incidence of illiteracy in the 10-14 age groups was also high. Not only this, in fact, the literacy figure went down in rural areas.

This paper attempts to briefly analyse the situation and present the views of the author, in context of the views of some known authorities on the subject.

1. Introduction and Review:

After independence, the state of UP has continued to make investment over the years in all the sectors of education and has achieved significant success in overcoming general educational backwardness and illiteracy. The increase in overall literacy rate is due to persistent multi-pronged efforts made by the state Government to enroll and retain children,

---

* *Student of B.Ed, Faculty of Education, Unity Degree College, Lucknow*

especially of weaker sections, in schools; to effectively implement the adult educational programmes; and to establish centers of higher education. As a result UP is ranked amongst the first few States to have successfully implemented the Education For All Policy.

The following is indicative of the gradual progress:

In 1981, the literacy rate in UP was 28% and it increased to 42% in1991. In 1991, the adult literacy rate (percent literates among those aged 15 and above) was 38% and it increased to 49% in 1998, an increase of 11 percentage points in the seven-year period. But, the differential between female and male literacy remained high: while in 1991, male literacy was 56% and female literacy was 25%, eight years later in 1999, as per survey estimates, the male literacy rates became 73% and female literacy rates 43% (NFHS II) One more notable feature in the state has been the persistence of higher levels of illiteracy in the younger age group, more so in females, especially in the rural areas. In the late 1980's, the incidence of illiteracy in the 10-14 age group was as high as 32% for rural males and 61% for rural females; and more than two-third of all rural girls in the 12-14 age group never went to school. Only 25% of the girls in 7+ age group were able to read and write in 1991 and this figure went down to 19% for rural areas: it was 11% for the scheduled castes, 8% for the scheduled castes in rural areas and 8% for the entire rural population in the most educationally backward districts in terms of the completion of basic or essential educational attainment. In 1992-93, only 50% of literate males and 40% of literate females could complete the cycling of eight years of schooling.

The problems of state education system are complex. Due to public apathy the public schools are run inefficiently. Privately running schools (including those run by Christian missionaries) are functional, but beyond the reach of ordinary people.

As we have read above in the educational level estimates; it is quite well reflected that males are gaining more education than females. The literacy rates reported above from 1991 to today's era it is quite clearly shows that education is granted to great deal to males only. Despite of so many government schools the girls prefer to stay at home and attend to household work. When they are asked the reason for not going to school they say it is worthless to go to school and the reason for them is that girls are not meant for knowledge but for marriage. If we compare 19th century educational system to today's educational system we will find a huge difference. Earlier, most of the girls never gave more emphasis to study, while in today's era girls are eager to gain education but yet some fail to do so.

Well why only girls but boys too lag behind in education and the reason put forward by them is poverty or lack of time. Hence, it is said that it is never too late to learn, so they should also try to gain education without any disturbance in their lives as it would help them to build their future.

2. Three views:

1) The greatest single factor which can incredibly improve the status of women in any society in education.

- Sambangi, D[1]

Yes I agree, with Sambangi. Until and unless women gain education, they won't have a high status in society or an identity of their own. How long can we women be grabbed in the arms of household work it is high time whether it is rural or urban area the women needs to come out and gain education without any shame.

Women also have the right to be identified by their own names and personalities, why always to be hidden under a veil? One should live life to the fullest and gain education to a great level and show the world that women are not less than men in the field of education.

2) Education is the cornerstone of women's empowerment because it enables them to respond to opportunities to challenge their traditional roles and to change their traditional roles and their lives.

- Kaur Sukhpal[2]

The idea put forward by Sukhpal Kaur is well supported, a

---

[1] *Education is the foundation for women's empowerment in India. By: Sambangi, D*
[2] *Education and women empowerment: challenges and remedies. By: Kaur Sukhpal*

girl plays an important role in society, she is first a daughter who gains education by birth then she is a wife and she is a mother too but above all she is a woman who even after marriage has the right to gain education, and do a job according to her wish. For a woman to gain education is very important because there are some roles which she plays in society as well as her traditions in which education is important so one should understand the importance of gaining education.

3) It is unfortunately true of our society that children are sent to school not because of their intelligence or aptitude but according to their sex.

- *Hussain Yuman*[3]

It is well said by Yuman Hussain that children are sent to school because of their sex but not because of their intelligence level.

Individuals who are male have the benefit to inculcate more and more education but the same is not true with females. Why so? The answer is - because of their sex! As some people even today are against female education whether we see in rural areas or urban areas all over only one thing is reflected that is lack if education if we see in practical life it is also found on roads where beggars leave their children to beg, small children are nowadays trolley pullers and workers. In this tender age when children need to study they are doing these kinds of activities. We all should help them to be benefit from education.

3. Following are the solutions for backwardness of education:

1) People should give huge donations for study purposes in schools.

2) Citizens should help these children especially girls in studies by giving them free education.

3) People should help poor children to gain education.

4) People should provide maximum help to poor girls.

5) People should not give money to poor children or family but provide free tuition to them.

---

[3] *Educational problems of women in India. By: Hussain Yuman*

30 ECONOMIC GROWTH WITH JUSTICE
(By: Mr. Ajatshatru Singh *)

Abstract

" "*W*ith most problems now-a-days the economic answers are only political questions.*"[1]*

Experts from all over the world say that the Indian economy is poised to take off and enter the league of developed nations over the coming decades. Slow but steady growth rate of the economy, along with the unflinching faith in democratic principles has contributed much to the growth and development of our country as a powerful developing nation.

India is a vibrant democracy which is gaining strength day by day. If we consider the achievements made by India during the last few centuries, we at once become aware of the economic opportunities and entrepreneurial avenues that exploded in our country. Factors such as strong GDP growth, along with the growth of service sector and a well-defined financial system contribute to the backbone of the Indian economy. The demographic dividend also plays an important role in shaping the economy of our country.

This paper tries to look on the situation of growth in the Indian economy and raises a few questions which need answers.

---

* Student of B.A,LL.B (HONS), Faculty of Law, Unity Degree College, Lucknow
[1] given by Joan Robinson

1. Introduction:

India being the second most populated country, the need for accelerated economic growth is a prime concern in India. In a country where a fiercely independent media and a population that prefers democracy to other forms of government thrive, failure to satisfy the needs and necessities of the common asses involves chaos of instability and political conflicts. Economic development can be measured in various ways. Ideology followed by a country, types of population residing in it, and the extent of foreign aid available to it can be considered as yardsticks for economic development. Currently, economic situation is not rosy in India, even though we can point out various strong areas of economic growth, on the whole. Low productivity along with inflation, fiscal deficit, poverty and inequality combine and contribute to the eroding nature of Indian economy.

Democracy gives due preference to humanitarian concerns. People abiding by democracy are supposed to live within the framework of a free society and achieve economic growth by respecting the fundamental rights and duties. Our Constitution is designed in such a way that it envisages the functioning of an economic system that restricts the amassing of wealth and the means of production by a few people. It is in this context that the concept called social justice has its significance.

In a developing country like India, social justice can be related to distributive justice. The main problem in India is not the scarcity of resources, but the unjust distribution of resources among the people. Many of the people are not getting their deserved lot; at the same time wealthy groups are becoming richer in every sense. Elite groups are competing among themselves to erect luxury apartments and shopping malls. They never hesitate to spend an implausible sum of money on ceremonies such as marriages and house warming.

Much of the shares of means of production which is meant for the effective modernisation of our economy is concentrated in the hands of wealthy people. At the same time, most of the people who are relegated to the lower ladders of society are amid poverty. Many of them live in slums with ration cards showing 'Above Poverty Line' (APL) in it. This is an evident example of poverty amidst plenty in India.

2.   Economy of India:

The Economy of India is the seventh-largest in the world by nominal GDP and the third-largest by purchasing power parity (PPP). The country is classified as a newly industrialised country, one of the G-20 major economies, a member of BRICS and a developing economy with an average growth rate of approximately 7% over the last two decades. Maharashtra is the wealthiest Indian state and has an annual GDP of US$220 billion, nearly equal to that of Pakistan or Portugal, and accounts for 12% of the Indian GDP followed by the states of Tamil Nadu (US$140 billion) and Uttar Pradesh (US$130 billion). India's economy became the world's fastest growing major economy from the last quarter of 2014, replacing the People's Republic of China.[2]

3.   Sixty years of fighting Indian poverty:[3]

India's government is well aware that poverty is a giant barrier to overcome if it is to fully develop the nation. A wide range of anti-poverty policies have been introduced since the 1950s, which nonetheless took effect after 20 years of implementation.

If the decline in poverty went from 60% to 35% between the 70s and the early 90s, globalization and liberalization policies have made this trend go backwards in the 90s. How? And why? Weren't the effects of joining the global market place supposed to create growth? Why has India lagged behind China for so long? What went wrong?

4.   Poverty in India - Statistics

- 50% of Indians don't have proper shelter;

- 70% don't have access to decent toilets (which inspires a multitude of bacteria to host their own disease party);

- 35% of households don't have a nearby water source;

---

[2] *https://en.wikipedia.org/wiki/Economy_of_India*
[3] *http://www.poverties.org*

- 85% of villages don't have a secondary school (how can this be the same government claiming 9% annual growth?);

- Over 40% of these same villages don't have proper roads connecting them.

5.   The Government Schemes:[4]

Scheme	Ministry	Start	Sector	Brief Detail
Deen Dayal Upadhyaya Gram Jyoti Yojana	MoP	2015	Rural Power Supply	It is a Government of India program aimed at providing 24x7 uninterrupted power supply to all homes in Rural India
Digital India Programme	MoC & IT	July 1, 2015	Digitally Empowered Nation	Aims to ensure that government services are available to citizens electronically and people get benefited from the latest information and communication technology
radhan Mantri Suraksha Bima Yojana	MoF	May 9, 2015	Insurance	Accidental Insurance with a premium of Rs. 12 per year.

---

[4] *https://en.wikipedia.org/wiki/List_of_government_schemes_in_India#cite_note-15*

Pradhan Mantri Jeevan Jyoti Bima Yojana	MoF	May 9, 2015	Insurance	Life insurance of Rs. 2 lakh with a premium of Rs. 330 per year.
HRIDAY – Heritage City Development and Augmentation Yojana	MoUD	Jan 2015	Urban Development	The scheme seeks to preserve and rejuvenate the rich cultural heritage of the country.
Sukanya Samridhi Yojana (Girl Child Prosperity Scheme)	Mo WCD	Jan 2015		The scheme primarily ensures equitable share to a girl child in resources and savings of a family in which she is generally discriminated as against a male child.
Smart Cities Mission	MoUD	June 25, 2015	Urban Development	To enable better living and drive economic growth stressing on the need for people centric urban planning and development.

Atal Mission for Rejuvenation and Urban Transformation (AMRUT)	MoUD	June 25, 2015	Urban Development	To enable better living and drive economic growth stressing on the need for people centric urban planning and development.
Pradhan Mantri Awas Yojana (PMAY)	MoUD	June 25, 2015	Housing	To enable better living and drive economic growth stressing on the need for people centric urban planning and development

This list shows that a number of schemes are being run by our government. But one cannot desist from asking whether different political parties ruling India have been able to, or will ever be able to complete these schemes within their period of rule? Today we have a beautiful slogan of Make in India. Will India ever make it? Will India ever match the European nations? And if yes then how many generations it will take? And if no, who will be responsible for it!

India has fought against many social injustices and any oppression will not deter the courage and spirit of the citizens of India that will let down its nation or its citizens.

The economic inequality is threatening to ruin the nation and the development of the Republic of Indian Union will be meaningful only when it runs on the lines of equality for which the nation fought in the past and it will be a real tribute to the leaders of the Indian independence who shed their blood for mother India from the bondage of slavery by foreign invasion.[5]

---

[5] *Taken from "The Indian Front"*

On the other hand for the globe as a whole what Ban ki – Moon has said is worth sharing here:

"Saving our planet, lifting people out of poverty, advancing economic growth... these are one and the same fight. We must connect the dots between climate change, water scarcity, energy shortages, global health, food security and women's empowerment. Solutions to one problem must be solutions for all". [6]

Education is the most powerful weapon we can use for changing the world and also use to fight for any kind of poverty and injustice around the world.

---

[6] *given by "Ban Ki-moon"*

From Here We Begin

www.ingramcontent.com/pod-product-compliance
Lightning Source LLC
Chambersburg PA
CBHW072301200526
45168CB00014B/79